Routledge Revivals

Morals in the Melting Pot

First published in 1948, *Morals in the Melting Pot* is an important historical reference work addressing some of the age-old moral dilemmas prevalent in society. Edward Griffith discusses themes like contraception, sex and religion, divorce, homosexuality, abortion, adolescent problems, preparation for marriage, and extramarital relationships. The author argues for having the capacity to appreciate moral truth and give integrity and purpose to actions which can otherwise become isolated and devoid of meaning and says that this requires a degree of spiritual awareness which many people seem to ignore or don't even possess. This book will be of interest to scholars and researchers of sociology, ethics and moral philosophy.

Morals in the Melting Pot

Edward F. Griffith

First published in 1948
by Methuen & Co. Ltd.

This edition first published in 2024 by Routledge
4 Park Square, Milton Park, Abingdon, Oxon, OX14 4RN

and by Routledge
605 Third Avenue, New York, NY 10017

Routledge is an imprint of the Taylor & Francis Group, an informa business

© 1948 Edward F. Griffith

All rights reserved. No part of this book may be reprinted or reproduced or utilised in any form or by any electronic, mechanical, or other means, now known or hereafter invented, including photocopying and recording, or in any information storage or retrieval system, without permission in writing from the publishers.

Publisher's Note
The publisher has gone to great lengths to ensure the quality of this reprint but points out that some imperfections in the original copies may be apparent.

Disclaimer
The publisher has made every effort to trace copyright holders and welcomes correspondence from those they have been unable to contact.

A Library of Congress record exists under LCCN: 49004675

ISBN: 978-1-032-61128-0 (hbk)
ISBN: 978-1-003-49617-5 (ebk)
ISBN: 978-1-032-80273-2 (pbk)

Book DOI 10.4324/9781003496175

MORALS IN THE MELTING POT

by
EDWARD F. GRIFFITH
M.R.C.S., L.R.C.P.

METHUEN & CO. LTD. LONDON
36 Essex Street, Strand, W.C.2

Originally published by Victor Gollancz, Ltd.
First published (entirely re-written and brought up to date) by Methuen & Co. Ltd.
in 1948

CATALOGUE NO. 3583/U

THIS BOOK IS PRODUCED IN
COMPLETE CONFORMITY WITH THE
AUTHORISED ECONOMY STANDARDS

PRINTED IN GREAT BRITAIN

To
L. A. G. STRONG
in gratitude
for many years of
encouragement and friendship

" To be in love," said the Count, " is to suffer a perpetual torment for the sake of relieving it, from time to time, with a dab of delicious ointment. It is a ridiculous state of affairs, and the only cure for it is to grow old. But you have to grow very old."

ERIC LINKLATER

Private Angelo (Jonathan Cape), 1946

CONTENTS

Chapter I.	The Moral Situation	*Page*	1
II.	Contraception		32
III.	Sex and Religion		47
IV.	Mental Deficiency		58
V.	The Social Problem		73
VI.	Divorce		100
VII.	Getting Married		130
VIII.	Extra-Marital Relationships		140
IX.	Homosexuality		169
X.	Frigidity and Impotence		183
XI.	Abortion		190
XII.	Sterility and Artificial Insemination		195
XIII.	Preparation for Marriage		211
XIV.	Adolescent Problems		231
XV.	" The Wages of Sin "		248
	Epilogue		281
	Index		294

CHAPTER I

THE MORAL SITUATION

THE Canon leaned forward aggressively towards his audience, wagging his finger in condemnation. " Some of you are parents with daughters who are growing up with all the freshness of youth. Are you aware of the temptations that beset them ? There is an evil knowledge abroad—an encouragement of vice disguised as knowledge, a loosening of moral standards and a weakening of moral fibre, due in part at least to the changes wrought by science in a civilisation which has altered more rapidly in the last fifty years than throughout all the preceding nineteen centuries. The dreams our grandfathers dreamed are the commonplaces of to-day. The extraordinary achievements, discoveries and inventions of this age demonstrate how the forces of nature are being harnessed for the benefit or destruction of man. But these advances bring with them new problems and new conditions of life. This is particularly apparent in the realm of social morality. There has been a general speeding up of life during the last fifty years and an increase in nervous tension that was commented upon by Erb as long ago as 1893, in a striking passage.[1] ' The demands on the ability of the individual have enormously increased and he can meet them only by putting forth all his mental powers. The demand for enjoyment has increased in all circles. Unprecedented luxury is displayed by classes hitherto wholly unaccustomed to any such thing ; irreligion, discontent and covetousness are spreading widely through every degree of society. All is hurry and agitation. Night is used for travel, day for business and even " holiday trips " keep the nervous system on the rack. The exhausted nerves seek recuperation in increased stimulation, in highly seasoned pleasures, only thereby to become more exhausted than before. There is a craving for sensuality coupled with a

[1] Freud, "Collected Papers", Vol. II, p. 78.

total disregard of fundamental principles. The theatre captivates the senses and our ears are over-stimulated by incessant music. Even the creative arts turn also by preference to the repellent, the ugly and the suggestive.'

"If this was true then, it is doubly true to-day. I like that bit about 'incessant music'. How often does one visit houses in which the wireless blares forth for hours at a stretch, so that one has to raise one's voice to a scream in order to be heard. But the emotions are being over-stimulated and there are signs that nature is beginning to strike. Even our children are expected to enter this competitive field at an age when all their energies should be used for the purpose of growing into healthy men and women.

"We live in an age of fear, and the books we read, the dances we dance and the amusements we indulge in are, for the most part, an escape from reality. Is it to be wondered at if there is over-emphasis in the sexual sphere? Sex is a strong, imperative urge: and how do we deal with it? Do we control it? Do we repress it? On the contrary, we say that it must be used; that we must express ourselves. And what is the result? Sexual immorality stalking through the land; leaving behind it a cruel trail of disillusionment, remorse and illegitimate children.

"There are people who say that sexual morality is improving, and give as an instance the decline of prostitution; quoting figures to prove that the number of convictions for this offence has decreased within recent years. But is this the right inference to be drawn from these figures? I think not; in fact, I would go so far as to say that I know not. There is an evil far more insidious, far more dangerous, creeping into the homes of *every* section of the community— yes, even into our own homes. And what is that?"

Once more the finger wagged dangerously as the Canon altered his position.

"Our young people—your sons and daughters—have a knowledge of sexual matters far and away beyond anything that we dreamed of in our day. And this knowledge has created a new menace to society; a new menace to the sanctity of marriage; a new menace to the very foundations of family life. I refer, of course, to that product of modern civilisation, the amateur prostitute; an individual far more dangerous and far more devastating than her elder sister. And the manner of her creation—her very existence, in fact—is dependent upon the fact that science has made discoveries which enable us to gratify the desires of the flesh without reaping the rewards thereof. Large numbers of young people are making experiments in sexual experience of so advanced a nature that they are little removed from actual physical union. In many cases pre-marital relationships do occur; indeed, I hesitate to use the term 'pre-marital', for marriage is the last thought that enters the minds of these people. And the result is to be found in our medical consulting-rooms, which, I am given to understand, are thronged with neurotics; with those who have been prematurely awakened and are sexually over-active. Our police courts are filled with an ever-increasing number of sexual offenders, juvenile criminals and couples pleading for separation; whilst our law courts are overcrowded with divorce cases.

"And how does this affect the nation as a whole? Not only is the moral standard falling, but we are told that the population, which now numbers about forty million, will almost certainly decline. If the present conditions continue, the population of this country may be reduced to twenty millions or less in a hundred years. That there has been improvement recently I am well aware, but I believe that authoritative opinion is not convinced that this is likely to be of lasting value. That the problem is urgent can be better understood when we realise that whereas there should be about four children in every family to maintain our present population, there are, in fact, only one or two, and those very often coming from parents whose health and background are of little value to the nation.

"What is the reason for this state of affairs? The causes are numerous and varied. We seem to be suffering from some kind of social malaise which, by encouraging luxury and amusement, favours fewer children. There are those who say that if the conditions of life were improved there would be more children. But this I believe to be a false argument: it is precisely among those sections of the community who have a high standard of life that family limitation occurs most drastically.

"Then again, many people are genuinely worried about the future of civilisation and feel doubtful as to the wisdom of bringing children into this troublesome world. That these people have a genuine sense of responsibility, however misguided, must be admitted, and we must respect their attitude. They do at least think. But they are wrong—terribly wrong—and are essentially selfish. I wonder if there is a single person in this audience who would rather have never been born.

"Others say that food, clothing and education are so expensive that they cannot afford to have children, but talk of this sort is frequently a cloak for more selfishness. It entirely depends upon what we mean by 'afford'. Some people with incomes of well over £1,000 a year cannot 'afford' more than one young hopeful. But they can run a car, keep a week-end cottage, own a small yacht, keep a couple of servants—if they can get them these days—and so on. Theirs is a selfish existence, and retribution will come to them eventually in the shape of a troublesome, over-fed, over-pampered, over-emotionalised child, rebellious of parental authority and sapped of all vigour by a variety of complexes."

The speaker paused, and Dr. Hansell, sitting next to his old friend Mrs. Bellamy, shifted uneasily in his chair. The scene was one of the evening meetings of the Society for Human Betterment which was holding a post-war Conference in Wagstaff College, conveniently situated in attractive country near London and usually devoted to the training of teachers. Now, however, its large hall was crammed with about two hundred people of various ages and sexes who seemed anxious to acquire as much knowledge as possible of the social problems which six years of war had done nothing to abate. The Chairman of the Conference, Lady Mary Burr, J.P., was conducting the proceedings with her usual cheerful ability, and Canon Heathcott, a tall, ascetic-looking parson, was the principal speaker at this particular session.

"I thought you said this fellow was very provocative,"

THE MORAL SITUATION

Dr. Hansell whispered to Mrs. Bellamy, who smiled back at him and murmured, " You wait."

" What are the remedies suggested for this state of affairs ? " Canon Heathcott continued, coming nearer to the edge of the platform. " Reduction of income tax; taxes on bachelors; marriage allowances; encouragement of parental responsibility; cheaper houses; higher wages, and more domestic help are some of them. But will these things get to the root of the evil ? Did Mussolini increase the Italian population by all his bribes and promises ? No ! He did not. And why not ? Why are these things ineffectual ? Because we are suffering from a moral disease rooted in irreligion and selfishness. The movement that is afoot to-day to popularise the artificial interference with births is leading to race suicide and the abominable murder of the unborn. The practice of these noxious methods reached unprecedented heights during the war and is still increasing. It is bolstered up by a section of the community which should know better. Birth control is sapping the very life-blood of the nation, destroying our self control, outraging the sanctity of our homes, violating the honour of our daughters and decimating our population. How else is it that people marry and live for years in childlessness ? Do these people exercise that natural self-control which is the only rightful way of managing these personal matters ? Are they incapable of creating new life ? Of course not. Birth control has created a social and economic problem of immense importance and one that is likely to destroy the whole fabric of the nation. Unfortunately it is practised most effectively amongst that section of the community from whom we should expect the production of a large number of healthy, virile children: among the thinking people of the community, the professional classes, business people, doctors, lawyers and so on. But marriage without children is a mockery. Children are the purpose of marriage and the inspiration of family life. Refusal to have them is a wicked misuse of the natural powers of man and, if persisted in, will upset the whole structure of national life and even lead to race suicide. The Prayer Book tells us that marriage was ordained for ' the procreation of children to be brought up in the fear and nurture of the Lord ', but young people seem to look upon the marriage relationship as something which can be broken at the least provocation, and do not pay much attention to the Lord.

"Christian civilisation has been built upon the sanctity of the marriage bond; destroy that and you destroy the very foundations of society. I would go so far as to say that the whole conception of parenthood is being lowered, and the minds of our people perverted, by the noxious sensuality bred by this fascinatingly immoral doctrine of birth control.

"But this is not all. I am told on good authority that the use of these noxious contrivances gives rise to pathological conditions in women. Those who marry with the deliberate intention of preventing children often find that, when their artificial methods are discarded, conception cannot occur. Could anything be more devastating?

"I know that it is often stated by the supporters of this movement that the economic condition of the poorer sections of the community makes some limitation of their families necessary, and with this point of view I have much sympathy, although I am inclined to think it would be wiser to alter the economic conditions than to prevent the coming of children. What is even more unsatisfactory, however, is that it is just these very people who cannot use the methods prescribed and will not be bothered with all the troublesome and disgusting processes involved. The woman's health should, of course, be considered, and if the husband is unable to control his sexual urge—if he is emotionally unbalanced, in fact—the wife should refuse union. Birth control, by removing every check to licence, makes the position of these women infinitely worse; they are reduced to the level of the brothel. The only proper birth control is the practice of continence. This is morally right. Artificial methods are morally wrong. There is a profound value in the practice of restraint and abstinence. I repeat that the object of the sexual urge is procreation; if you frustrate that object you are committing sin.

"I am told that, from a medical point of view, sexual union in marriage has a general tonic effect upon the woman, through the absorption of the beneficial products from the man. This is lost by the use of these abominable articles.

"Finally, let me take another point. The sale and distribution of these articles have reached alarming proportions. I read recently, in a book devoted to the dissemination of these immoral ideas, that the sale of one particular article in America has reached the colossal figure of over a million a day. The towns of this country are strewn with objectionable shops which not only display their disgusting products in the most flagrant manner, but sell a type of literature which, by pandering to the emotions of the people, is undermining their moral fibre. What are our authorities doing that they permit the open sale and display of such degrading nostrums? These are the things that are destroying our national life, undermining our morality, and perverting the minds of our young people. Let us not shirk the issue. If we are to prevent the further fall of our population; if we are to save our souls and indeed preserve the fundamentals of family life, we must reorganise our social morality, abolish this insidious propaganda, encourage the desire for parenthood and create an ideal of married life based upon mutual love and affection, toleration and self-sacrifice, and, above all, self-control. If we do none of these things; if we continue in happy complacency, our nation will lose those qualities which have stood us in such good stead in the past and enabled us to venture into the farthest corners of the earth and make our name respected throughout the world. We shall become decadent as those other great civilisations, which have long since departed and lie moulding in the dust of antiquity, have become decadent; destroyed by their own moral perversity."

Considerable applause greeted the Canon as he retired to his chair and began mopping a somewhat heated brow.

"Phew!" said Dr. Hansell. "You were certainly right, Meg. I haven't listened to such a clever distortion of facts for a very long time. A most insidious doctrine, full of half-truths bolstered up by an excessive play on the emotions. I had hoped for something better from a man of his knowledge and sincerity. What a pity it is that so many people muddle up their science and religion so appallingly. Aren't they going to have any questions?"

"Oh yes, I expect so; they usually do. Are you going to ask any?"

"No, I would prefer to meet the Canon later on when we shall have more time. He needs more drastic treatment than a few rapid questions fired at him during a public meeting if he is to see the error of his ways. Ah!"

A middle-aged woman with closely cut grey hair and dressed in a well-cut coat and skirt had risen to her feet.

"There is so much in what you have said with which I find myself in disagreement," she said, smiling quietly, "that I scarcely know where to begin. I hardly think you will convince young people of the error of their ways—if they are in error—by merely condemning their behaviour out of hand as you have done this evening. Some of your statements are open to serious criticism by anyone who has studied these matters with a fair degree of impartiality. I will mention but two. You suggest that the use of contraceptives does harm to the female genital tract and that beneficial male products are absorbed by the woman. Before making such a statement I think you should give chapter and verse for your source of information because, whilst it is true that some authorities do make these assertions, you will find that they are often made by people who do not approve of the use of contraceptives on religious grounds, as indeed appears to be your own attitude, and whose views must, unfortunately, be suspect on that account by anyone who is considering the problem scientifically and dispassionately. If you will refer to the October number of the *Eugenics Review* of 1935, you will find there an open letter from the medical committee of the National Birth Control Society [1] to one of the chief exponents of these doctrines which the committee regarded as scientifically inaccurate. The letter was published in this fashion because the individual concerned refused to answer personal letters addressed to him. So far as I am aware there has never been a reply. There is much evidence—overwhelming evidence, in fact—to show that such statements are completely inaccurate, and if

[1] Now the Family Planning Association.

you are interested in the matter and care to apply to the committee in question, I have no doubt they will supply you with much valuable and detailed information.[1]

"Secondly you suggest that contraceptives cause sterility. Here again there is no evidence that properly applied contraceptives cause sterility. That people who are infertile use contraceptives and then, when they want a child, discontinue the use of the contraceptives and, finding themselves unable to conceive, blame the contraceptives, is of course a common occurrence, but who is to say that they were not sterile from the first day of their marriage? The incidence of sterility amongst married couples is far more common than the public is aware, and the investigation of these cases is extremely difficult, and by no means perfectly developed as yet. There is sufficient evidence, however, to show that those who use adequate contraceptive methods have more live births than those who do not and, in addition, there is evidence from the women's welfare clinics to show that the majority of healthy women become pregnant almost directly they discontinue their contraceptive methods. As long ago as 1930 the Walworth Clinic showed that out of 116 women seen there who had practised contraception for times varying from one to five years, 113 became pregnant immediately on stopping the method.[2] I would suggest therefore that you do your cause more harm than good by making such statements."

This speech was greeted by applause from various parts of the hall.

"I would not like you to think that I make these statements without due thought and consideration," Canon Heathcott said in reply. "My information is largely derived from the publications of the League of National Life—a body of some standing, I believe——"

"It was to a former President of that Society that the letter was addressed," the lady said, rising again for a moment.

A general laugh, in which the Canon joined, reduced the

[1] See also Griffith, Edward F., "Sex in Everyday Life", p. 308, where the matter is discussed at length.
[2] Malleson, Dr. Joan, "The Principles of Contraception".

emotional tension, whilst the Chairman hurriedly called on another speaker, who discoursed at some length on the value of vitamins in the treatment of various female ailments.

"I should like to cross swords with you over one small point," a man said from the back of the hall. "You said in the course of your remarks that science, by perfecting the use of contraceptives, enabled women to 'gratify the needs of the flesh without reaping the rewards thereof'. Those were your exact words because I wrote them down at the time. By this I take it you mean to suggest that the only proper purpose of sexual activity is the production of children, and that any other use is low or immoral, and, in any case, pandering to the less dignified aspects of man's personality. But do you seriously suggest that every time a man performs the sex act with his wife the result should be a child and that the couple should always be desirous of achieving pregnancy? Reduced to its simplest form such an argument means that a man and woman need only have connection about once a year, because there is no reason why a healthy woman should not become pregnant after one act of sexual intercourse. In that case the couple would only need to have eight connections in as many years to more than satisfy your population demands?"

"If you care to put it that way," the Canon said, "then I must agree that that is what I do mean, although I see no reason why they should not have connection during the early months of the pregnancy, as I am given to understand that this will have no harmful effect upon the woman."

"But you are illogical," the man said, springing to his feet. "If the woman is pregnant, why have connection? There is no longer any purpose in it according to your argument; indeed I judge it to be a mere gratification of the flesh which you condemn so wholeheartedly."

"In that case I should say that as soon as the woman is aware of her condition union should cease and abstention should be practised," the Canon replied.

The questioner persisted. "And you really mean to say," he said, "that you believe this intense urge was given to man for the sole purpose of being used once or twice a year for procreative purposes?"

"That is how it is used by animals," the Canon retorted, "and I see no reason why we should not behave at least as well as they do."

"But that is just the point," the man exclaimed. "We are not animals. We are human beings with souls and minds which ought to raise us far above the animals so that the sex relationship becomes the expression of all that is highest and best in man, and not a mere copulating activity. As such it becomes of profound psychological importance to the life of man. Would you not accept that?"

"Oh, yes, of course I recognise its psychological value," the Canon said, "but I see no reason why that should not be expressed by the couple in the way I have indicated. Besides, there are other ways of achieving psychological harmony; one must learn to exercise control."

"But why condemn sex activity all the time? You and people like you degrade the whole subject. And as for your vaunted control, you are merely encouraging licence. You——"

At this point the Chairman rapped on the table.

"I'm afraid you must continue your argument afterwards," she said sweetly. "The subject is a most interesting one, but there are others wishing to speak, and we cannot remain here all night. You have a question, I think," she said, pointing to a red-faced little man sitting on the other side of the room.

"Well, it really follows on from the last question," the little man said. "You suggested, sir, that a man is emotionally unbalanced if he is unable to control his sexual urge. I really must protest against such a statement. It seems that you think a man can go for months at a time without exercising his sexual function, but I must remind you that we are talking of marriage, and not celibacy. I would suggest that the sexual urge in man works rhythmically much in the same way as it does in women. This rhythm varies in different people, being more intense in some than in others. Satisfy it by adequate sexual expression at weekly or fortnightly intervals, as the case may be, and the individual is likely to be emotionally healthy and stable, other things being equal. Dam it back and give it no adequate outlet, and he becomes emotionally unstable. Thus the course you recommend will eventually lead to the very condition of unbalance that you are trying to avoid. I agree with the last speaker, sir, and deprecate the tendency I find in your remarks to reduce the sex act to a mere biological activity."

" Good point that," Dr. Hansell said to Mrs. Bellamy.

" Your point is an interesting one," the Canon said, " and I recognise its force. Naturally, as a priest, I do not regard sexual activity in the way you suggest."

" You may not in theory, but that is what it comes to in practice, you know."

Again the hammer sounded. " I am sorry," the Chairman said, " but you have made your point and must continue your discussion at a later date. We have over-run our time as it is. Next, please."

A few more less exciting questions brought the meeting to an end, and Dr. Hansell and Mrs. Bellamy made their way to a smaller room for the usual coffee and bun. Here they ran into Canon Heathcott and the Chairman.

" You two should know each other," Lady Burr exclaimed, introducing them. " Dr. Hansell is going to speak later on in the week, Canon, as I expect you know."

" I couldn't help wondering as I listened to you talking," the doctor said after they had exchanged greetings, " whether your views about birth control were gleaned at first hand—whether, in fact, you had ever visited a clinic to find out what is really being done there; the type of person who visits these places and the conditions they are up against."

" I must admit that I have not the first-hand knowledge of which you speak," Canon Heathcott said, " but I have read a great deal on the subject, including one or two of your own works, doctor."

A twinkle came into the Canon's eyes as he delivered this little thrust.

Dr. Hansell laughed. " Then I can only say that I'm sorry my pen has not been more persuasive. If, however, whilst you are here, you would like to visit a clinic I should be happy to take you to the one I run. Indeed, I have to go there tomorrow evening. Why don't you come along? I expect the Chairman will forgive us if we miss a session."

" Well, I hardly think —— ! "

" Oh, but you must go, my dear Canon," Lady Burr exclaimed. " There is nothing like first-hand information. I'm sure you will be converted. I took the Chairman of our Health Committee to our local clinic when we were trying to get a grant from the local authority, and he completely changed his opinion. You shouldn't miss the opportunity." She smiled sweetly at the Canon and patted him on the shoulder.

" Besides," she added as an afterthought, " it will do you good."

" Well, if you think I need doing good to —— ! "

" I do, most certainly. And I shall be most interested to hear your views when you return."

" Very good. I shall be very pleased to come with you, doctor," the Canon said. " And now I think I must go to bed."

" Well, really, Lady Burr," Dr. Hansell said as they watched the Canon disappear, " I think you managed that very well."

" There is plenty of good stuff in that man," Mrs. Bellamy said, " if only he will get his facts straight. I thought the questions were good, didn't you ? And I agreed most wholeheartedly with that woman. I wonder who she is—some doctor, I imagine."

" Dr. Alice Minor," Dr. Hansell said. " I know her well ; she runs an excellent practice in Bournemouth or Torquay or some such place as that."

" She is one of our speakers," Lady Burr said, " but I forget for the moment what it is she is going to talk about."

" Sterility and artificial insemination," the doctor said, after looking at his programme. " Ah, yes, she should be interesting."

. . . . .

Canon Heathcott was as good as his word, and joined Dr. Hansell in the drawing-room next day for a cup of tea before motoring to the clinic.

" We needn't leave for a quarter of an hour or so," the

doctor said as he poured out some tea. "It's good of you to come, Canon. I think I can promise you an interesting evening."

"I'm sure you will," the Canon said, as he sat down in a large armchair. "I'm one of those people who believe that the problem of social morality is one of the more pressing issues of the day. As I said last night, there's an insidious propaganda abroad that is undermining our social structure. I cannot believe that the widespread discussion of sexual subjects which is so prevalent amongst young people to-day is either healthy or desirable."

"But surely it's better than the veiled innuendoes with which most of us were brought up."

"I'm not so sure. We at least had some standards to which we could conform; nowadays there are none."

"Largely because people are thinking and reading more," Dr. Hansell said. "They are dissatisfied with the old conventional standards, which have very little relationship to modern conditions."

"That may be so, but there are fundamental truths which the younger generation have cast aside. As a result, they have no sheet anchor. This is particularly apparent in the realm of social morality. Matters will not be improved until there is a revival of spiritual feeling—a return to moral principles. Of course I appreciate the difficulties of the situation. We clergy are often accused of narrow-mindedness, I know, but I don't think the criticism is altogether fair. Many of us are only too willing to learn, but we can't be expected to surrender all the ground; there must be an equal willingness on the part of those who differ from us to concede something. I am particularly disturbed by the widespread knowledge of birth control. I cannot help feeling that it is undermining the whole principle of family life."

Dr. Hansell smiled. "So I gathered from your remarks last night," he said. "And that brings us to a fundamental question—the relationship between science and religion. Perhaps it might be helpful to find out how far we can agree on that point."

"I think that would be a very good idea," the Canon said, filling his pipe. "What are your views?"

"With much of what you said last night I am in entire agreement. That our moral standards are altering is obvious, and there can be little doubt that there is a general speeding up of the emotional mechanism leading to much nervous tension. The war has merely accentuated a situation which has been developing for years. The increased interest in sex matters which you seem to condemn appears to me to be not only inevitable but, on the whole, healthy. A critical searchlight is being turned on to such matters as marriage, divorce, prostitution and abortion; and the unaccustomed illumination doesn't reveal a very pretty sight. If I say that we aren't tackling the problems of social morality in a really constructive spirit, you will probably agree with me, but if I go on to suggest that this is largely because the Church—organised religion—call it what you like, will not recognise the essential relationship between science and religion, I wonder whether you would still agree."

"How do you mean?"

Dr. Hansell began walking up and down the room.

"The man in the street," he said, "is intensely interested in modern scientific advancement, but the upholders of orthodox religion are frightened of it, because science makes men think for themselves, which is contrary to the authoritative position which religion assumes. Thus, to many people, there seems to be an inevitable antagonism between religion and science. Yet, in reality, there should be no conflict between them. Neither can stand still; both are progressive and evolutionary. The discoveries of the one must be fitted into the fundamental beliefs of the other."

"That may be so," the Canon said, "although I think we shall have difficulty on agreeing about the fundamentals. You must agree that our traditions are being overthrown and our moral beliefs no longer accepted."

"I do agree—because the traditions are outgrown and the moral beliefs are not really moral," Dr. Hansell replied. "Isn't it possible that the retreat from organised religion is simply due to the excessive emphasis placed upon traditional teaching? Aren't we inclined to confuse theology with religion? Most people aren't particularly interested in traditional teaching nor yet in doctrine; but they are certainly concerned with the practical application of religious principles to everyday life, both personal and national. And that doesn't mean that they haven't got a religious sense, or that they don't feel the need of a religious basis to their lives."

"I can agree with you there," the Canon said. "I believe that the majority of people find a purely materialistic interpretation of life unsatisfactory because they recognise, consciously or unconsciously, that we all possess, in the highest part of our nature, something which we may call spiritual or religious feeling; it is part of our make-up. When people say that they don't believe in this or that creed, they are really rejecting a particular form of religion rather than religion itself, just as when we say that we don't believe in some particular scientific theory we are not rejecting a belief in science, but only in that particular presentation of it. A materialistic interpretation of life only provides an imperfect outline. There is something deeper and higher in all of us which concerns the personality and finds expression in ideals of truth, beauty and justice."

"True, but it's just because these ideals seem to be lacking from orthodox religion that people are so dissatisfied. They feel that the Church is entirely concerned with the subjection of the individual to a certain code of moral behaviour."

"But that is inevitable," the Canon said. "There are very definite standards of behaviour which Christians have to obey."

"I know, but those standards don't always give any weight to the discoveries of science, and yet a belief in science by no means rules out a belief in a spiritual existence."

"Certainly not."

"Then why can't the Church accept the discoveries of science in the realm of social morality as part of the divine interpretation of God's spirit, and act accordingly; teaching people constructively and insisting on the development of a moral order that is just and merciful? If you liken the religious experience of the last two thousand years to a Roman road, with sound foundations, but with its surface all cluttered up with rubble, doesn't our present task consist in removing the rubble of dogmatic traditionalism and resurfacing the foundations with the constructive discoveries of science?"

"I like your simile, Doctor, but I foresee great difficulties."

"I daresay, but doesn't the problem present a challenge to the Church to do some really creative work? If only she would have the courage to come out whole-heartedly in favour of real moral reformation based on a sound and widespread system of sex education, instead of tinkering about with moral platitudes, I believe she would find an immediate response on the part of the ordinary individual. If she doesn't face the situation, I'm afraid she'll find that society will take matters into its own hands. If that occurs I doubt whether anyone can say what sort of moral code will eventually emerge, or on what ethic it will be based."

"I think Christian principles will always hold the field. The foundations of your Roman road will remain."

"Well, let us hope so," Dr. Hansell said, sitting down on the edge of his chair and beginning to fill his pipe.

"You are a bit hard on the Church, you know," Canon Heathcott said. "I should say that much good work has been done, and is still being done, behind the scenes. Many church people are well aware of these problems and have endeavoured to tackle them in a constructive spirit. Listen to this statement, for instance, issued by a conference on Christian relationships as long ago as 1924. 'We regard sex as a divine endowment of the human race, to be used, not to be feared. The satisfaction that it yields may be amongst the highest that can be experienced by human beings, involving not only physical and emotional delight, but the further bliss of the mutual self-surrender of the married lovers, and the self-satisfying and self-realising joys of parenthood. In this way sex ministers to the highest moral and religious development of mankind.'[1] Then again in 1930 the Lambeth Conference said: 'Sex is a God-given factor in the life of mankind, and its functions are therefore essentially noble and creative. Correspondingly

[1] "The Relation of the Sexes", Vol. IV, p. 20. Conference on Christian, Political and Economic Relations to Citizenship (C.O.P.E.C.), Birmingham, 1924.

great is the responsibility for the right use of it.' There is nothing wrong with that, surely?"

"Nothing at all, except that they are mere statements of opinion by certain sections of the Church, and do not appear to be implemented by the Church as a whole."

"Perhaps not, but you will agree that they are progressive and healthy?"

"Oh yes, certainly. I only wish we could get a few more like them. Whether you like it or not, sex and sin are synonymous in the minds of many people, and this attitude is fostered by the Church services we have to listen to every day."

"How so?"

"Well, all this business about 'In sin did my mother conceive me'."

"Ah, but that is a misinterpretation of the word 'sin'," the Canon said. "The Commission on Christian Doctrine in the Church of England had something to say about that in 1938. 'The belief that the process of human generation is in itself sinful, or that sin is conveyed to the offspring because of any sinfulness in the process, is not a necessary part of the doctrine of original sin, and we are agreed in repudiating it. We believe that it is wholly unwarranted, being part of a profoundly unsatisfactory view of sex and of sexual relations.'"[1]

"But that is only another opinion, however eminent the members of the Commission may have been. Nothing is done by the official Church to implement these ideas. The Mothers' Union can scarcely be said to hold them, and what about the Baptismal Service: 'Dearly beloved, forasmuch as all men are conceived and born in sin'? What do you think of that?"

The Canon looked at Dr. Hansell for a moment, and they both began to laugh.

"It is pretty awful, I admit," the Canon said.

"Awful! It is a disgrace to the intelligence of any right-thinking person. The perpetuation of these ideas—and they are to be found in one form or another throughout the whole of church worship and teaching—do the Church an

[1] P. 63 of the Commission's Report.

immense amount of harm. It is no use trying to say that it all means something else; to the ordinary man in the street it means what it says, and the sooner it is all done away with, the better."

"Well, it isn't quite as easy as all that," the Canon said. "The only point I wished to make was that the Church is doing something. The more advanced thinkers will have a good deal of converting to do amongst their own flock before agreement can be reached and definite action taken. Besides, the trouble isn't confined to the Church authorities as such. I should say that much of the opposition to progressive thought comes from people in authoritative positions in local government, or amongst the 'high-ups' who have rigid opinions based on old or inaccurate knowledge of which they are unable to rid themselves. They are never willing to admit they are wrong."

"True! And where sex is concerned, their actions are largely regulated by fear of upsetting someone and stirring up a local rumpus, or having questions asked in Parliament."

"Yes, you are right there," the Canon said, laughing. "Authority is almost always fearful, and therefore tends to sit on the fence."

"Do you know that there are still many booksellers up and down the country who won't allow a single book on sex to be placed on their shelves, and yet their shops are full of a most pernicious type of literature about film stars, gangsters and so on which are sold at a very cheap price."

"But you can't prevent that sort of stuff being sold," Canon Heathcott said.

"Perhaps not, but they might at least have the courage to display and sell some decent literature on these matters."

"And let the two fight it out together, I suppose," the Canon said. "I'm afraid the gangster would win."

Dr. Hansell laughed. "I'm not so sure," he said. "People want decent scientific information—young people in particular—and they ought to be able to get it easily."

"I don't see why the Church should accept every discovery of science with open arms," the Canon said. "These things must be tested by time and experience. After all, that is how the scientists work. They too are always changing their ideas. We must go slowly and prove the worth of some of these things."

"Very true," Dr. Hansell said, beginning to pace up and down the room again. "It all boils down to this," he said. "Both religion and science are necessary for a true understanding of life. Scientific discoveries may be used morally or immorally in the sense that gas may be used for the benefit or destruction of man. What we do with these facts depends upon ourselves. The trouble is that man has not developed a sufficient sense of moral responsibility to manage either his life or his own scientific discoveries; he has run away with himself."

"That's very true."

"When you relate all this to the problem under discussion—namely, sexual morality—I think you must agree that the Church is still unwilling to admit that some of the modern discoveries concerning our sex lives can be used beneficially. If it is true, as Professor Macmurray points out, that religion is concerned with the emotions, is it not also true that the Church has always endeavoured to suppress the emotions by ignoring the physical and over-emphasising the spiritual? Consequently, sexual emotion has been condemned, and a sense of guilt has been firmly implanted in our minds whenever we have to deal with sex matters. One of the main problems to-day is to rid ourselves of this guilt sense, and replace it by a belief in the creative purpose of sex in our lives. Would you agree with me so far?"

"Yes, I think so."

"Good. Now, there was a time when this desire to subject the body reached such a pitch that its very sight was looked upon as a vice, and, as Havelock Ellis points out in his 'Selected Essays', the cult of dirt became a virtue. He tells us that sex was regarded as a destructive force ready to crush the soul [1] and repression became an essential ingredient of the Christian character. But whenever you get repression you develop licence or abnormality; we only reach a true balance in life through moderation and freedom."

"Yes, I agree," the Canon said. "The Church has done harm there, I fear."

[1] "Selected Essays: St. Francis and Others" (Everyman's Library).

"Only recently," the doctor continued, "have we come to see that a healthy and clean body are essential for a contented mind; that mental, physical and spiritual health are necessary for perfect development, to which science and religion should make an equal contribution. If a man's moral outlook is warped, his spiritual life goes by the board. If his physical make-up is distorted in some way, his emotional life is affected, as has been well shown by Adler. I fail to see how you, as a parson, can avoid a consideration of the physical when dealing with spiritual matters, any more than I, as a doctor, can avoid a consideration of spiritual factors when dealing with the physical condition of my patients. Spirit and body are so closely allied that we need a far greater co-operation between doctor and parson."

"There I entirely agree," Canon Heathcott replied warmly. "And I think the rank and file of Church people can show a very good record when it comes to dealing with problems of social morality."

"I agree that they have done a great deal, but I think they have still a long way to go. They still won't face facts. Take this problem of birth control, for instance, which you condemned so roundly last night. Many people, both church and lay, won't find out what are the underlying principles of contraception." Dr. Hansell broke off and looked at his watch. "I say, we shall have to be going, or we'll be late."

The Canon got up and went towards the door. "I'm quite ready," he said. "We can continue the discussion in the car."

.   .   .   .   .

Having settled themselves comfortably, the doctor resumed the discussion. "Where were we? Oh yes—birth control."

"It is an extremely difficult subject to think about dispassionately," the Canon said. "Of course, I am aware that family limitation has been practised by most civilisations in one form or another, but I cannot help feeling that the modern attitude towards the subject is based on insecure foundations. I'm not sure, for instance, that the abolition of the large family, with all its potential influence for good and its capacity for training people in unselfishness and service, is not hostile to the individual and the State and will not, in the long run, do us greater disservice than the many evils of our present system."

"But, my dear Canon; the advocates of contraception don't wish to abolish the large family. They would like to see a social order in which families of four to six healthy children were the rule rather than the exception; we only wish to put the whole affair on a constructive basis. The small-family system has come about as the result of economic conditions, not moral ones, and contraception is only the means by which this is achieved. By all means let a woman have a dozen children if she wishes, provided she and her husband come of good stock and her health does not suffer in the process, and provided further that the State sees to it that there are adequate facilities for upbringing and education."

The Canon laughed. "You are demanding a good deal."

"You mentioned 'family limitation' just now," Dr. Hansell said. "I wonder if it has occurred to you that there are only three ways of limiting families. You can destroy the child after birth by such methods as infanticide; you can destroy it by abortion after it is conceived but before it is born, or you can prevent the sperm from ever reaching the egg. This latter is an entirely different principle from the others, and is the basis on which modern contraceptive technique is founded. There is obviously a great difference between the destruction of a fertilised cell and the prevention of fertilisation."

"Yes, I realise that."

"You referred to birth control the other night as though it meant birth prevention, but, as a matter of fact, it means nothing of the sort. Birth spacing might explain its meaning better. The suggestion is not to abolish children, but to space them properly."

"But it can be used selfishly so as to prevent the coming of children."

"So can abstention, for that matter."

"True. I hadn't thought of that."

"Can't we agree that it is the motive behind the action which counts rather than the action itself? If the motive is wrong, any form of sex relationship is really wrong. If selfish considerations are uppermost in people's minds and there is no consideration for the other, the motive must be wrong."

"Yes, I can agree with that. Even abstention could be put to unworthy ends."

"Quite so. Can't we also agree that there are two purposes in marriage—reproduction and mutual satisfaction?"

"I think that there is considerable danger of people avoiding the reproductive purpose and merely enjoying themselves selfishly."

"Perhaps so; but can't we agree on the principle?"

"Yes, I think we can."

"Well, then, you cannot really mean what you said in your lecture, about reproduction being the only purpose of marriage."

"It's the most important purpose."

"Yes, but is it the only one?"

"No! I agree that the other has its place—indeed, the Church has always insisted on it—but it must not be abused. You see, I feel very strongly that if people have a sex relationship at all, they should be willing to take the consequences. If they are not willing, they should abstain from any intercourse."

"Yes, that is what you said last night in answer to one of the questions, but surely you are subjecting them to a very unnatural strain by so doing, and are at once going back on the admission you have just made that coitus is valuable as a means of satisfaction quite apart from the reproductive aspect. Indeed, I would go farther than that, and say that it is a necessary part of the development of the personality; it is a means of emotional release and psychological adjustment."

"I am willing to accept that now, and therefore find myself in a dilemma. I am forced to the conclusion that the practice of coitus interruptus is the best way out of the impasse."

"But you are illogical, Canon. You start off by saying

that coitus should never occur except when children are wanted, and you end up by saying that a man can have a sex relationship without the intention of creating a child; because that is what you imply if you allow the practice of coitus interruptus, which is designed solely for the prevention of pregnancy."

"I think it would be wiser to abstain; but I realise that the flesh is weak, to use an everyday phrase, and that one must legislate for that contingency."

"But that isn't a very good reason, and you were taken up on it last night. Aren't you really dodging the issue? Either coitus is good for its own sake or it is bad. I feel that this is a fundamental point about which you must make up your mind. After all, you agreed a little while ago that it was bad to repress the emotions and that there was something good and valuable in the sex life."

"Yes, I do; but I think that by admitting this fact—broadcasting it, as it were—we are running a very grave risk of being misunderstood, and are opening the door to considerable abuse."

"But the door is wide open as it is. You surely don't suppose that the average couple practise abstention, do you? If they don't use some contraceptive, they practise coitus interruptus and persuade themselves that it is a safe method, whereas in reality it is very unreliable. Isn't it possible for us to agree that, except for a small minority, whom we will consider in a moment, abstention and coitus interruptus are not to be recommended?"

"I scarcely think——"

Dr. Hansell held up his hand. "One moment, please. Let me explain myself more fully. Abstention is not really a birth-control method at all, because coitus cannot occur, whereas all real contraceptive methods presuppose that coitus does occur. Quite apart from all that, however, abstention is an impracticable method for the great majority of people, owing to variations in sex needs. What is perfectly possible for some people is a practical impossibility for others. Besides, it doesn't permit a free relationship between the couple and is liable to set up a severe strain on one or both partners."

"I understand that, and am willing to concede that point. Nevertheless, I don't think the method should be entirely disparaged; it has its place in the social structure and is of use to many couples."

"I don't wish to disparage it; merely to indicate its limitations. If two people find that it doesn't lead to undue strain, then I see no reason why they shouldn't practise it, although I think they are missing a great deal in life and will regret their decision later on. However, I will grant its possibility for certain couples."

"Very good."

"Now let us consider coitus interruptus for a moment, since it is a method which is still widely practised and was, at one time, universally recommended. It has several grave objections. It doesn't prevent conception, as is proved by the numberless women who have had large families and have always had connection in that way; it doesn't provide the woman with that normal satisfaction which we have agreed upon as being desirable, nor does it encourage a really free relationship between the couple, because the woman is always afraid of becoming pregnant and the man is keyed up to restrain himself the whole time. This tends to bring the act to a rapid conclusion, which is unsatisfactory for both partners. Finally, its constant practice often leads to the development of an unhealthy condition in the woman's sex organs, owing to the fact that the tension which she normally experiences during the sex relationship is not relieved, as in the case of the man."

"Is that so? I admit that I hadn't realised that point," the Canon said.

"It is really quite obvious when you come to think about it, and is simply a question of physiology. When any organ in the body is used, it requires and receives more blood in order to enable it to do this extra work. Many people tend to forget that the female sex organs, when they are used, must receive more blood, although they readily accept the fact in so far as the male is concerned. It is essential that this blood should be returned eventually into the general circulation after the organ has fulfilled its function; the engorgement must be relieved, otherwise an unhealthy condition of over-engorgement will eventually develop. This relief of engorgement and tension is brought about by the orgasm. The better and more satisfactory the orgasm the greater the relief of tension—both physical and emotional. Hence the great importance of the orgasm from a physiological point of view. Coitus interruptus, by interfering with this mechanism, usually prevents the full expression of the female orgasm and the consequent release of tension, thus having a bad effect on the female organs."

"I see."

"In order to be perfectly fair, however," Dr. Hansell continued, "one must admit that a very small proportion of couples do seem to practise the method satisfactorily; the woman doesn't become pregnant and does derive proper satisfaction. But such people are usually practised lovers. I think you must agree, therefore, that, generally speaking, the method doesn't provide a true expression of sex feeling. Indeed, it is one of the few conditions about which you will find most doctors in agreement, and you must admit that it is a rare thing to find the medical profession agreeing about anything."

Canon Heathcott laughed. "Are they worse than the parsons?"

"Oh, I think so!"

"Is it really true that there are many women who do not experience sex feeling by this method?" the Canon asked. "I have often seen it stated, and have been told so on occasions by women themselves, but I've never been able to convince myself of the truth of the statement."

"I don't think there can be any doubt about it," Dr. Hansell replied. "The percentage is very high. You see, sensation should coincide in both partners, but if they are bound to separate at the critical moment, the woman is naturally left in a state of tension which cannot then be relieved normally, and that is bad."

"I see. But if we rule out both abstention and coitus interruptus, we are forced to consider the use of some appliance."

"That is so. We will discuss them when we get to the clinic, if you don't mind. There is, however, one other method to be mentioned, and that is the " safe period ".

"Ah, yes. I had forgotten that. It is advocated by many people, I believe."

"That is so, but it too possesses several serious objections, one of which is that coitus has to be regulated by the calendar, and, in many cases, can only occur when the woman is least desirous of having a physical relationship and therefore least likely to derive real satisfaction. Besides, it takes several months of careful record-keeping before a woman can determine her own ' safe period ' accurately, and even then is liable to be upset by illness or emotional disturbances. The method is welcomed by many people, notably the Roman Catholic Church, because it allows normal coitus to occur with a reasonable chance of pregnancy not following the act, and without using any appliance."

"I see. It is a pity it isn't more accurate. Perhaps scientists will find out more about it."

"Perhaps, but I doubt if it will ever become really reliable. All one can say at the moment is that in most women there may be some days when they are less likely to become pregnant, but that is quite different from saying that there are days when they cannot become pregnant."

"Yes, I see that."

"The chief interest in its acceptance by the Roman Catholic Church lies in the fact that, by admitting its practice, the Church acknowledges that coitus can be beneficial in itself, quite apart from any question of reproduction. This is a distinct advance from their earlier and more uncompromising position. As a matter of fact it is only in the use of appliances or chemicals that there remains any real difference between the Roman Catholic point of view and that advocated by the upholders of what I may term ' scientific contraception '."

"But the safe period is based upon scientific findings."

"Exactly. And if the Roman Catholics will admit the use of science in one direction, I don't see why they shouldn't admit its use in another, especially if there is evidence to show that the one is more satisfactory than the other. No! I'm afraid the supporters of the ' safe period ' are still being illogical. They object to the use of appliances and chemicals."

"Why is that?"

"I don't quite know, unless they think the destruction of germ cells sinful. Even so I can't quite follow their reasoning, because germ cells are constantly being destroyed in large numbers, as are all other body cells. There isn't any real difference between a germ cell and a skin cell, except that they have different functions. The germ cell cannot even reproduce itself; it is only the fertilised cell that can do that, and we are agreed that its destruction is wrong from many points of view. I'm afraid they haven't really thought the matter out."

"I have known cases," the Canon said, "where a Catholic has married a non-Catholic and the non-Catholic has used an appliance of some sort although the Catholic has refused to use anything. How does that fit in with what you have just been saying? Suppose, for the sake of argument, that the man is a Roman Catholic, and the woman uses the chemical or whatever it is; isn't it wrong for him to allow his germ cells to be destroyed, or isn't he, or rather his Church, concerned with their fate once they have left his body?"

"That is a bit of a poser, Canon," Dr. Hansell said, laughing, "but it is a very good point. In so far as I understand the Roman Catholic position, nothing must be done to interfere with the natural order of life, so I suppose they would say that when a man uses a sheath he is interfering with life by preventing the natural deposition of semen in the woman's body. If he uses nothing it doesn't seem to matter in so far as he is concerned, although he must know perfectly well that the chemicals in the woman's body are destructive to the germ cells. Logically he appears to be committing murder. However, their whole attitude to the non-Catholic partner is quite extraordinary. For a Roman Catholic to use contraception is mortal sin, and no doubt the sinner will eventually suffer for it in the next world, if not in this, unless, of course, he is pardoned for his sin by going to confession—I don't know about that. But for the non-Catholic individual to use contraceptives, and therefore become a mortal sinner every time he or she has connection with the Catholic individual, doesn't seem to worry them. It seems strange, when you come to think of it, that the man can enjoy himself with the woman he loves, and yet every time he does so she, presumably, by using these immoral things, is damning her soul, whilst he, surely, must be condoning her misdeed. But perhaps the Roman Catholics are not concerned with the welfare of the non-Catholic, although they do all they can to convert them. The whole thing seems to be profoundly callous and extremely selfish."

The Canon laughed. " Yes, it sounds bad when you put it like that. It looks as though the Roman Catholic has no right to exercise his sexual function under those circumstances, no children being intended. It hardly seems fair that he should drive his loved one to perdition. To my mind his only logical behaviour would be to practise abstention."

" Yes, I agree."

" Of course, the matter doesn't arise when both partners are Roman Catholics," the Canon said, " because the woman has to chance to luck, unless they abstain."

" Yes, but even that is a pernicious doctrine, and doesn't work in practice. The average man won't abstain, in spite of everything the priest says. I had a case like that once in which the woman was so ill that a further pregnancy would have endangered her life. As a matter of fact, I had two just at the same time. One woman was a Roman Catholic and the other wasn't. Both had had a serious illness with their last baby, and both had damaged their kidneys so severely that further pregnancies would have been dangerous to life. I explained the matter to the husband and wife in both cases and suggested that the women should learn a proper contraceptive method. The non-Catholic agreed; the Catholic asked the priest, who forbade it and advocated abstention. This the husband refused to observe, and the woman soon became pregnant and died. The other is still alive."

" Dear me! What a shocking tale! "

" Yes, it is," the doctor said, changing his gears with a bang. " That sort of thing makes you think, you know. I'll tell you another thing. A Catholic was having an affair with a non-Catholic girl, and the man, who incidentally had a wife somewhere or other, used to go to confession regularly. One day the girl asked him if he confessed the fact that he was living with her and what the priest had to say about it. 'Oh yes,' the man replied, 'but having regard to all the circumstances he thought I was justified'!"

"Dear me! And what about the girl? Wasn't he injuring her, or was that equally justified?"

"Exactly. That is what she said, but as far as she could make out the point hadn't arisen."

"What did she do?"

"Well, being a girl of some spirit, she said that she didn't like having her immortal soul endangered every time the man went to bed with her, and so she left him."

"Perhaps that was what the priest thought would happen."

"My dear Canon—you're becoming too subtle."

They both laughed.

"But seriously," Dr. Hansell said, "these matters are most important. Most of the methods we have been talking about cause some degree of mental strain which ought to be avoided. That being so, which is the best method? Coitus interruptus, from which the woman derives little or no satisfaction, has no sense of insecurity and is mentally and physically aroused without being satisfied—or a normal sex relationship in which there is no fear of pregnancy, no need for haste, no anxiety, and every chance of the couple deriving proper satisfaction? If the latter state of affairs can be brought about by the use of a scientific method, carefully taught, why not use it? Besides, the result is so satisfactory to both partners that their relationship takes on a deeper significance and is only practised at regular intervals, whereas coitus interruptus is often practised far more frequently just because real satisfaction isn't obtained."

"You make out a very good case, Dr. Hansell," the Canon said, "but I'm doubtful whether your suggestions are really practical. For instance, the sale of these articles has reached such colossal proportions that only the minority of people can be using them under the conditions you suggest."

"I agree. But that is the fault of society, and not of the principle. Once establish the principle and the rest will follow. We are only just beginning to look upon our sex relationships in a constructive manner. I agree that we still have very far to travel, but if the principle is right we must work for its acceptance. I'd prohibit the indiscriminate sale of the various articles you so rightly condemn, because they are, for the most part, unreliable or unsafe, but I'd provide a far greater number of clinics, staffed by competent people, where the whole population could get proper help and information *and* reliable appliances at reasonable prices—as is done in Sweden, for instance."

" Well, you may be right, but I'm by no means convinced. You would have to do an enormous amount of educative work."

" Of course. That is just the point; we haven't started to educate people yet. But we can't start on that subject now because we have arrived. Here is the clinic."

CHAPTER II

CONTRACEPTION

AS soon as they entered the clinic, Dr. Hansell introduced the Canon to the secretary and then began to show him round.

"You must realise that these clinics are intended for women who can't afford private fees," he said. "The charges are kept as low as possible, most people being asked to pay a shilling or half-a-crown as consultation fee and something towards the cost of any articles they may require. Each woman is seen privately by a doctor, our aim being to provide her with as reliable information as it is possible to obtain. This is the waiting-room." He indicated a small airy room, in which half-a-dozen women were sitting. "And this," he continued, opening a door, "is the room where the women are seen by one of the trained voluntary workers whose duty it is to make some enquiry into their previous medical history, economic condition and so on. Not too much, but sufficient to give the doctor an indication of the type of woman and her circumstances. After that the woman is passed on to the doctor, whom she sees in here."

Dr. Hansell led the way into a small room furnished very simply with one or two chairs, a table and a gas fire. Taking off his jacket, he donned a long white coat and sat down at the table, inviting the Canon to take a vacant chair beside him.

"You'd better sit here," he said. "The women won't mind your being in the room. We frequently have doctors down here to see the work, although we try to limit them to one or two at a time. You'll get a pretty good idea of the type of case and the problems people are up against if you stay here for an hour or two. When I've finished my preliminary conversation with a woman, I pass her on to a nurse, who gets her ready for examination in one of those little rooms through there. Having decided on the most suitable method for her particular case, I leave it to the nurse to teach her the necessary technique, after which she comes back here for a final interview. She then returns to the worker she first saw, who makes certain that she understands everything she's been taught and isn't bothered about anything. It occasionally happens that a woman learns so quickly that it seems unnecessary to bring her back again to the clinic, but in most cases we try to get them to revisit the clinic at the end of a week, to make sure that everything is satisfactory. All patients are provided with the necessary appliances and chemicals at the cheapest possible price, and a careful follow-up system is maintained, so that the clinic keeps in touch with its patients and can assess the value of the various methods employed. Women are often found to be suffering from some physical condition which needs treatment."

" Do you find many such cases ? "

" Oh rather; about 25 per cent., I should say off-hand. That's one of the chief values of the clinics. Hundreds of women seem to suffer from some minor ailments, which they put up with for months, and which can be cleared up very quickly by a little simple treatment. Occasionally, however, the condition is more serious, and the woman is then referred to her own doctor, or to a hospital, for the necessary attention."

Dr. Hansell rang a bell: the door opened to admit a neatly dressed little woman with a pale, anxious expression. She handed the doctor her card and sat down opposite him. " You seem to have done your duty by the State, Mrs. Jones," he said, after a quick perusal of the card. " Eleven children in thirteen years is pretty good."

" Yes, Doctor, and quite enough too, I'm sure; I'm only thirty-five now and I feel wore out."

" I should think so indeed. Are they all alive ? "

" Two of them died in the first year, Doctor. Sickly little mites they were from birth. I'd no trouble in having them neither, excepting a few stitches with the first. I had to have the last took from me. But one can't go on like that for ever, not on £3 a week."

" Is that all your husband gets ? "

"Well no, Doctor, he generally takes about £5 by working overtime, but he pays the rent and the clubs and gives me the £3 clear."

"I see. Even so, you must find it pretty difficult to make ends meet."

"I do, and that's a fact. But what can one do? A man must have his way and the babies just come. Not that I think it's right, mind you, because I don't, and that's why I'm here. A woman can't bring up all them children properly, not as they ought to be brought up. It's more than human nature can stand."

"Quite so, Mrs. Jones. Now tell me, what have you done to try and prevent having all these children?"

"Nothing, Doctor; although I did try one of them cap things once after Albert was born—he's the third, you know—but I couldn't rightly manage it. Not that my husband isn't a good man, because he is; no one could be more careful and considerate."

"I see what you mean, Mrs. Jones," Dr. Hansell said. "I think we shall be able to help you all right. It's a pity you didn't come here earlier."

"Never heard of the place until a friend told me about it, a week or two back; said it had made all the difference to her life, she did, so I thought I might as well come along and see for meself."

A few more questions and Mrs. Jones departed in charge of the nurse, while the doctor rang his bell again.

"Wouldn't it be possible to do something with the husbands, in cases like that?" the Canon asked.

"What can you do? They have implicit faith in coitus interruptus. It's useless to suggest that they should practise abstention, and they won't be bothered to buy sheaths even if they had the money. Come in."

A tall, fair-haired young woman came into the room. She too was neatly dressed, and would have been good-looking had she not been so pale. Dr. Hansell looked at her card.

"Three babies and one miscarriage in five years is rather much, isn't it, Mrs. Bean?"

"Yes, and I nearly died with the last two. I had puerperal fever with both of them and was in hospital nearly three months each time."

" So I see. How old are you ? "

" Twenty-three."

" And the miscarriage ; what was the cause of that ? I see it happened only two months ago."

" Well, Doctor, I'm afraid I took some pills which made me very ill. You see, the doctor told me that I oughtn't to have any more children."

" But didn't he tell you what to do ? "

" No, he didn't, and neither did the doctor at the clinic I went to after the birth, although I asked him about it. He told me to go home and tell my husband not to have any more babies."

" But surely he told you to go to a birth-control clinic ? "

" No, Doctor, he didn't ; when I asked him point blank if he couldn't teach me some birth control, he told me that it was too early to do anything. I heard of this place through a friend."

" Well, Mrs. Bean, I'll see what I can do for you, if you will go along with nurse."

Dr. Hansell turned round in his chair as the woman disappeared. " That's the type of case which makes my blood boil ! " he exclaimed angrily. " There you have a woman who has twice nearly died as the result of puerperal septicæmia ; twice, mind you, and yet she's given that sort of advice by people who ought to know better. I shall make further enquiries into the case, and if the woman's statements are correct—and I see no reason to doubt them—I shall endeavour to bring the matter to the notice of the Authority concerned. Medical officers in charge of welfare clinics have power to refer such cases to a birth-control clinic, but they very often won't bother. What would be your attitude to such a case, Canon ? Would you say that it was more Christian to teach the woman a suitable contraceptive method, or send her home to tell her husband not to have any more children ? "

" Teach her a contraceptive method, undoubtedly. I'm amazed that people should hesitate in such a case."

"Ah, but that's the sort of difficulty we're always up against. However, we must get on."

Several patients came in quick succession. Two women who had recently had babies and wanted to make sure of not becoming pregnant again at once; two or three "return visits"—women who had visited the clinic a year ago and had been written to and asked to come back for a check up—and one or two who wanted some particular point made clear. Their cheerful attitude and the complete absence of any anxiety were in marked contrast to that of the new patients.

"Is everything satisfactory?" Dr. Hansell asked one of them.

"Yes, thank you, Doctor. My husband and I are so happy that we don't know ourselves. So different to what it used to be. We're thinking of having another baby next year."

"That's fine. I'm so glad everything is all right."

One woman, who had been trying to have a baby for two years, wanted to know if anything could be done about it.

"Done about it? I should say so indeed," Dr. Hansell exclaimed. "It's a pity we don't get more people like you here. The country is full of women who want babies and can't have them and don't know what to do. It's a complicated problem, and we shall need the co-operation of your husband. Do you think he'll be willing to help?"

"Oh yes, Doctor, I'm sure he'd do anything."

"He must be an exceptional fellow, then," Dr. Hansell said. "Most of them are far too conservative. If you'll go along with nurse, I'll find out as much as I can to-day; and then you must both come here next week if you can manage it, and I'll explain the problem to you in detail." [1]

The next patient was a girl of eighteen who already had two children; whose husband was out of work and practised coitus interruptus very frequently.

"What would you do in that case, Canon?" Dr. Hansell asked when she had departed.

"I should like to give the man a good talking to; he ought to learn a little self-control."

[1] See Chapter XII.

" I agree with you, but don't you think he might be able to control himself better if I taught his wife a suitable contraceptive method so that they could have a normal sex relationship ? At present their whole life is a misery. He's never satisfied, and she's in constant fear of becoming pregnant again."

" But wouldn't the knowledge that she was safe from pregnancy encourage the husband to indulge himself even more recklessly ? "

" That argument is often advanced. I am frequently coming across such cases, and find that the provision of a suitable method, together with a little elementary instruction in sex hygiene, allows the couple to have a normal relationship. That means that they both derive real satisfaction instead of none, as in the present instance, so that the number of times coitus occurs is immediately reduced to normal proportions and they become happier. If something isn't done there pretty quickly, the marriage will be wrecked ; the girl appears to be at the end of her tether."

" I see your point. I hadn't looked at it in that light."

" Good ! I must leave you for a moment and go and see some of these cases," Dr. Hansell said, ringing the bell for another patient, with whom he nearly collided as she came into the room. " Why, Mrs. Jackson, how nice to see you again ! you haven't been here for a long time. Sit down, will you, and tell this gentleman all your troubles ; I won't keep you long."

" Thank you, Doctor ; I shall be pleased to tell anything I can."

" Have a look at this," Dr. Hansell said, passing her card to the Canon as he left the room.

" Dear me, Mrs. Jackson," the Canon said, after reading the notes. " You do seem to have had a lot of trouble. Eight children in ten years and you only thirty-four."

" That's right, sir ; eight it is, not to mention two miscarriages into the bargain. But three of them are dead, and no harm too—they were too weakly to live. Tuberculosis of the bowels it was in two of them, and pneumonia with the third. My baby's just over a year and is in hospital with the mangyitiss or something, and the doctors don't think he'll live. My husband has been out of work these five years. He has the consumption. I'm sure I didn't want all these children, but what can one do?"

"Can't you speak to your husband?"

"Speak to him! I've been speaking to him for years, but what's the use? I left him once, but he minded the children so badly, I had to go back. And the doctor spoke to him several times too, but it isn't any good talking to the likes of him. Besides, his mother tells him that I'm his lawful wife and it's my duty to consider him. He gets like a maniac at times, and comes into my room day and night, he does—he has a room to himself because of the consumption, you see—most tempestuous he is."

"Dear me. He seems to have no sense of responsibility at all."

"Responsibility. Not him! I fear for the children. After a time, when I couldn't stand it no longer, I said to myself I'd put a stop to it, in spite of what his mother said; and so I came along here and asks the doctor if he thinks it right for him to go on like that and if he can help me, which he did. But my husband found out where I kept the things the doctor gave me and threw them on the fire and hit me cruel."

"But why didn't you refrain from any union?"

"I was afraid for the children, sir. You see, he would take it out on them, because he knows that they keep me to him."

"I see."

Dr. Hansell came in again. "Well, has Mrs. Jackson been telling you her history?"

"She has indeed."

"Did she tell you that the first time she came here, she had to walk for half-an-hour in the pouring rain, and then travel for another hour or so by bus, to get here at all?"

"No, she didn't say that."

"Well, she did. How are you getting on, Mrs. Jackson?"

"Quite well, thank you, Doctor. I'm doing just as you tells me."

"I'm so glad. You'd better let me make sure everything is all right."

"Very good, Doctor."

CONTRACEPTION

"What a terrible case!" said the Canon when the woman had left the room.

"Pretty bad, isn't it? We hear more tales like that than you would imagine. I consider we are just making life bearable for her. She has only been coming here for a year, but she looks quite a different creature already."

The next patient was a large, pasty-faced woman of about forty-five, who had had six children, three miscarriages and two serious operations, the last one two years previously.

"I asked the matron to ask the doctor to sterilise me when he did the operation," she said, "but she wouldn't do nothing about it—she said she thought it was disgusting."

"Why didn't you ask the surgeon yourself?" Dr. Hansell enquired.

"I never saw him but the once before the operation, and then I was too frightened. My husband's a good man too, and we had separate rooms for two years at a stretch before the last two came, but of course the chances of escape are worse after such a long time. I hope you can help me, Doctor, because I don't know what will happen if I become pregnant again."

"I'm sure we can, but you must remember that your security really depends on yourself."

"I know that, Doctor; I will do whatever you say."

"What do you think of that?" Dr. Hansell asked when the woman had disappeared.

"It sounds extraordinary to me. Why shouldn't she have been sterilised?"

"I'm sure I can't say, but it wasn't the matron's job to decide the question; she should have reported the matter to the surgeon."

"Why didn't she?"

Dr. Hansell looked at the Canon, and they both laughed.

"Disgusting indeed!" Dr. Hansell exclaimed.

"But is the medical profession against helping these women?" Canon Heathcott enquired.

"No, I don't think it is really. But doctors are a conservative crowd and have to consider their reputations and all that. This business—sterilisation and so on—is illegal, or at least its legality is doubtful; so you can't blame the doctors if they take the safest course, or the hospitals if they refuse to deal with such cases. Of course some doctors muddle up ethics with their professional judgment, but I think many of them would welcome a more constructive and liberal attitude towards these problems."

" You are referring to sterilisation, I suppose."

" Partly, and to abortion as well. Our position there is very difficult—almost impossible. It is high time something was done. But we mustn't embark on a consideration of the abortion question, or we shall be here all night." He pressed the bell again, and a pale, timid little creature with a dull, sullen expression, came into the room.

" Sit down, will you ? " Dr. Hansell said kindly. " You needn't pay any attention to this gentleman; he's only here to see how the clinic works. Tell me now, what can we do for you ? Your name is Corder, I see."

"Yes, Emily Corder. I'm twenty years old and going to get married next month and want some help."

" I see. What do you know about things ? "

" Nothing."

" But you must know something, surely; how you were born, for instance ? "

" I can't say I do."

" And you don't know how babies are made ? "

" I'm not certain."

" Have you any brothers and sisters ? "

" Yes, two."

" How long have you been engaged ? "

" I'm not engaged; but we've decided to marry for the last year."

Dr. Hansell shuffled slightly in his chair.

" Have you talked things over with your young man ? "

" Not much."

" What is his job ? "

" He's in the confectionery."

" I see. You can't have gone out with him for a year without talking to him a bit, or making some kind of physical contact. Don't you do any love-making when you're together ? "

"Not much," the girl said slowly.
"But he kisses you, doesn't he?" Dr. Hansell insisted.
"Kisses me! He's all over me sometimes. And he's—well—I want to get rid of it."
"I see! But if you're going to get married, it doesn't make very much difference whether you're pregnant or not, does it?"
"I don't want to marry. I can't marry. What would people say?"
"But you said you were going to marry next month?"
"I know, but I don't want to. We can't afford it, besides he has to keep his mother, and it would mean my living with her, and I can't do that. We don't get on. If he could leave her and come and live with me and give her an allowance, but this——! Oh dear! I've took medicine and all, but it doesn't seem to have done no good." Her head dropped and the tears began to fall on to the table.
"Well now, Miss Corder," Dr. Hansell said, getting up, "you run along with nurse, and we'll see whether you really are pregnant."
"You see," he continued, as the girl departed; "the same old story. We get quite a lot of them here. All due to ignorance. If that girl had been told a few things properly a couple of years ago, she never would have got into this mess."
"I'm inclined to agree with you," Canon Heathcott said.
"I'm sure of it," Dr. Hansell said, ringing the bell vigorously. "This sort of thing is occurring all the time—on the increase, in fact. In almost every case you will find that the girl knows nothing and has been told nothing. It is really ridiculous that parents are so stupid in this enlightened age. Taking all these pills and things, too, and just making herself ill. Still, the majority of attempted abortion occurs amongst married women, you know."
"Really."
"Yes, it has been discovered by workers in similar clinics to this that most women admit to making some attempt—however inadequate—to end every pregnancy after the third or fourth. It is my opinion that the most frequent reason women come to this clinic is fear of pregnancy. Not that

they mind having babies, mind you, but that they don't want them so rapidly. Adequate contraceptive advice would stop all that."

The next woman had a letter from her doctor saying that she had five children and a bad heart, and would the doctor kindly give her some contraceptive advice.

"That's the sort of case I like," Dr. Hansell said. "A straightforward medical case sent by a doctor. Besides, we shall probably be able to get a grant for her from the local authority, which means that she's more likely to persevere with her method. Paying for these things is a constant drain on the family resources, however small the amount is; the women don't like charity, although the clinic is perfectly willing to forego payment altogether in suitable cases."

A small, intelligent-looking woman came in next, with a letter from the medical officer of a neighbouring child welfare clinic.

"This is an interesting case," Dr. Hansell said, passing the letter over to Canon Heathcott. He turned to the woman. "So you have two hæmophilic children, Mrs. McTavish? That must be a great worry to you and your husband?"[1]

"It is indeed. I shall be thankful not to have any more. We wouldn't have had these two if we'd understood a bit more when we were married. Not that we don't like children, because we do, but it's cruel to see them suffer. When I learned all about this hæmophia from the doctors, I made up my mind to come here straight away. ' It isn't no use messing about with things we don't know nothing about,' I said to my husband, but I'm afraid he doesn't hold with me altogether, and so I persuaded him to come along too in the hope that you will kindly see him, Doctor, if you have the time, and explain things to him."

"That I will, and gladly."

"Not that he's unkind or anything like that, because he isn't, but he has some mighty queer ideas sometimes and is a bit stubborn like."

"I'll get him in now, if you'll go along with nurse."

---

[1] Hæmophilia is a hereditary blood disease usually passed through the female to the male in which the blood does not clot properly so that cuts go on bleeding for hours or days.

" Thank you, Doctor, I'm sure."

" What's that ? " Dr. Hansell said, as the nurse whispered something to him.

" Oh ! Excuse me a minute." He hurried out after Mrs. McTavish, leaving the Canon alone, but returned again shortly, his face wreathed in smiles. " You remember that girl who was in here a minute or two ago—Miss Corder ? " he asked.

" Yes ! "

" Well, she isn't pregnant after all. All fright. I've known it happen before. Now we shall be able to do something really constructive. Teach her some elementary sex hygiene ; give her some contraceptive advice and, I hope, get hold of the young man and talk to him. Most important that." He opened the door leading to the waiting-room and summoned Mr. McTavish—a thin-faced, alert little man, with a mop of flaming red hair.

" Take a seat, please, Mr. McTavish, and make yourself at home. I'm sorry to hear about your children. The condition is comparatively rare."

" So I gather, Doctor, but we didn't know nothing about there being anything like that in my wife's family when we married ; but now we find that several of her relations suffered from it. My wife has made up her mind not to have any more children."

" And very wise too, I think, under the circumstances, but I gather from her that you're not altogether in agreement with her."

" Oh yes, I am, Doctor. I don't want to run no more risks, I assure you, but I'm not sure that these new-fangled notions are the best way of doing things."

" How do you mean ? "

" Well, all these appliances and chemicals and things ; are they really necessary ? My pals tell me they don't always work. Besides, it's doing a man out of his rights, from what I can make of it."

" Well now, let us take one point at a time, McTavish," Dr. Hansell said quietly. " You suggest that the methods may not be safe, but that depends upon the method and how it is learnt. The indiscriminate purchase of contraceptives is unwise, because they are frequently unreliable and not always suitable for the individual case. But a proper method, efficiently learnt at a place like this, and carefully carried out, is safe in about 95 per cent. of cases,—possibly more. I think I can guarantee that, provided your wife always does as she's told, the chance of failure will be very small indeed and very much less than the methods your friends are probably referring to."

"That all right as far as it goes," the little man replied, "but what about the man? Doesn't all this fussing and meddling interfere with what I may call his natural feelings?"

"Well, McTavish, if you don't want any more children, what is your way of preventing them?"

"A man can be careful, Doctor."

"You mean coitus interruptus? That's very unsatisfactory for you, isn't it? Nor is it safe. You'll find that the information given to your wife here will enable you to have a perfectly natural sex relationship without either of you being aware that anything is being used."

"If that is so, Doctor, I'm satisfied, because I only want to do what is best for the wife."

"I'm sure you do."

"Can't these things do any harm to the woman?"

"No, McTavish, they can't. There isn't a scrap of evidence to show that the methods we teach here can do any harm whatsoever."

"Then I've nothing more to say. I'm sure we shall both be most grateful to you."

"If you'll wait here a moment, I will see if your wife is ready," the doctor said, going out of the room.

"It's a pity there aren't more places like this," Mr. McTavish said, addressing Canon Heathcott. "It's very difficult for the likes of us to get proper help and information. Life is quite difficult enough without people being worried by these questions. There ought to be more education, I'm thinking. It would do a power of good for some of my mates to hear some of these things."

"Tell me, Mr. McTavish, do many of your friends believe in self-control?"

"How do you mean?"

"Well, refraining from union if that appears to be unwise."

"Oh! I get your meaning. Why, mister, that sort of thing ain't self-control. How many people do you know of what's doing it? Precious few, I fancy. 'Tain't natural, neither. A decent man respects his wife and her him. That's self-control. But they must act natural now and again—Ah!"

The door opened and Mrs. McTavish reappeared with the doctor.

"Get on all right, my girl?" the little man enquired eagerly.

"It's easy as falling off a log."

"That's fine. And the doctor here has assured me that everything will be all right, so you needn't have no more worries on that score."

"Always providing that you do as you're told," Dr. Hansell added.

"Never fear, Doctor; we'll do that."

"Good. Mind you let me know if you're worried about anything." He turned to Canon Heathcott. "I've still got one woman to see; then we shall have finished." The door opened as he spoke, and a woman came in crying.

"Sit down, my dear, and let's talk this out. Didn't you realise that you were pregnant when you came here?"

"Yes, Doctor, I did, but I thought you could do something for me, because I've already got three children and we really can't afford no more."

"But don't you realise that it's illegal for me to take your baby away? I could be put in prison for doing it. I'm afraid you will have to make up your mind to have this one. If you come back here one month after the baby is born I can teach you birth control."

"Thank you, Doctor. I suppose I shall have to do as you say," the woman said, drying her eyes.

"It's an extraordinary thing," the doctor said, when she had gone, "how many women seem to think that abortion and birth control are the same thing: in reality they are the exact opposite."

"I'm afraid a good many people don't understand the

difference," Canon Heathcott remarked, as they prepared to leave. " Tell me, are all birth-control clinics run by voluntary organisations ? "

" Oh dear no. The Ministry of Health authorised Local Authorities to provide facilities for giving contraceptive advice to women in 1930 ; since then a good many Authorities have established their own clinics. Others have set up a special type of clinic particularly recommended by the Ministry of Health, called ' gynæcological ' clinics, where women receive advice and treatment on a variety of other minor conditions. Others refer cases to voluntary clinics such as the one we have here, or to private doctors doing this type of work, in which cases they usually pay a fee for the patient. Others again allow their medical officers to give advice, but have started no special clinics. Some Authorities lend, or hire, premises of a Maternity and Child Welfare centre to a local branch of the Family Planning Association."[1]

" There seems to be a variety of different methods of spreading the information."

" That is unavoidable so long as the Government refuses to make the clinics part of the ordinary health services of the country. At present there are not nearly enough, and even those are hampered by lack of funds."

" So I imagine."

The doctor looked at his watch. " We shall just get back in time for the coffee if we hurry and then, if you are not too tired, we might finish our discussion before going to bed."

[1] All information concerning these clinics can be obtained from the Family Planning Association, 69 Eccleston Square, London, S.W.

CHAPTER III

SEX AND RELIGION

"YOU have partly converted me," Canon Heathcott admitted, as they settled themselves down in Dr. Hansell's room later that night. " I can see that the work done in the clinics is good, and that there is much to be said for their extension."

" I'm so glad," Dr. Hansell said. " I felt sure that you would change your views if only you could see what is actually being done."

" I'm not at all sure," the Canon continued, " that I can go as far as you would like me to in regard to some of the other matters. I'm by no means convinced as to the value of such a widespread system of education as you seem to favour."

" But you would agree that some constructive teaching is necessary, wouldn't you ? "

" Oh yes, but I don't think we know enough at present to say what form it should take, who should do it ; at what age it should start and so on. Nor, for that matter, have we sufficient people to impart the information."

" I agree with all that," the Doctor replied, " but before discussing ways and means we must get down to bed-rock and decide what it is we are going to teach. We are not going to solve the problems of social morality until we make far greater use of the sciences—of biology and psychology, for instance."

" Well, you may be right, but I think it will be difficult to prevent an over-emphasis of the sexual functions."

" If we had a proper system of teaching that would not occur," Dr. Hansell replied, " because the knowledge would become part and parcel of the general educational system. The truth of the matter is that education in sex and marriage has never been attempted in this country. Any over-emphasis that occurs in the sexual sphere is always put down to licence, whereas in actual fact it is usually due to deprivation, misuse and deviation of the natural instinct from its proper purpose. Teach about it naturally, allow it to have natural expression in an early, well-thought-out marriage, encourage those in difficulties to seek advice, and you will find that the sex function takes a much more normal place in the life of the family and the nation. In a well-organised intelligent society there would be no need to have abortions, illegitimacy, venereal disease and all the rest for the simple reason that society wouldn't tolerate that sort of behaviour, and so the incidence would be reduced to a minimum. But so long as we go around with our heads in the sand pretending that the conditions don't exist, so long will we have our present moral system. I'm not advocating sexual licence; on the contrary, sexual licence is an indication of immaturity and ill-thought-out social laws. What we need is a fine balance between expression and suppression. Not until we have learned to understand ourselves shall we be able to discipline ourselves. The point has been stressed by people like Havelock Ellis for years." [1]

"I quite agree with all that."

"Then I don't see why you are still hesitating. Either this kind of approach to life is right, in which case you and I and people like us have to accept it and preach it, or else it is wrong."

"Yes, I see that too, and agree with it, but I think that one of the reasons why the Church is afraid of committing herself whole-heartedly is over the contraceptive issue. On the one hand it is obvious that the work of such a clinic as yours is of great value, but many people think contraception may place too great a temptation in the way of young people, and encourage a still greater increase in indiscriminate sex relationships."

"That may be so, but the fact remains that everyone knows about contraception nowadays, so that our problem is to encourage its rightful use rather than attempt the hopeless task of abolishing it, but you must make up your mind about the principle first of all, just as you must decide whether the

---

[1] See, for instance, "St. Francis and Others" in Affirmations. Recently re-issued in Selected Essays. (Everyman's Library.)

use of any other scientific invention—such as gas or morphia—is morally justifiable. The fact that the invention may be misused is beside the point."

" I see its value, but I see its dangers."

" So do we all. Will you not, however, agree with the principle ? "

" Yes, I have already."

" Then must we not teach about it more positively ? "

" Yes, I think so."

" Good ! May I now turn to another matter ? "

" So long as we don't sit up all night ! " the Canon said.

. . . . .

Dr. Hansell laughed. " Tell me, Canon," he said, " what do you think Christ really taught about marriage ? "

" Well, because he was mainly concerned with man's personal relationship to God, I think his teaching about marriage differed profoundly from that of the Jewish law which existed at that time."

" In what way exactly ? "

" Their law didn't forbid a man from having several wives ; it acknowledged the principle of polygamy for man, but not for woman. It permitted divorce ; but the power to make the divorce rested with the husband, and the wife had to agree to his decision. Adultery was a crime against the husband, not against the wife. That is to say, a married man could have sex relationships with an unmarried woman if he wished and there would be no adultery, but a married woman could not have an extra-marital relationship without committing adultery. The only exception was that a man would commit adultery if he went away with another man's wife. Christ condemned all this as being cruel and unjust, putting in its place the ideal of equality between husband and wife."

" And what about divorce ? "

" I don't think Christ ever approved of divorce. The ideal that he set before people was to marry and accept what came, but I agree with you that he made no law on the subject. It is only in later Christian history that we get the idea of absolute law. Christ always taught that the administration of any law was to be tempered with the idea of God as being merciful and loving."

"That's very interesting," Dr. Hansell said. "Tell me another thing. Am I right in supposing that there was no special religious marriage service in the Christian Church earlier than the sixth century?"

"Quite right. It was the custom to attend church after the civil service, but any development of a special religious service came very slowly; it was not until the tenth century that it became customary to celebrate a special mass in church."

"Would you agree, then, that this attitude was not altogether beneficial, because, by doing away with the idea of a purely business transaction, and insisting that the marriage ceremony, performed under any other jurisdiction than a religious one, was sinful, it created a wrong impression as to the meaning of sex?"

"I think one could put up a good argument along those lines."

"Would it be fair to say that the idea that sexual enjoyment was a sin had its origin in this way?"

"I don't think that Christ ever suggested that sexual enjoyment in its right setting was a sin, nor, for that matter, does the Church teach it to-day."

"But the idea is very prevalent."

"Yes, but it arose, I think, because the early Christians were firmly convinced that the world was soon coming to an end and that the things of the body were of little concern compared with those of the spirit."

"An unfortunate decision."

"Certainly, and one which I am sure all sensible people deplore."

"Would it be equally fair to say that all irregular unions —those not blessed by the Church—came under the heading of 'licence', whereas all marriages performed in church were 'sacraments' and on a higher plane?"

"Yes, I think you can say that."

"And so the form gradually superseded the motive, and the idea of personal responsibility towards the other individual was lost sight of. What was done in marriage was right, however low the conception of sex might be; and what was done outside marriage was wrong, however high a conception of the sex relationship existed between the two."

"I suppose you could say that is the logical result of the teaching of those days."

"Good. That clears the air a lot."

"The trouble with you scientists," the Canon said, "and especially with a certain section of psychologists, is that you are far too materialistic both in outlook and treatment, especially in regard to sex and the emotions. Everything is analysed and dissected to such an extent that people hardly know whether they are standing on their head or their heels. You seem to forget that man is a composite being endowed with various qualities that are difficult to define scientifically —moral and spiritual qualities, for instance—which are of immense importance in that they raise the human being above the level of the animal. You will remember that this point was brought out last night, and that I agreed with the questioner that the sexual element in human beings differed from that of animals in that it is on a higher plane."

"I couldn't agree with you more," Dr. Hansell said warmly, "but you must define more exactly what you mean by the higher plane. If you mean that the sex life of the individual must become so spiritualised that it is practically non-existent, and that in order to attain perfection in after life—if there is an after life—the individual must forget that he has a body, then I cannot agree with you, because it is just that kind of attitude which has done so much harm in the past. If, on the other hand, you mean that sex is only rightly used by a couple when it is an indication of some spiritual relationship between them, when, in fact, it is the outward expression of a mental and spiritual oneness, then I think we might get somewhere."

"It is in the latter sense that I was thinking."

"In that case we must consider the nature of the sex instinct more fully and see how it is that it is related to the spiritual, because I think that it is here that we shall find at least one source of difference between science and religion. Most people, if asked what is the purpose of sex, would reply that it is for reproduction, an interpretation which, in my opinion, is only partly accurate. I would suggest that the sex instinct has three co-equal purposes which may be used together or separately as occasion may arise, but of which one should not be used to the complete exclusion of the others; it can be transferred into other creative channels; it can be used for reproduction or for purposes of mating. In other words, sex has a meaning and purpose which is not only reproductive but psychological and spiritual as well. In addition, it must act in accordance with the needs and principles of man's other fundamental drives, the most important of which are those relating to social adjustment and self-preservation. Man must live in harmony with his neighbours unless he wishes to destroy them or be destroyed —he must be co-operative. But to be co-operative he must be unselfish and thoughtful; his fundamental drives must be socialised. There must be a balance between the needs of others and the needs of the self. A philosophy of life which encourages the development of the State at the expense of the individual acts in direct opposition to the principle of co-operative unselfishness. Developed to its logical conclusion this barren philosophy shows itself in the sadistic outbursts we have witnessed in Nazi Germany and in earlier periods of history."

"Yes, you are right there; man is still a very imperfect being."

"Let us consider these three functions of sex more fully," Dr. Hansell said. "The transference of sex energy into other channels is a positive activity rather than a negative one. Our forefathers, unfortunately, concentrated on the negative side and used their power to repress the instinct by minimising its importance; pretending it didn't exist; condemning it as sinful, and teaching that only by subduing the lusts of the flesh could man rise to spiritual perfection. All this is quite contrary to the facts as we know them to-day. It can hardly be suggested that a happily married couple cannot enjoy as rich a spiritual life as a celibate, indeed in some ways their experience must be fuller than his. It is invidious to make comparisons, however. The true celibate has his place in the world just as the married couple. He is conscious of sex activity and knows how to manage it. Even so he has his difficulties."

" That is very true. One has only to read the lives of the early saints to understand that."

" Yes, living in the desert didn't seem to help much. They didn't know as much as we do now-a-days. The modern celibate manages so much better because he accepts the fact of sex in his life and doesn't struggle against it all the time. Quite apart from this, however, it should be recognised that transference has a definite place in marriage. It is often necessary to refrain from sex intercourse for considerable periods of time in marriage, and this may be just as difficult for one used to regular sex experience as for the celibate. On the other hand, if the couple have experienced a really satisfactory relationship they are likely to be adjusted and poised and able to wait contentedly for the time when they can return to something which is so abundantly creative. Only the few are capable of a real creative celibacy. Far too many restrict it and deny it adequate outlet, thus producing the neurotic, the unbalanced, the aggressive and the fanatically ascetic."

The Canon laughed. " I know the type well," he said.

" Good. Well, that deals with the first function of sex. The second function—namely, that of reproduction—can be dismissed very quickly because it is obvious that life must be continued. This aspect of sex has been over-emphasised to such an extent in the past that the other two have often been ignored or overlooked. It is when we come to the third function—namely, the mating one—that we are on new, and to some extent controversial, ground ; it is round this aspect that the present battle is really raging. Until quite recently it has been presumed that provided the reproductive function was well catered for, the mating one would look after itself. Indeed, I would go farther, and say that when people were married it was the reproductive function which was uppermost in the minds of their friends, relatives, society and the Church, but not, I think, in their own. The idea of enjoying the relationship for its own sake was not accepted—it wasn't quite nice, whereas, if we are honest with ourselves, we know perfectly well that when a couple marry they are really concerned with the mating aspect; indeed, I would say that if they aren't there is something wrong with them."

"You put it bluntly, but you are quite right," the Canon said.

"Of course I am. It is ridiculous to suggest that every time a young, newly married couple have intercourse they are hoping to create a new life, even if they intend eventually to have a dozen children. They are not. On the contrary, they wish to express their mental and spiritual oneness in a physical manner. It by no means follows that the result is always as satisfactory as they hoped, but that isn't the point. Their intention is to enjoy the relationship for its own sake, and children are a secondary consideration for the moment. And my point is that this instinctive feeling is based on an important psychological principle, which is that the relationship should be mutually enjoyed. There are a hundred and one things that may happen to the couple in these early days which may interfere with the true expression of the mating function. Time must be allowed for its achievement. But this so rarely happens. Before they know where they are, the woman is usually pregnant, and the mating aspect, never having been properly established, has to take a back seat for months or even years. Indeed, it may never be established. Almost all the cases you saw this evening were examples of this situation—of conflict between the mating and the reproductive principles only solved by adequate contraceptive practice. I must stress again that it by no means follows that because a couple have sex intercourse and the woman becomes pregnant, the relationship has been properly enjoyed by either party, and certainly not by the woman. They may have had some temporary pleasure, but nothing deep or lasting. It is round this situation that so much marital disharmony is produced, and yet this is the one department of life that no one will investigate or attempt to clear up. It is always glossed over or minimised, both by the individuals themselves and the doctor, nurse or parson who is trying to help the couple."

"I must admit that is a new idea to me," the Canon said, "but I see its force now that you explain it like that."

"Let me put it in another way by taking an analogy from

the fishes," Dr. Hansell said. "You will agree, I think, that the herring has not reached a very advanced stage of development. Nevertheless the reproductive function of the female herring is prodigious, and she lays about six million eggs a year, of which only about two are fertilised. At the other end of the scale, however, we find that a woman produces perhaps a couple of dozen eggs a year, of which one or two are fertilised. So her reproductive activity is less, although, of course, her concern with the fertilised egg lasts much longer. But what of the mating aspect? No one can say that a pair of herrings have a very important love life, indeed the mating aspect is practically negligible. In human beings, however, the love life is profoundly important and occupies a great part of the personal lives of men and women."

"You mean that as we rise in the scale of development the mating aspect becomes of increasing importance, whereas the reproductive is less important and looks after itself to a large extent?" the Canon enquired.

"Precisely. Let me remind you of what was said last night about a man only needing coitus once a year to produce eight children in as many years. Suppose six times a year would be sufficient to produce a pregnancy. In ten years, therefore, a couple need only have intercourse sixty times in order to produce five healthy children if they voluntarily spaced them at a two-year interval. Although the reproductive principle would be more than satisfied by this means, you surely don't believe that the couple would be satisfied with so small a number of connections—six a year. Sixty would be more appropriate and healthy."

" I hadn't realised that this aspect of sex was so important."

" I think all those in a position to judge are agreed that the mating principle is profoundly important for human beings. It is precisely because we do not recognise this fact and do not legislate for it in our social structure that we find ourselves in our present dilemma. Society—the man in the street—has always recognised this need; authority—Church or State—has always tried to limit its expression and bring it under control."

" Yes, I recognise that," the Canon said.

"Owing to the fact that woman has never been able to give expression to the mating aspect of sex without the possibility of becoming pregnant, she has never been on an equality with man in the sexual sphere; she has always been at his mercy, and he could disrupt her whole life by one physical act which, ten to one, meant nothing to him. But now, owing to the discovery of modern contraceptive methods, the whole position is altered. Now for the first time in the history of civilisation woman finds herself sexually independent of man."

"And man doesn't altogether like it," the Canon said.

Dr. Hansell laughed. "That is true. He has to think again and adjust his ideas to an entirely different set of values. His relationship to woman will have to take on a new meaning in the future. No longer is he the dominant personality, indeed the reverse is very often the case. By virtue of her new power, woman has the capacity to hurt man quite as much as man has hurt woman in the past. She can, if she is not careful, disrupt his emotional life, destroy his respect for her, turn him into a cynic and hurt him profoundly. Thus she too has to readjust herself to these new values and learn again the meaning of love and the proper use of power."

"Yes, I should say that was very true."

"We have to ask ourselves, therefore, whether or not the Church will accept these new facts and graft them on to her life. Is it morally right that woman should be sexually at the mercy of man, or is it wrong? Is woman on the same personality level as man, or is she a step or two lower down the ladder? Must we not accept the fact that the sex act should never be used between man and woman unless it is mutually desired and has a creative end? Is it right that the mating aspect can and should be separated from the reproductive aspect on occasions and in the context of marriage, or is it not? If it is, does not contraception, by making these things possible, become a factor of profound social value likely to contribute greatly to family stability? These are the sort of questions that are still not answered frankly by many people because the dangers of accepting them appear to be so great that they have not the courage to face the issue, and vacillate in uncertainty, as indeed, my dear Canon, you have been vacillating!"

"Yes!" the Canon said, laughing heartily. "I see your point very clearly and I must say that I agree with you. The idea that marriage subordinates a wife to a husband and renders her person his property has never been taught by the Christian Church and should be repugnant to every thinking person."

"And yet because of these facts it has been widely accepted and taught by Church and State for years."

"I know, I know. But I don't believe that it is either right or Christian."

"Well, that's fine. We seem to have reached a considerable measure of agreement. We are agreed that contraception has its place in married life and abstention is of very limited value; that coitus interruptus is unsafe, and that the mating aspect is of profound importance. And further, we are agreed that a strong educational policy is essential and that the relationship between sex and religion is positive."

"Yes, I think I can agree to all that, but I shall have to think it over. However, I must go to bed now; it must be long after midnight."

"One fifteen to be exact," Dr. Hansell said, laughing.

CHAPTER IV

MENTAL DEFICIENCY

ALTHOUGH well past forty, Mrs. Bellamy retained a neatness of figure and a natural beauty of complexion that were the envy of many a younger woman. She was so tiny that Dr. Hansell always wondered how she had managed to produce any children at all, let alone three. A vivacious sense of humour, coupled with a directness of speech, completed a personality which made her much sought after by all sorts and conditions of people.

Being one of Dr. Hansell's oldest friends, and therefore knowing his habits pretty well, he was not surprised when she caught him having a late cup of tea in one of the small conference rooms set aside for speakers.

"Well, Jerry," she said, settling herself in a comfortable chair, "how did you get on with the Canon? I've been dying to hear. Did you convert him?"

"I made a little progress, I fancy," Dr. Hansell said with a smile. "We talked till long past midnight."

"Good gracious! you must have had a pow-pow."

"We did. I expect you will hear about it later on, as I feel sure he will want to discuss it in public. Tell me, how is Wendy?"

"Very well indeed, and very happy with David. I have just left them. I hope you approve."

"I do, most certainly. He seems a delightful young man."

"I hope they are coming to see you; I told them to, but you know what young people are."

"They have already got in touch with me."

"I'm so glad. Oh, by the way, I have persuaded a friend of Wendy's to come and see you too—at least, I hope I have —Betty Romney. Do you know her? No? Well, it doesn't matter. She is a charming girl, but running around with an objectionable young man of whom no one seems to approve—Montague something-or-other. Stupid of me, but I've forgotten the name. However, that doesn't matter either. The point is that Betty told me she was worried, and so I persuaded her to come to see you. You will see her, won't you?"

" Of course. As a matter of fact I am seeing her the day after the conference ends."

" Oh, good! I'm sure you can help her. I'm so glad you agree about Wendy and David. Some people seem to think that Wendy is too young to know her own mind—after all, she is only twenty—but I don't agree. I think young marriages are a good thing provided you are lucky enough to meet the right person. Not that I want people to rush into marriage; there is far too much of that sort of thing going on; some people hardly give themselves time to think. A sudden infatuation, a hurried marriage, a tiff, a refusal to understand the other point of view, and the affair is over before it has well begun. But I don't think Wendy and David are rushing things, do you?"

" No, I don't. They have had time for consideration and seem excellently suited to each other."

Mrs. Bellamy sat back and looked out of the window. The doctor watched her quietly whilst drinking his tea.

" Is anything the matter, Meg?" he said at length; " you look worried."

Mrs. Bellamy continued to gaze out of the window. At length she turned and said quietly:

" Yes, I am worried, Jerry. Shall I bore you if I talk to you?"

" Of course not."

" Well, as you know, Tom is no good with the children; no good at all. Wendy laughs at him and Christopher ignores him. I have to do everything, and make all the decisions. You know what he says: ' Have it your own way, my dear, and don't worry me '; but that is no great help to me, is it? I can't help getting a bit down now and again."

She pulled out a small handkerchief.

" I know, my dear; but crying! I haven't seen you cry for years."

"I'm not really crying, Jerry, although I can't see what you doctors are for if women can't drop the mask of pretence with you."

"But you don't pretend, do you?"

"Of course I do. All women pretend. If they didn't they would give up the unequal struggle. How many perfect women do you see, Jerry? Physically perfect, I mean, with clear complexions, fine bodies, happy faces and so on. A few of the younger ones certainly, but for the most part we are acting all the time, covering things up, pretending that something doesn't exist; that we aren't as fat as we look or as thin as we feel; that we have no spots on our faces or wrinkles under the eyes. A woman has so short a time in which to be young, Jerry, whereas a man isn't thought much of until he's forty. It isn't altogether fair."

"Perhaps not, but there are compensations. Women are differently constituted from men; they get different satisfactions from life; they suffer more in many ways, but they also experience greater depths of joy—their compensations are fuller."

"Oh, I don't know about that! What a thrill it must be to write a great book, or pull off a large deal satisfactorily, or achieve high distinction in politics."

"But women can do all those things. Besides, I'm not at all sure that the 'thrill' they experience is not one of relief rather than of joy, and certainly doesn't compare to the joy that a woman has when she sees her new baby."

"Joy! My dear Jerry. I thought my babies looked terrible!"

"Yes, for a day or two perhaps, but after that——?"

Mrs. Bellamy smiled. "Well, perhaps you are right. However, I didn't come here to discuss women. Tell me——!" She fidgeted in her chair.

"Well?"

"I'm worried."

"So I see, my dear. Wouldn't it be better to get it off your chest?"

"Yes, of course. You won't tell Tom or Wendy or anyone, will you?"

"My dear Meg——!"

"I know. I'm sorry, Jerry. The truth is that no one knows about this. I wouldn't mention it now were it not that Wendy is getting married, and one has a duty to one's children. One hears so much about these things nowadays that one doesn't know what to believe. I wouldn't do anything to spoil the child's happiness——!"

"Come, Meg," the doctor interrupted kindly. "This isn't like you at all. I don't think I have ever seen you so upset. What exactly are you talking about? There can't be many happenings in your life that I don't know about."

"This happened before you knew me—before Wendy was born."

"Yes. Well——?"

There was a silence, during which Mrs. Bellamy twisted her handkerchief into a tight ball.

"Wendy isn't my eldest child, Jerry," she said at last. "I had an affair with another man before I married Tom. I was a fool, I suppose, or rather my people were. They told me nothing, and I had a baby. I was never more surprised in my life than when it arrived."

"Does Tom know?"

"Oh dear no! I never told him and he never guessed. The man was a rotter. Luckily he was killed at the end of the war."

"I see. But why rake all this up now, my dear? It's past and done with."

"But it isn't, Jerry. You see, the baby was all wrong; he has the brain of a child even now, and has to have everything done for him. He gets fits, too, and has to live in an institution, where I visit him occasionally. I suppose you would call him an idiot. Luckily I have money of my own, so there was never any need to tell anyone except Mother. But now I'm afraid, because I can't help wondering if there may be something wrong with me which can be passed on to Wendy and her children, although the doctor assured me at the time that it wasn't me. But I can't help wondering if he was wrong."

"And you have been carrying this terrible worry about with you all these years? Why didn't you tell me about it?"

"I couldn't; I was afraid you would tell me that the children couldn't marry."

"But that is ridiculous, Meg; you and Tom are perfectly healthy, and there is no hereditary disease on your side of the family—or is there?"

"Oh no, but I've discovered that the father came from very bad stock; there's quite a lot of insanity in his family."

"But that can't be passed on to any children you and Tom may have."

"I thought he might have infected me in some way."

"Of course not. Didn't the doctor explain all this to you at the time?"

"Yes, Jerry, he did. He said that it was probably due to excessive pressure on the child at birth. He had some difficulty, I believe."

"And so did you, I imagine?"

Mrs. Bellamy smiled. "Yes, I had a bad time, but one forgets that sort of pain very quickly."

Dr. Hansell nodded. "Let's get this straight," he said. "Your child is presumably mentally deficient, but you must realise that mental deficiency may be of two types: primary, which is usually inherited, and secondary, which is usually due to some outside cause, such as illness or injury at birth. Supposing for the sake of argument that Tom had been the father of this child and a birth injury resulted in its being mentally deficient. That is not a hereditary condition; the mental deficiency is due to some accident to the child which has nothing to do with heredity, and so the child would be suffering from a mental deficiency which is secondary.

"Suppose, on the other hand, that the child did come from bad stock; suppose that the father was himself mentally unbalanced and that his father before him was mentally unbalanced and there was a long family history of mental instability—even supposing all that, he couldn't possibly have 'infected' you, as you call it, although he could have passed the condition on to the child, who would be a primary defective."

"Oh, I see. But there are diseases which can be passed from one to the other during the sex act, aren't there?"

"Yes, of course; but those are the venereal diseases—

MENTAL DEFICIENCY 63

syphilis or gonorrhœa. They are transmitted from one person to another by a definite organism which can be seen under the microscope, just as the tuberculosis or pneumonia germ is passed from person to person."

"Then how is mental disease passed from parent to child?"

"That is more difficult to explain. You realise that the sex organs—the testicles in the male and the ovaries in the female—make the sex cells which have to unite to form a new baby; the male sperm has to fertilise the female egg."

"Yes, of course."

"Well, those cells—in fact all cells—contain what is known as a nucleus, and the nucleus contains special bodies called chromosomes. The simplest cells reproduce themselves by dividing into two, during which process the chromosomes divide into exactly equal portions, half going to one cell and half to the other, so that each new cell has the identical form and constitution of the original cell. This is known as asexual division. The chromosomes contain bodies called genes, which are so small that they can only be seen through the most powerful microscope. You can imagine them as a series of beads on a string. There are hundreds of genes in each chromosome, and each gene is the bearer of a particular characteristic. When mating occurs the male and female gene for each particular characteristic meet and join according to certain complicated laws. Some genes are the bearers of good characteristics and some of bad ones. If two 'bad' genes meet, the result is that the 'bad' characteristic comes out in the child. It is thus that the individual characteristics are passed from cell to cell, and, in the higher animals, from parent to child. The process is, of course, more complicated than that, but I'm giving you the general principles. The number of chromosomes varies in different species, but is always constant for that species."

"I see; it all sounds very complicated."

"It is, and very wonderful too."

"The sex cells in human beings divide in a special way during their early division, so that each new cell contains only half the original number of chromosomes. Thus, when the male sex cell unites with the female sex cell, the chromosomes in the new individual are brought up to the correct number. The fertilised cell which results has obtained half its chromosomes, and thus half its characteristics, from one parent, and half from the other. The sex cells cannot produce new individuals by themselves, but only after they have united with a cell of the opposite type; in other words, after fertilisation has occurred. If I have made myself clear you will see that it is quite impossible for you to have ' caught ' any hereditary condition like mental deficiency from the man, or for you to pass on any taint that he may have had to any children you and Tom had."

" Yes, I see now. I can't think why I didn't ask you about it before."

Dr. Hansell laughed. " You're not the only person going about with hidden fears that they won't get cleared up. I constantly come across people with similar worries which could be so quickly dispelled by a little explanation."

" Tell me some more about mental deficiency. Is it a very serious problem ? "

" Well, it's a complicated subject about which those who know most are by no means agreed. Mental deficiency seems to be on the increase, and the general level of national intelligence is in danger of being lowered. There are two broad lines of approach to the problem. In the first place you can investigate the health and conditions of those people whom we know to be mentally deficient, or who are bordering on mental deficiency, or, alternatively, you can estimate the intelligence of the whole population, or of sections of the population. Let us consider the first method. Our knowledge of mental deficiency was so inadequate in 1924 that Sir George Newman, the chief Medical Officer of the Ministry of Health at that time, appointed a special committee to investigate the whole problem. This came to be known as the Wood Committee, after its chairman, Mr. A. H. Wood. It reported in 1929, and came to the conclusion that there were about 300,000 mentally deficient people in the country. Many of these came from the same families and were part of a still larger group known as the ' Social Problem Group '. The Committee found that this ' Social

Problem Group' contains a large proportion of insane people, epileptics, paupers, criminals, unemployable people and so on. It comprises roughly 10 per cent. of the population—about four million people."
" That's a very large number."
" It is, and the problem of how to deal with them is very complicated, not only on their own account, but because the majority of them are breeding freely, and therefore reproducing their own type."
" But surely mentally deficient children don't always have mentally deficient parents, do they ? "
" No, many of these children, of the primary or hereditary type, come from parents who, while not being mentally defective themselves, are below the average in intelligence, stability, perseverance and other characteristics which go to make up the good citizen. These people are carriers of mental defects; they possess the bad genes in their sex cells and can pass them on to their children. The Committee divided these cases into three main groups :—

(1) Idiots, who have a mental age up to two years and comprise about 5 per cent. of all defectives.

(2) Imbeciles, who have a mental age from two to seven years and comprise about 20 per cent. of all defectives.

(3) Feeble-minded persons, who have a mental age from seven to ten years and comprise about 75 per cent. of all defectives.

" It was found that the children in the first two groups were born of parents who, for the most part, hardly differed from the average of the population. In other words, the parents seemed to be normal people. Those from the third group, however, often came from families whose standard of living was well below the average for the community. The explanation is that the majority of idiots and imbeciles owe their defects to birth injuries or accidents, as in your own particular example, whereas the feeble-minded are more likely to inherit their condition. The Wood Committee came to the conclusion that two-thirds of the mental defectives could live in the community under supervision, but that the remaining 100,000 should be placed in institutions."

" But should those who live in the community be allowed to breed ? "

" That's the problem. One of the difficulties is that it would be very difficult to stop them. Some of them could probably learn and practise contraceptive methods satisfactorily, especially if these methods become safer and simpler. Others, however, could not. In which case it would probably be wise to allow them to marry, provided they were sterilised. However, don't let us wander off on to the problem of voluntary sterilisation now. If you are really interested you should read Dr. Blacker's excellent book ' Voluntary Sterilisation ', from which comes the greater part of the information I have given you."

" Then it would not be right to say that all these defective conditions are inherited ? "

" No, but it's difficult to determine how much is due to hereditary conditions and how much to accidental causes. Some authorities place the hereditary factor at over 75 per cent., others would say that 75 per cent. of cases were non-hereditary. The reason for these wide differences of opinion is that different investigators use different standards. Take mental deficiency, for instance. Some authorities say that only 5 per cent. of mentally deficient children have mentally deficient parents. Others would place the figure much higher.

Dr. Hansell opened a book he had with him.

" Let me read you an extract from Dr. Blacker's book," he said. " The Brock Committee which was appointed in 1932 to investigate the problem of sterilisation seem to think that ' a slight modification of standard may result in a large increase in the number of persons regarded as mentally deficient among these borderline cases. Clinically, there is no definite line separating mental deficiency from dullness ; one condition merges gradually into the other '. In summing up the position, Dr. Blacker says that ' taking all the defectives into consideration, it is probably legitimate to say that no more than 10 per cent. of all defectives have one or both parents certifiably defective within the meaning of the Mental Deficiency Acts '.[1]

[1] Blacker, C. P., " Voluntary Sterilisation ", O.U.P., 1934, p. 52.

"You must bear in mind, however," Dr. Hansell continued, laying down the book, "that up to the present we have only been considering the inheritance of mental defect, and have not touched on the inheritance of mental disease."

"Yes, I realise that. What about the second method of investigation?"

"You mean the estimation of the intelligence of the whole population?"

"Yes."

"Some recent work has been done by Dr. R. B. Cattell and reported on in his book 'The Fight for Our National Intelligence'. He was investigating the possibility that the average mental capacity in this country may be declining owing to the differential birth rate; that is to say, that the production of children is not evenly distributed throughout the population."

"Yes."

"Two population groups were tested, one in the city of Leicester, with over 200,000 inhabitants, and the other in an unspoilt rural area of twenty scattered villages and townlets in Devonshire, varying in population from 300 to 6,000 people. Nearly 3,000 ten-year-old children were tested in the urban area and about 1,000 in the rural."[1]

"You mean that they came from ordinary schools and were presumably normal children?"

"Exactly. He found that 75 per cent. of the children are feeble-minded when *both of the parents* are feeble-minded. He puts the percentage of mentally defective children higher than the figure of 1 per cent. suggested by the Departmental Committee in 1929, and thinks it is nearly 4 per cent."

"But that looks as if the condition is getting worse."

"That may be, but only a small fraction of the population was investigated, so that it would not be right to make any dogmatic statement. His findings are certainly sufficiently serious to warrant a more widespread investigation."

"How can one test intelligence?"

"There are specially devised tests to enable this to be done quite easily, without the individual knowing what is happen-

[1] The actual figures were 2,873 children in the urban area and 873 in the rural.

ing; children are easier to test than adults. In this way the whole population can be divided into groups according to intelligence. Some people are imbeciles and idiots, incapable of learning anything; others are mentally retarded, but capable of being taught something in special schools; others have a normal intelligence; whilst others again are clever. A few are brilliant. The result of these tests is expressed in intelligence quotients. I have Dr. Cattell's figures here," Dr. Hansell said, picking up another book. "Have a look at them for yourself. You will see that he divides the distribution of intelligence into five parts." [1]

Intelligence quotient.	Class.	Per cent. of population.
40–60	Feeble-minded	About 4
60–80	Dull, subcultural	20
80–115	Average	50
115–135	Able	20
135–180	Brilliant, highly gifted	5

"He points out that the intelligence quotient does not vary very much as one grows older; one cannot acquire more intelligence, although one can be taught to develop the intelligence one possesses. Mental capacity is inborn; one cannot buy it. Higher intelligence is found among the children whose parents are in more complex occupations. He thinks that the children with intelligence quotients of over 140 are being materially reduced, and that there will be an increase in mental deficiency in the next generation. The cost of educating these mentally backward children is extremely high—about £36 per child, as against £12 for the normal child.[2] We are already spending about £11,000,000 a year on the certified defectives. There are, of course, many children who are on the border-line, attending ordinary schools."

"Is it fair to expect teachers to cope with children who can't really benefit by the instruction provided?" Mrs. Bellamy demanded, as she returned the book to the doctor.

"No, I don't think it is. A lot of their work is wasted in consequence."

[1] "The Fight for our National Intelligence", p. 106.
[2] Cattell, "The Fight for our National Intelligence", p. 47 (pre-war money values).

"But surely no one wants children who are either mentally or physically warped?"

"The fact remains that we are breeding them. Children of small mental capacity are more liable to criminal behaviour and lack of judgment, and have anti-social tendencies. They make discontented members of society, always ready to stir up trouble, and easily led by agitators who are cleverer and less scrupulous than themselves. They aren't fit to enter the skilled trades of the country."

"How can we expect people to have good characters if they are so lacking in mental capacity?"

"That's just the point. Listen to this: 'Every new and hopeful thing in social progress, every step towards greater happiness and freedom requires, for its success, the support of an adequate number of people capable of appreciating the significance of the new truth, and that generally involves grasping some abstract principle in place of traditional practice. This, of course, applies to Art, Morals and Character'."[1]

Dr. Hansell turned over another page or two. "Here's another good remark," he said. "'Democracy is only just possible at the level of intelligence we now possess'."[2]

"The problem is a serious one because we shall never reorganise society and build a community based on mutual respect and appreciation unless we enlist the brain power of the country on the side of reconstruction. It seems that only 5 per cent. of the population possesses that high measure of intelligence which is so greatly needed in industry to-day. Here is a passage from another book I have just been reading: 'Intelligence is the supreme gift which raises man above the level of the beasts, and when this is defective, retarded or unstable, it is at least conceivable that the resulting lack of balance or adjustment may declare itself in more than one form. Intelligence, moreover, is the quality most essential if men are to get on together as members of any kind of social group; those who fail to reach a certain standard of intelligence are liable to becomes a "social problem group"; a group dependent on society'."[3]

[1] Cattell, "The Fight for our National Intelligence", p. 57.
[2] *Ibid.*, p. 61.
[3] Dr. Caradoc Jones in "A Social Problem Group?" edited by Dr. Blacker, p. 224.

"Are these sub-normal people only to be found among the poorer sections of the community?"

"No. I've already said that certain conditions, such as idiocy, are found to exist in a greater proportion among the more cultured groups of society.[1] It has been pointed out by Professor Carr-Saunders somewhere, that in each social group there is sound material at one end of the group and bad material at the other end.[2]

"You've concentrated on the hereditary side of the problem. Doesn't environment play an important part?"

"Of course, but it's difficult to say how much influence such conditions as bad food, unhealthy surroundings, squalor and poverty have on intelligence. Probably better conditions will help people to use what intelligence they have to better advantage. Some authorities are of the opinion that there is a large pool of untapped intelligence in the population which for one reason or another has never had the opportunity of being developed. It is possible that one of the effects of the new Education Act will be to bring this untapped source to light and give it an opportunity of being properly developed."

"Is it true that physical development is influenced by environment?"

"Yes, I think it is. Sir John Orr recently published some rather striking figures on this aspect of the question.[3] He records the results of measurements of the heights of boys taken from schools of different social grades; a 'public school', attended by boys of well-to-do parents, Christ's Hospital, which caters largely for boys of the middle class, two elementary schools in London and a group of wage-earning boys in actual work; in all about 70,000 boys. The results show that the boys from Christ's Hospital are, on the average, considerably taller than boys of the same age group from the elementary schools; but that they themselves are

---

[1] 9·5 per cent. in the superior families, as against 5·4 per cent. in the very poor.

[2] *Eugenics Review*, April, 1935. "Within each class of Society at one end of the scale there is material of the highest value and at the other end material which is poor and worthless. There is evidence that families are largest within the classes at the wrong end of the scale."

[3] "Food, Health and Income."

not so tall as the boys from the 'public school'. There seems to be a similar relationship between average weights of children from the rich and the poor. The Coles, discussing the matter in one of their recent books say: 'There is little doubt that a comprehensive investigation would confirm the conclusion that the rich, age for age, are taller and heavier than the poor, as a result, partly, of heredity, but also in part of better nutrition in childhood and of being born of better nourished mothers'." [1]

" It makes one think, doesn't it ? "

" It certainly does. One of our present troubles is that if you move people from slums to municipal housing schemes, the rents of the latter are so much greater than those of the slum dwellings that the people have to cut down on their food in order to pay the increased rent.[2] Because the people are having smaller families, there is a big demand for smaller houses, and of course the housing problem is appalling. Quite apart from the lack of accommodation, there are still thousands of houses all over the country that are a positive disgrace. Thousands of people still live in overcrowded, insanitary, ill-repaired and back-to-back houses. Give them more income, time to adjust themselves to their new surroundings, social amenities which they can afford to enjoy, and they might become healthier and happier, provided you teach them how to use their leisure. But it is a slow process, and one often has to wait for the next generation to grow up to see any real improvement."

" And meanwhile they breed like rabbits."

" You can't exactly blame them."

" They might at least practise birth control."

" In theory I agree, in practice I see many difficulties. There are nothing like enough clinics in the country, and where there are clinics it is difficult to persuade the people to go to them; not only because they do not appreciate their value, but because of the expense. Even a few pence is a large item out of some people's weekly budget. If they haven't enough money for the necessities of life you can

---

[1] G. D. H. and M. I. Cole, " The Condition of Britain ", p. 111.
[2] This has been clearly shown by Dr. M'Gonigle in his book, " Poverty and Public Health ".

hardly expect them to spend money on contraceptives, especially when they have such faith in their own particular method of coitus interruptus, or ' being careful ', which costs nothing."

"Surely they realise that it fails over and over again."

"They do; but they don't understand the reason for its failure. Quite apart from all this, however, I doubt if you would bother to use contraceptives under the conditions that some of these people have to endure."

"I dare say not, but if they are really incapable of practising the present methods, I should have thought it would be a good thing to sterilise them."

"I hardly think you could do that. You can't force people to do this or that. Besides, it is the conditions which are at fault rather than the people. When you start to consider the ' social problem group ' I admit that its a different matter, but that is too large a subject to embark on now."

"Of course not, but I find it all very interesting."

"The main thing we have to do is to encourage parenthood among those who are biologically healthy, no matter to what class of society they belong, and discourage the breeding of unsuitable stock. If we are to improve the physical and moral condition of the nation, we must pay more attention to quality than quantity."

"Yes," Mrs. Bellamy said as she got up, "I shall remember that quite easily. Quality rather than quantity. It has been one of the guiding principles of my life; I impressed it on Wendy when we were buying the new sheets for her house, but unfortunately one has to take what one can get these days. Thank you, Jerry; you have taken a load off my mind. I must go, or I shall miss the lecture. Dr. Alice Minor is talking about psychologist development during the first five years of life. Are you coming? It ought to be interesting."

Dr. Hansell laughed. "No doubt," he said, "but I shall stay here and think over what I am going to say to-night." He took her hand for a moment. "You won't worry any more, Meg, will you?"

"No, certainly not, Jerry. I feel much happier now that I have got it all off my chest."

CHAPTER V

THE SOCIAL PROBLEM

THE evening meeting was packed when Dr. Hansell rose to speak.

"I'm not sure how much use I shall be to you to-night," he said. "I'm not going to give you any magic key that will unlock the door of some wonderful garden of knowledge, where life is easy; because that is impossible. Life is not easy, and I doubt whether it was ever intended to be so. The most valuable people in the world are those who have found life difficult and have managed to overcome difficulties, thereby developing character. But character itself can vary. There are those whose character is such that their influence is positive and good; there are those whose influence is definitely bad, and there are those whose influence is nothing in particular. The majority of people belong to this latter group, unfortunately. For the most part they are unconcerned with life around them except in so far as it affects their peace and comfort. Their inertia forms a dead weight against progressive idealism. Their attitude to life is purely individual—largely materialistic. They move with the masses, uninstructed, and uninterested. Their motto is 'Leave well alone'. This attitude is particularly apparent when we come to consider the subject of social morality. The vast majority of people cannot see that the problems of our sex lives affect the whole structure of our civilisation; that our attitude to sex colours the whole of our outlook on life. If our attitude to sex is creative, our attitude to life is positive. If our attitude to sex is negative, our attitude to life is warped, and may even become callous, brutal and harmful.

"If the war has done nothing else, it has presented the social problem in a new light, illustrating the barrenness of our moral structure, the hypocrisy of our behaviour and the confusion of our thinking. It would, however, be inaccurate to say that the alteration in sexual behaviour which can be observed both here and in America is only due to the effects of war; there are deeper causes to be considered.

"War, by encouraging a materialistic outlook which pays little attention to the deeper values of life and often ignores the personality of those around us, merely accentuates selfishness and the desire to live in and for the present; materialism is the curse of this age. I doubt if progress will be made towards a fuller and more satisfying social morality until the individual is accepted for what he is—a unique personality, worthy of respect and understanding, and not just a cog in a great machine, whether that machine is the State, the large business combine or the tiny village community. The question that affects us all to-day is whether we are simply State servants obeying the laws which it sees fit to promulgate, or whether the State is intended to be the servant of the people, its laws being designed for their welfare. Some say that the individual is paramount, others that the State must regulate everything. The truth is, of course, that the State is not just an abstract thing, but is composed of individuals, and the individual has his responsibility to the State. In other words, we each have an individuality which must be respected and encouraged to grow in an atmosphere of freedom and healthy competition, whilst at the same time the individual can never reach a full maturity until he becomes a co-operative citizen working for the good of his neighbours and ultimately for the good of the State. There are six unsatisfactory conditions in social morality which, owing to the fact that they have never been tackled satisfactorily by the individual or the State, are undermining the family. They are: divorce and separation, sex relationships before marriage, extra-marital relationships, illegitimacy, abortion and venereal disease. To all of them we have turned a blind eye in the past and a myopic vision in the present. Our refusal to understand them and deal with them intelligently causes an immense amount of preventable misery, unhappiness and mental and physical ill-health.

DIVORCE AND SEPARATION

"An analysis of the statistics of the Registrar-General's report shows that there were about 42,000 applications for divorce or separation in 1944. By 1947 the number of divorces alone will probably be in the region of 50,000, and this does not take into account the applications for separation, which run into many thousands a year.[1] All this may be explained in part by the unsettlement occasioned by the war ; by the enforced separations and hasty marriages which have occurred during the past ten years. At the beginning of the century the number was about 500 a year. During the reign of Queen Anne there would not have been more than a dozen a year. In 1857 jurisdiction in matrimonial causes was transferred from the ecclesiastical courts to the civil courts, and this enabled more marriages to be dissolved.[2] But this is not all. The number of divorces begun reflects only a fraction of the marital disharmony which exists throughout the entire country—the whole world, in fact. The reports also show that from 1938 to 1943 nearly one in three of all first maternities were conceived outside marriage, and it may be safely estimated that one in ten of all women in this country have sex relationships outside marriage—the number is probably as great or even greater in other countries. In Sweden, for instance, one of the major social problems is the enormous number of sex relationships which occur amongst young people and the consequent high illegitimate and abortion rates. In this country in 1938 40 per cent. of all girls marrying under the age of twenty were already pregnant ; 30 per cent. of those aged twenty, and 20 per cent. of those aged twenty-one.[3]

"In most of these ' cover-up ' marriages the seeds of future emotional conflict are already sown, and ignorance of the basic principles of the sexual function, together with feelings of fear, guilt or shame engendered in one or both

[1] Mace, David R., "The Outlook for Marriage", Marriage Guidance Council, 1945.
[2] Denning, Mr. Justice, "The Divorce Laws", The Churchman Publishing Co., 1947, p. 6.
[3] Mace, David R., "The Outlook for Marriage", Marriage Guidance Council, 1945.

partners, will soon produce a rich crop of disharmonies. Resentment with the other partner often lies dormant to start off with, but springs to activity when things begin to go wrong. All this encourages the development of anti-social tendencies in the grown-ups and delinquency in the children. It will be seen, therefore, that thousands of unhappy or disillusioned people are being returned into the social pool every year, all of them having to readjust and many, no doubt, having to form fresh relationships which may or may not be of a more stable nature. We shall not be far out then if we say that the annual marriage breakdown rate in this country is round about 20 per cent. and in America the figure is even higher.[1] As for those countries which have been ravaged by the war, no one can say what the figures are, but they must be far worse.

Legal separation is but a method of escape, and if continued too long must, by its very nature, encourage further unhappiness and, very often, further unsatisfactory relationships. As a temporary expedient which will give the couple time to think, readjust and perhaps obtain some specialised help and advice it has a definite role to play in the sphere of marriage reconciliation. One of the crying needs of the time is a complete overhaul of the divorce system; the introduction of conciliatory machinery as suggested by the Denning Committee, and the elimination of the sexual factor from most of the cases. To condemn divorce root and branch, as is done by such organisations as the Mothers' Union, on the ground that it is immoral and unchristian, is inhuman and, in my opinion, contrary to the whole spirit of Christ's teaching. If divorce is immoral, so are all the arrangements or lack of arrangements which permitted the original marriage, which, so far as I can see, can scarcely be said to have been made in heaven."

Dr. Hansell paused for a moment to look at his audience. That they were interested was shown by their concentrated attention and the absence of noise.

[1] See Burgess and Locke, "The Family", American Book Co., 1945.

SEX RELATIONSHIPS BEFORE MARRIAGE

" So much for divorce," he continued. " What of the next problem—sex relationships before marriage ? It is not easy to assess with any accuracy the proportion of people who are conducting these relationships to-day. All that can be said is that they have markedly increased within recent years. There are five fairly easily distinguishable types :

    (*a*) The casual.
    (*b*) The friendship.
    (*c*) The affection.
    (*d*) The changing.
    (*e*) The premarital.

(a) *The Casual Type.*

" The casual affair often arises between people who hardly know each other but who meet after a party or a dance and ' feel that way ', as one girl put it to me. The couple may or may not meet again. Such affairs are far more common than is generally supposed, and, being ill thought out and badly prepared for, frequently end in disaster. There is a type of young man in our big cities who limits himself to this type of relationship and frequently boasts of his ' conquests '. And there are plenty of girls to aid and abet him. Both frequently exhibit other traits of an anti-social nature and are often on the border-line of problem cases. Some men, in all social groups, still seem to regard women as fair game for the satisfaction of their physical needs. They copulate with all and sundry without considering the consequences of their action and without taking adequate precautions to prevent a pregnancy. I suppose such people will always exist in every community, however well educated and knowledgeable we all become, but that they should run the risk of introducing an unwanted child into the world seems to me to be profoundly immoral, and little short of criminal. I would like such people isolated from society and given a course of re-education, and would not allow them to mix with the general public until they presented evidence of knowledge and stability.

(b) *The Friendship Type.*

"Relationships of a slightly more stable nature, there being some kind of mutual interest between the couple other than that of sex, may be termed the friendship type of relationship. The general increase in freedom between the sexes encourages this sort of behaviour, especially when that freedom is not accompanied by knowledge and understanding. Such affairs may go on for weeks or months, but usually come to an end almost as soon as they have begun, leaving one or both of the partners unhappy and disillusioned. This is particularly true of the girl, who, if it is her first experience, feels besmirched and ashamed—a state of affairs which she often covers up by excessive bravado. Their contraceptive technique is usually limited to coitus interruptus or the occasional use of a sheath.

(c) *The Affection Type.*

"A different type of affair in which there is considerable affection and understanding between the couple may be termed the affection type. They try and think things out as well as possible beforehand, but owing to the fact that they do not know very much about sex, and will not seek advice, make rather a muddle of it. They may meet fairly regularly; go away for week-ends or holidays together, or even inhabit the same house or flat. They are usually young—often of the student type—and are to be found in most social groups. The reasons that prompt their behaviour are legion: propinquity and certain mutual interests, loneliness and unhappy or unstable family backgrounds, lack of money with which to marry combined with a need for affection and physical activity, and many other similar conditions. Their contraceptive technique varies from indifferent to good. Only rarely is marriage seriously contemplated, and one of the tragedies that is almost certain to occur is that one of the partners, usually the girl, falls deeply in love with the other and really wants to marry and settle down, whilst the other is quite satisfied with the relationship as it is. Thus they begin to quarrel and hurt each other. Finally they part. Such affairs are very common indeed.

(d) *The Changing Type.*

"There is a small but important group of people—usually women—whose psychological life-pattern is such that they seem to desire, and even thrive on, change. They are so made that they cannot settle down with one partner for very long. The family background of such people is frequently unsatisfactory. Deprived of love, affection and security in childhood and adolescence, they seem to be constitutionally incapable of growing up emotionally, and their sexual pattern is immature. Some are just incapable of more than a butterfly existence, others, having become conditioned that way by circumstances not altogether under their control, have developed this particular life-pattern, which is really that of an abnormal adolescent. Constant change and excitement are as necessary to them as drink is to the semi-inebriate. Nothing less than a severe shock will jolt them out of their present mode of behaviour. Occasionally they manage to break away and grow up to the acceptance of mature responsibility. More often they just drift from one affair to another, becoming more and more maladjusted in the process. Alternatively they give the whole thing up and regress into unhealthy instability.

(e) *The Pre-Marital Type.*

"The last group is of a different nature, and is the only one to which the term pre-marital should be given, because the intention of the couple is to see if they are really suited to each other physically before marriage, in which case they do marry. Their reasons are usually well thought out, and they often seek expert advice beforehand, and the woman usually acquires a suitable contraceptive technique. The main argument in favour of this behaviour is that sex relationships are a purely personal affair so long as no children result; that the sex life of a married couple is of supreme social as well as personal importance, and apparently goes wrong with such appalling frequency that they do not intend to be caught out in that way. Such relationships cannot be dismissed as mere immorality or classed with those we have already considered. They are practised all over the world, and are greatly on the increase. Many of them are satisfactory in so far as they go; that is to say, the couple are confirmed in their opinion of each other and eventually marry. Others do not end in marriage for the simple reason that the couple find they are not suited to each other, and therefore separate—frequently without recrimination and often remaining friends. Such behaviour is an indication of the changing attitude on the part of the public to the whole function of sex and to the changing social morals of our present civilisation. That they are contrary to the accepted rules of social behaviour and to the religious conception of marriage has little significance with the couple, who are frequently high-minded, intelligent people who maintain that their attitude is more sensible than that of those who wait until the marriage service gives sanction to an act of such supreme importance to their future happiness. 'Why,' they ask, 'should it be presumed that the marriage service will make everything right when, in fact, it is very well known that the reverse is often the case and thousands of couples find to their regret that the sexual function is by no means so easy to manage as their forefathers pretended?' This is not the place, nor have I the time, to discuss this attitude at length.[1] I would only suggest that this particular type of relationship cannot be lightly dismissed simply because it does not conform to the accepted social conventions. There are, however, a few observations I would like to make about the whole situation.

" 1. In the first place, the couple, whom we will presume have not had previous sex experience, make the great mistake of presuming that the sex act will function perfectly almost at once—in a night or a week-end—or a week. But this is not so. Even though the girl should go to a doctor and be fitted with a contraceptive device and they both learn as much as possible about technique, indeed though they both should receive all the teaching that goes under the heading of marriage preparation, it by no means follows that they

[1] See Chapter XIV.

will achieve perfection in the time they allow themselves. Broadly speaking, I should say that even when a couple have received adequate marriage preparation it will take them anything from two to six weeks or six months to achieve a mutual orgasm, the average being about two months. And if any extraneous circumstance such as' fear or anxiety should enter into the relationship the time will be much longer. Indeed, I would say that no woman will get a proper orgasm until she is willing to completely let herself go emotionally, and very few women will really do that in the circumstances we are considering. They always hold something in reserve, and this is apparent even in those more experienced women who have had several affairs before marriage. I have made careful inquiries from many women who made this kind of 'pre-marital experiment', and almost all of them admit that it was not entirely satisfactory and that they might just as well have waited till they were properly married and prepared for marriage.

" 2. Secondly, I think that most of those who are in a position to know would say that the number of people who have had sex relationships with their married partner or someone else before marriage is very high. Personally, I would put the figure at about 75 per cent. In many cases actual coitus does not take place, although everything else is permitted. This behaviour is technically known as petting, and is profoundly unsatisfactory from every point of view. Emotional stimulation should always end in emotional release. This cannot occur in these cases, and so the individual remains in a state of emotional tension which, if persisted in for some time, leads to over-excitability, frustration and various physical and psychological ills.[1] Such behaviour prohibits a true emotional development and retards those creative powers which are so essential to the fuller development of the personality. Indeed, it may eventually lead to a type of individual who can never take his or her matrimonial responsibilities seriously. It may even produce frigidity and sexual inability later on. Such an irresponsible attitude to one of the most sacred functions

[1] See Chap. VIII.

of life will never make a constructive contribution to our present-day problems.

"3. Should physical relationships occur, a more subtle situation may arise. Once begun, physical activity rouses a desire which needs constant fulfilment. If this is not achieved with the person with whom the relationship was started—if something goes wrong and the relationship does not prove satisfactory—there is a tendency for the individual to seek other adventures of a similar nature in the hope of finding this real fulfilment. Thus the individual becomes conditioned to an immature life-pattern in which there is a constant seeking for new adventure and new fields of conquest. He or she passes from one to the other, changing without rhyme or reason—ever in search of the ideal. The physical is over-emphasised at the expense of the other elements of the personality. Such people say that when they do find the right partner everything will be all right and they will settle down, but in my experience this happens but rarely, and the pattern laid down often persists in marriage, and causes much unhappiness. There are exceptions, of course, but in so far as my experience goes, I should say that this was the general result. I could give you many examples of marriages being wrecked because of the establishment of this type of life-pattern in one of the partners. There is an inherent instability that persists. The physical having been over-emphasised, the pattern of monogamy disappears or is repressed, and something else reigns in its stead. If this is recognised by the couple, all may be well, but there will need to be very strong ties of another nature to keep the marriage stable.

"4. Should the pre-marital relationship I have already mentioned progress to marriage, the picture is different. There can be no doubt that in a certain small number of carefully-thought-out relationships the result is satisfactory, but—and it is a large but—the initial situation must be carefully thought out and planned. We may well ask ourselves, therefore, whether this particular type of relationship is the answer to our moral problem. Will it work for the whole of society? Is there no other alternative? I will try and give an answer to these questions later on.

"5. Finally I would remind you that it is much easier for a person who has never had sex experience to remain continent than it is for one who has had various affairs to stop having them and return to a celibate life. This is not to deny that the practice of celibacy for the young man or woman is not difficult; it is—profoundly so—especially at the present time, when the trend of social opinion is to regard such behaviour as strange—I was almost going to say unnatural. But it is much more difficult for the person with experience to pull himself up.

Sex relationships before marriage are but one aspect of the whole picture of sex relationships outside marriage. The other—extra-marital relationships—is even more complicated, and a whole lecture could be devoted to this one subject alone. I can only say that the effects of these relationships are often very devastating. I hope to have the chance of discussing the matter later on.[1] Nor can I do more than draw your attention to the remaining three groups—illegitimacy, abortion and venereal disease. They all have a profoundly unsatisfactory effect on our social life. The illegitimate rate of about 50,000 per annum does not diminish, and is a subject about which society is becoming increasingly anxious because of its evil effects on the child, who is usually sent to some institution, unless adopted or kept by the parents, and so loses security and love. Abortion is an even greater evil.[2]

Venereal Disease.

"As for venereal disease, this, too, has increased enormously within recent years, although its effects are not so great as they were fifty years ago, owing to the great advances that have been made in treatment and prevention. The position on the Continent is worse than in this country, although it is bad enough here, when we remember that several thousand new cases occur each year. But even if there was not a single case of venereal disease in the country, the problems that I am considering would still remain. It is cheering to find that people are at last realising that the

[1] See Chapter VIII.
[2] See Chapters XI and XV.

problem of venereal disease is not the whole sex problem; indeed, it is a very small part of a great whole. If people had a right outlook towards sex, the V.D. problem would diminish in intensity, as would the other conditions we have been considering to-night."

Dr. Hansell paused for a moment before continuing:

"The truth is that we are a hypocritical nation where sex is concerned, and will not face facts. So many people imagine that we can live to a set pattern that they will not make allowances for those who, for one reason or another, cannot conform to the rigid code they demand. How often does one not see an over-emphasis of the sexual element which often blinds the couple to the many deficiencies that exist in the other partner. You will agree, I think, that when you add together these various unsatisfactory situations, the sum total weighs heavily against the family. These social evils, affecting as they do both the individual and the State, must be combated. We cannot afford to allow them to persist with such intensity in our society. But their abolition cannot be brought about unless society recognises their gravity and takes positive steps to minimise their evil effects. Nor must it be thought that they are the only factors impinging on the stability of family life. There are many others more closely related to our economic life which are so serious that many people fear they will overthrow the whole structure of the family. Personally I do not hold this view, and whilst agreeing with Westermarck that marriage is rooted in the family, and when we disrupt the one we endanger the other, I do not think we should be afraid of change either in the one or the other. When everything else around us is changing and altering we must not be surprised if there are changes in marriage and family life. I would like to mention nine further factors which are having a profound influence on the family at the present time. 1. Changing family pattern. 2. Separation. 3. Equality of sexes. 4. Contraception. 5. Insecurity. 6. Mechanisation. 7. Altering standards. 8. Individualism. 9. Greater knowledge of sex.

"1. *Changing Family Pattern.*—In the first place the family pattern is changing. Where we had the large united family ruled by the father as the head of a group, we now find the small family system taking its place, and the internal relationships between members of the family altering and becoming looser in some ways, broader in others. Towns are taking the place of villages, and the young people tend to migrate to the former and live their own lives and go their own ways outside the family circle. At the same time this greater freedom does allow for the development of a far more emotional relationship between parent and child if the parents are prepared to accept the changing conditions and act positively and intelligently. I say parents advisedly, because I am convinced that if they are forthcoming and understanding, the children will be equally so.

" 2. *Separation.*—The war, by separating families for months and years, has put an intolerable burden on the emotional life of many people. Only a day or two ago I saw a woman whose marriage was in danger of breaking down because her husband had been abroad for several years and formed a liaison with some girl he met on his travels and now finds it difficult to settle down to the humdrum life of home, wife and two young children who get on his nerves. Now, for the first time possibly, he is beginning to realise that marriage involves responsibility, and that the good time he had with the attractive and unattached young woman does not mean that he can walk out on his wife and children. But the process of settling down for this couple will be difficult, as it is for thousands more like them. Some cannot stay the course, and rush to the divorce court.

" 3. *Equality of Sexes.*—The changing attitude to women, allowing them to work outside the home and have lucrative and interesting occupations, has altered the whole relationship between the sexes, putting women on an equality which was never possible before.

" 4. *Contraception.*—This is made more possible by the discoveries of science in relation to sex, and in particular to the perfection of contraceptive methods, which, by enabling women to regulate their pregnancies, has made it possible for them to become sexually independent of man for the first time in the history of civilisation. To my mind contraception is a scientific discovery equal in importance to that of X-rays or printing. By allowing greater freedom of choice, it places a greater burden of responsibility on the individual, and opens up many channels for positive fulfilment or dangerous misuse. The burden of decision in regard to any particular course of action becomes heavier and more important. More is expected of the individual: greater forethought, more understanding and a greater realisation of the dangers of the misuse of his or her powers. A greater responsibility devolves on the State to ensure that the citizens are well educated in these matters.

" 5. *Insecurity*.—A profound feeling of insecurity due to widespread and continuous world warfare during the past fifty years has made people disillusioned and anxious, encouraging selfishness and a need for momentary amusement. Life has become so complex, so frustrating, and for many people so dull, that they will do anything to escape, in the hope of throwing over the old ties and making a new start—very often in a new job, a new town or a new land. Why not, then, with a new partner?

" 6. *Mechanisation*.—Mechanisation and scientific invention, by raising the standard of living, have brought about a complete alteration in our standards of values. Until quite recently these changes were hailed with almost universal delight, but now there are signs that people are not quite so sure that true happiness is to be found that way. Constant change, movement and excitement; running from this place to that, doing everything on the material level, as Canon Heathcott pointed out in an earlier lecture, does not seem to bring the contentment and happiness people were hoping for. And why not? Because the occupations are often dull and soul-destroying, and compensation is sought for outside the home in amusement and gaiety. Many women who leave home at nine in the morning and return at six in the evening to cook the dinner have to spend the rest of the evening hurrying through the chores they should have been doing all day. Many of them seem incapable of settling down to the more fulfilling but less exciting task of home-making. Some, of course, aren't made that way. They have had everything provided for them by a beneficent Government for so long that they are incapable of fending for themselves. Others are just bored—bored with their jobs, their homes and their husbands! And the same applies to the man.

"7. *Alteration in Standards.*—A changing attitude to religion has contributed much to this alteration in our standards and values. Many have no other standard than that of personal gain. 'What is right is what I decide is best for myself.' This is not to say that people are not conscious of the need for spiritual expression. I think they are, but they find orthodox religion as taught by some people too difficult to understand and too much out of sympathy with present-day life. A religious revival is long overdue in this country, but it will have to be more dynamic and forthright; more positive, more willing to make allowances for the frailties of human nature and, in my opinion, far more sensitive to the difficulties of family life. When such attempts are made by the Churches the response is excellent and the results very encouraging. The truth is that people are looking for a new family pattern in which there must be equality and mutual respect, independence of thought and outlook; a refusal to accept the interference of other members of the family, co-operation and a right to decide for themselves. Children of the future will be planned and wanted, and not produced haphazardly and without due thought, and once in the family will have a say in the management of the family.

"8. *Individualism.*—There is too much individualism about to-day. One of our greatest difficulties is the extraordinary isolation in which individuals and families live. There is far too little corporate activity and not enough opportunity for people to meet other people, exchange ideas and receive encouragement and help. Youth clubs are all very well in their way, but they tend to take the children away from the family circle and separate parent from child, so that eventually they have nothing to say to each other when they are together. The corporate life of the village, the family and the small community is rapidly disappearing. The need is being met to some extent, and indeed the answer to our troubles is probably to be found in the wide extension of such group centres as the Peckham Health

Centre. Corporate activities of this nature breed contentment, toleration and understanding. They bring out the best in people and give encouragement to the weak and stability to the wayward. Isolation, whether individually or in the small-family system, breeds selfishness, jealousy and many similar ills. This is particularly true of sex, which, even to-day, is avoided, glossed over, exaggerated or never mentioned in many homes. The muddles and unhappiness which so often result from this policy are quite incredible. Another thing that isolation does is to make the young people too dependent on the parents and allow for the development of possessiveness and parent fixation which so often ruins the future married life of the children.

" 9. *Greater Knowledge of Sex.*—We are only just beginning to realise that our so-called morality bears no relationship to physiological facts or psychological principles, and that sexual activity must not take place without responsibility. The underlying purpose of sex has been defined by Havelock Ellis as including ' all the finer activities of the organism, physical and psychic ',[1] in which sexual pleasure wisely used, and not abused, may prove the liberator of the finest and the most exalted of our activities.[2] Sex energy, Freud tells us, should be regarded as a treasured possession by everyone, and is essentially creative. It deals with ' love ' in its widest sense ; and all-embracing love which concerns others than ourselves—our parents and children, our country and humanity in general. It possesses the power of being transferred into other and more creative channels. As such it differs materially from the instinct of hunger with which many people compare it. We still tolerate the idea that it is a safety-valve for sin and that it is only within the borders of matrimony that it can be rightly expressed. The idea that women should derive pleasure from the relationship, or that coitus without mutual desire is a desecration of her personality even in marriage, is still foreign to many people. Thus we cannot blame the younger generation for experimenting along new lines, although we may

---

[1] "Lovers and Art", in the book on Marriage by Keyserling, p. 388.
[2] Walter Lippmann, quoting Havelock Ellis in "Preface to Morals", p. 301.

criticise the extreme stupidity with which this is often done.

" It is time, too, that we asked ourselves seriously whether it is right to demand a long period of continence from all young people—this period often running into the thirties. In my opinion this attitude merely encourages the conditions it is designed to prevent.

" One of the most important matters that we have come to appreciate more clearly is the innate differences between the sexes. From the very moment of conception the female differs from the male; every cell is different, and every influence that comes to bear causes a different response. Indeed, the influences themselves are different because the physiologist has shown conclusively that the male and female hormones differ in themselves. The discovery of these hormones and the demonstration of their profound influence on our emotional and reproductive life have revolutionised our conception of sexual physiology. We know that women feel things differently from men and react in a different way. Their range of emotional variations is greater and alters according to the stage of their physiological cycle, rising and falling like the tides of the sea.

" These deep-seated influences are partly responsible for the dual purpose of woman's sexual life—of her need for satisfying both the reproductive and emotional side of her nature. Man's sexual lapses have always been tolerated by society, indeed they are more or less expected of him. Woman, on the other hand, has never been expected to have a sex life of her own, apart from reproduction. Her inability to appreciate sex feeling has been stressed for years, until many women have come to believe that they do not possess the capacity for sexual appreciation. If they admitted to such enjoyment, they were frequently looked upon as being of loose moral character. How such ideas originated need not concern us now, but they have done much harm. The only way in which it has been possible to enforce their acceptance has been by denying women knowledge of their own bodily functions and by shutting them away from the evil persuasions of man. As a result, they have been at the mercy of men who have not neglected to make use of their opportunities. It is only within recent times that we have come to view these matters in a more sensible light and to recognise honestly that a woman requires emotional satisfaction just as much as a man does, and further that the production of children is by no means the only way in which she can obtain this satisfaction. A woman who has had half-a-dozen children has probably satisfied her reproductive instinct, but it by no means follows that she derived any satisfaction from the physical relationship that was a necessary preliminary to their conception. The reconciliation of these needs with our social behaviour is one of the major problems which confronts us to-day. One cannot help wondering if it is mere chance that the science of contraception has been brought to its present state of perfection at this juncture in the history of the family, for here we have means by which woman can reconcile these two ends.

"These nine conditions are but some of the factors impinging on family life to-day. To many their influence appears to be entirely evil and likely to lead to the destruction of marriage and family life. I do not take that view; on the contrary, I think the influences we have considered, whilst being disruptive in certain directions, are profoundly positive in others, and taken together show us possibilities for constructive activity which will go far towards stabilising family life. Why should we be so frightened of disruption and change? To my mind we have a great opportunity for constructive activity if only we will take it. Human beings are more than biological exhibits. We possess the power of appreciating abstract qualities and are endowed with intellect and reason, which enable us to control and regulate our biological urges. In fact, it is only by the fine adjustment of our different forces that we can hope to achieve a balanced personality. We shall only understand sex in its fullest sense when we realise that, far from being a mere biological urge, it possesses a strong capacity for creative use, and is necessary for true mental and spiritual development as well as for physical growth. When the nature and purpose of sex is visualised in this way the sex relationship takes on a new meaning, assuming a positive character that is utterly removed from mere selfish satisfaction. It follows that the whole purpose and meaning of the physical relationship in marriage must be approached in a more constructive spirit. No longer can we contemplate our young people marrying without providing them with a firmer background to help them to avoid many of the pitfalls into which their elders have fallen. No longer should it be possible to say of marriage that it is a state into which we enter in haste and repent at leisure. Instruction in the principles of social biology, emotional variation and love technique should be looked upon as a *sine qua non* of marriage preparation. Indeed, a great deal of this information should be imparted during later adolescence. The truth is that until quite recently society has been more concerned with marriage as an institution than with the happiness of the individual marriage. We have paid more attention to the house than to its inmates. No matter what happens to the inmates, the house must not be allowed to fall down. And so we have propped it up with the beams of social convention and surrounded it with the girders of legal restrictions. But because the builders didn't pay proper attention to the advice of the architect, the house has been built on a quicksand of emotional instability and ignorant superstition, so that the whole structure totters in a most dangerous manner. One cannot help wondering what the architect would have to say about it were he consulted, because the house appears to have lost the bold and simple outlines that he originally gave it. However, there are signs that the inmates are beginning to strike. The public is becoming dissatisfied with the present moral chaos and is beginning to look upon the problems of sex and family life from a more constructive angle.

" *Quality*.—And finally let me draw your attention to the value of the word quality. Quality of health, quality of stock and quality of love. With regard to the first, I think we have a good deal to be proud of. How many of you realise that twenty-five years ago the Ministry of Health did not exist? During that time a wonderful organisation has come into being which has materially improved the lives and health of millions of people. And yet much still remains to be done. There are widespread conditions militating against the quality of our national health. When we come to consider quality of stock and quality of love we find a less satisfactory state of affairs. Quality of stock is a matter of supreme importance. Yet we are only just beginning to concern ourselves with the problem. The principle of planned parenthood has as yet only touched the fringe of the population. It is true that we are limiting our families, but we are not yet planning them so that the best and healthiest members of the community are encouraged to breed and the less healthy are actively discouraged, irrespective of their social status.

"The biologist has demonstrated the evolutionary processes of man, and has shown that we are born with certain characteristics which we inherit from our forefathers. These inborn qualities set a limit to our possibilities. We cannot, for instance, make a brilliant scientist out of a person whose mental capacity is below a certain level, however carefully we may regulate his education or his environmental conditions. We may improve and alter, but the degree of change is limited by a certain latent ability beyond which we cannot go. It is true also that by a process of selective breeding we might be able to produce individuals of a certain type, but we don't know all the laws governing this process, nor are we in a position to state which qualities are the most desirable. 'Men,' says Professor J. B. S. Haldane, 'differ as regards their innate characteristics. . . . It is doubtful whether we can say that any particular innate disposition is always desirable. The combination of intelligence and aggressiveness may give a great constructive statesman or a bloodthirsty tyrant. . . . It is perfectly conceivable that a sudden rise of 10 per cent. in the intelligence quotient of the rising generation in England would precipitate a bloody revolution.'[1] Neither can we state with any certainty how far environment influences the growth and development of our children, but it is probable that we have paid far too little attention to this aspect of the question in the past. Although we can say that certain traits and characteristics are manifestly desirable, we can give no absolute lead as to how these should be achieved.

[1] Professor J. B. S. Haldane, "Human Affairs", p. 30.

"By quality of love I mean that standard of behaviour which is entirely concerned with the value and personality of the other person; in which the self is subjugated to the welfare of the loved one, and in which every endeavour is made to ensure that a relationship will work when, as almost invariably happens, difficulties arise. People are far too willing to throw over a relationship without making any real attempt to overcome the difficulties. And yet true happiness will only be found in personal relationships as we learn to destroy selfishness or—if you prefer a more technical word —egocentricity. But when these difficulties become apparent they must be tackled at once—nipped in the bud, in fact. On no account must they be ignored or thought to be of little moment. Left to themselves they breed disharmony, and if disharmony persists too long, a time comes when it is impossible to undo the damage which has been done. For this reason young married people should be encouraged to seek help and advice early. This is one of the main purposes of such an organisation as the Marriage Guidance Council—to prevent the growth of disharmony.

"To sum up, therefore, we may say that in order to combat the negativism, frustration and egocentricity of our present moral state we must concentrate on the family. To do this we must prepare people adequately for marriage and for family life. This means that we must make a start at the beginning—with the baby, in fact, who must be planned for and wanted by two well-adjusted parents. He must live in an emotionally stable home and have a sufficiency of brothers and sisters. His education, which must embrace every facet of his being, must be steady and progressive without being restrictive or compelling. First things must come first; principles of goodness, beauty, justice and honesty must be inculcated early. This can only be learnt by the example of those who have to do with the child. Sex must never be ignored, but must be dealt with by the parents as simply and reasonably as any other subject. This you have already heard about from Dr. Minor. The relationship between parent and teacher must become closer, and the teaching already given must broaden out into school, university and youth group, where the implications and meaning of sex and family life must be taught in an enlightened way. Marriage must be encouraged by society, but those wishing to marry should receive adequate marriage preparation from competent people, and present evidence of their worthiness to marry and start a family, both to civil and religious bodies, before the marriage is sanctioned. Failures should be dealt with by conciliatory machinery, and there should be no victimisation afterwards. It is rare to find that one person is really the guilty party in a marriage breakdown. It is usually six of one and half-a-dozen of the other. These changing attitudes will, in my opinion, go far to abolish the insidious social evils I discussed to start off with. And that, ladies and gentlemen, is all I have to say to you at the moment. I hope to have the opportunity of discussing marriage preparation in greater detail later on in the programme."

Dr. Hansell sat down amidst considerable applause, which subsided as the Chairman rose to speak.

"We have listened to an excellent and provocative address," she said in her clear, strong voice, "and as I expect many of you have questions to put to Dr. Hansell, I will not stand in your way."

"When you were discussing sex relationships before marriage," a young woman said, "you suggested that in certain instances these carefully-thought-out relationships proved satisfactory in the sense that the couple eventually married and were satisfied with their preliminary try-out, if I may put it like that. Nevertheless, you were doubtful if such behaviour would be a satisfactory solution for our difficulties if it were practised by the whole of society, and you said you had an alternative suggestion which you have omitted to give us."

"Ah! I am so sorry," Dr. Hansell said. "Put as briefly as possible, I view the situation as follows. These pre-marriage try-outs don't work because of the reasons I have already given you: lack of time for adjustment, anxiety and so on. There are three alternatives. We can go on as we are, pretending that everything is satisfactory at one moment and complaining that the morals of the country are going to the dogs at the next. No one in their senses can surely wish to see the perpetuation of this attitude."

There was a murmur of agreement from the body of the hall.

"Secondly, we can, if we like, say that, as these affairs are so numerous and the sex relationship is so important to marriage stability, it would be well for society to recognise the fact and set up some system of betrothal which permitted sexual union—thought out and taught about, mind you—provided there were no children. That would be different from trial marriage, which never visualised any form of preparation or guidance. If at the end of an agreed time the couple were satisfied with each other they could take the final vows of Church or State, and would then be well and truly married and could embark on the creation of a family. If they were not suited they could separate without any very serious harm having been done."

"I hardly think you would ever persuade the Churches to adopt that suggestion," the young woman said, "quite apart from what the State might say. It is too revolutionary."

"I quite agree," Dr. Hansell said, "and I do not think it is necessary, because of my third suggestion—namely, adequate sex education, early planned marriages and marriage preparation. It is my belief that were this really tried out by society on a large scale—and you must remember that up to the present no such attempt has been made—the result would be most satisfactory and the incidence of marriage breakdown would be reduced considerably. Given the preliminary training, I am convinced that the majority of healthy young people would lead happy and balanced sex lives. In any case, this suggestion is in accordance with the principles of monogamy, whereas the other one—betrothal—is not. Not until it has been proved conclusively that marriage preparation is a failure should we consider other alternatives."

"One of the difficulties I foresee in your suggestion," another man said, "is that a large number of parsons, doctors and educationalists do not really admit that young people have any sex lives at all. In spite of what has been said at this conference by yourself and other speakers, the fact remains that the majority of parents fight shy of discussing sex with their young, and often deal with their childish habits of sex expression by repression and punishment. The majority of young people to-day are still frightened out of their wits at the very idea of looking at their own or anybody else's sex organs, let alone touching them. When they become emotionally conscious, they are told that on no account must they allow any sex thoughts to come into their mind, because that is evil and sinful. If they are boys they are usually assured that masturbation is weakening or sinful. Indeed, everything is done to try to turn them into mental eunuchs and make them believe that they don't possess any sex feelings at all. This attitude persists in one way or another until the individual begins to take a more definite interest in the opposite sex, when he or she is warned against emotional feeling, or even the slightest physical contact. Then, by some mysterious process which is never explained, the individual is expected to fall in love with the right person straight away. On the other hand, some people encourage him to have various affairs to give him experience. In any case, by the time he is ready for marriage he is presumed to have acquired all the necessary knowledge which will enable him to understand and manage this new and intriguing person. Engagement follows, and the attitude of the elders immediately changes. Instead of denying the couple any chance of being alone together, the grown-ups do everything possible to throw them together, retiring to bed at an unusually early hour, and everyone else in the house being warned off from the best sitting-room, where the couple are left alone for hours at a time. Even so, nothing must occur which can offend convention. They seem to forget that passion, once aroused, may run away with the individual. In fact, they are utterly hypocritical, pretending at one moment that sex is non-existent, at another that it is an unmitigated evil which must always be held on a curb and at another that it is good and valuable. Finally the couple are married, and are immediately encouraged to let loose all the emotions they have been expected to sit upon and ignore for the last twenty odd years. The result, of course, is emotional chaos and the production of a host of fears, worries and anxieties which destroy the spontaneity of the relationship. It isn't surprising that after such an upbringing marriages go wrong and the sexual disharmonies you mention occur. I doubt if your suggestions are going to relieve that situation."

A certain amount of laughter and clapping greeted these remarks.

"I can only say that I believe a proper educative system such as I have suggested would alter that attitude, which I agree is most deplorable and far too prevalent," Dr. Hansell said.

"You are always stressing the importance of an adequate sex relationship," a lady said. "Can you give us any idea of what you regard as the norm?"

"I would prefer to deal with that question after I have had an opportunity of talking about marriage preparation, if you will agree," Dr. Hansell said.

"My name is Wilkins," a tall, fair-haired man said, "and I am a doctor practising in the East End of London. Whilst I agree with you that education for marriage is essential, I fail to see how it can be of very much use until the housing question is improved. The majority of young people to-day have to share a house with their parents and hardly have a room of their own, let alone any privacy. I have asked dozens of these people if they have a key to their bedroom door, and they look at me in astonishment. How can a couple conduct a satisfactory sex-relationship together if they are liable to interruption at any moment from a mother, sister or younger brother? Then, again, I am far from being convinced that marriage preparation will solve our problems, as you seem to suggest. To my mind one of the most ridiculous things about our present marriage system is the presumption that because two people are in love with each other, the physical will necessarily work satisfactorily. Even if you provide them with an effective contraceptive method and teach them all you can about technique, it by no means follows that they will find each other satisfactory from a sexual point of view, and, as you yourself have very well said, if the sexual factor does not work well, the marriage is in grave danger, however well adjusted the couple may be in other ways. Sexual attraction seems to me to be a most elusive thing, and is by no means firm and solid. On the contrary, it is balanced on a knife's edge, and may easily be tipped in the wrong direction. If that occurs it may never regain a proper balance, and then where are you? Then, again, the achievement of mutual orgasm is not a mere matter of technical knowledge; it will not be achieved unless the emotional relationship between the couple is satisfactory, and so many little things will upset that spontaneity which is so essential to this relationship. All sorts of things, like bodily formation, the approach of the man to the woman, his method of love-making and even the unlocked door may affect the relationship adversely. How are these adjustments to be made unless there is some kind of preliminary try-out? I like your betrothal scheme, and would like to see it put into practice."

"It is not my scheme," Dr. Hansell said amidst laughter. "It has been mooted by various people for years. Whilst I agree with much that you say, especially about the housing difficulty, I do not think we have sufficient evidence to show whether the betrothal idea or the marriage preparation idea is best. My only point is that, as neither has been tried, we might at least give a chance to that which is most in conformity with our social pattern than attempt a complete social upheaval at this stage. You will agree with me, I think, that we have not enough evidence one way or another?"

"Yes, I do. My main point is that we must do something, and do it quickly."

"I'm afraid that whatever we do will take time," Dr. Hansell said.

"I would like to come back to the thorny question of divorce, if you will allow me to," Dr. Alice Minor said. "I don't think you said as much as you might have done——"

"I'm sure I didn't," Dr. Hansell said amidst much laughter. "It is a subject which we could talk about for hours."

"And we have about four minutes left," Lady Burr said from the chair. "As I think it a mistake to prolong meetings beyond the stated time, I shall bring this one to a conclusion, but I see no reason why those of you who wish to discuss divorce should not stay on. You won't get any refreshments for some time, so you ought to have plenty of time to settle the problem to your satisfaction. I shall stay in case I am needed to keep order."

CHAPTER VI
DIVORCE

"THE floor is yours, Dr. Minor," the Chairman said after a few people had left the room and the rest had shaken themselves up a bit.

"I am glad you have allowed us time to discuss this subject at some length, Madam Chairman," the doctor said, rising to her feet, "because it is one of great complexity and interest, especially now that the Denning Committee has issued its final report.[1] Whilst I feel that the Committee has done a fine piece of work in making such constructive suggestions about reconciliation, and has shown its appreciation of the work done by such organisations as the Marriage Guidance Council, I am sorry to see that the Committee seems to favour the retention of the idea of collusion, by which means—as was pointed out in the *New Statesman* at the time—most divorces are obtained.[2] I fail to see how we are going to get any sense into our divorce laws until we rid ourselves of the idea of a guilty and innocent party and continue to insist that all divorce must be based on some kind of sex misdemeanour. As a matter of fact, the sex factor is often merely a cover for some deep-seated psychological disharmony that dates back to early days and makes the couple incompatible. Whatever the original cause, psychological incompatibility should be recognised as a cause of matrimonial discord, and therefore for divorce. By all means let us do everything in our power to prevent the onset of divorce, but do let us have the courage to accept the fact that the psychological condition, and not the sexual one, is often the more important factor. In some cases the sexual disharmony that arises in the early days of the marriage through ignorance and so on may lead to the establishment of this unsatisfactory pattern, whereas in other cases

[1] Final report on divorce procedure. 1947, H.M. Stationery Office.
[2] February 15th, 1947, p. 126.

the disharmony is really there from the start, and the sexual difficulties are simply superimposed. Some people are so maladjusted and incompatible that no known methods of treatment, whether by medical, psychological or pastoral means, will put them right. They should never have been married, and should be allowed to dissolve the marriage and make a fresh start as soon as possible. And the social stigma attached to the proceeding should be abolished. They are ill, just as a person with a physical illness is ill, and they won't be well till the cause is removed. We don't ostracise the individual with the physical illness, so why do so in the other case? The trouble is that our whole attitude to divorce is based on sex, instead of on incompatibility. By making sexual infidelity the prime cause for divorce we degrade the whole sex relationship between man and woman and keep it at its lowest level. At present if we want to have any sex activity we must marry, in order to put ourselves right with Church and State. If, having married, we find the relationship intolerable and want to bring it to an end, we must commit some sexual misdemeanour or prove to the satisfaction of the court that one of us is incapable or unwilling to perform the sexual function adequately. It is sex, sex, sex, from beginning to end. Unless, of course, we care to hit our partner over the head with a bottle or knock him down two or three times—if we are strong enough—or desert him. But if two decent honest people go to the Judge and say, ' We have tried to make a go of this situation for so many years and have genuinely attempted to live together in true love and harmony, but find we are unsuited to each other and cannot do it, in spite of all the help and advice we have received from others '—the Judge has to say, ' I'm so sorry, I can't do anything for you; go away and commit adultery, and then I shall be very pleased to divorce you, providing, of course, that there has been no collusion.' Do you think that is right, Dr. Hansell?"

"I quite agree with you about the over-emphasis on sex," Dr. Hansell said, "and also over the question of the guilty and innocent party. I have been dealing with these problems for many years, and only rarely have I seen a couple of whom one can say that one is guilty and the other innocent.

There are always faults on both sides, even if the fault is only that of ignorance. At the same time I realise that the divorce laws would have to be altered and widened very considerably to meet your requirements, and I doubt if the public would stand for that just now."

"May I chip in here?" Canon Heathcott said from the floor of the hall. "I have naturally listened to this discussion with considerable interest, and agree that our attitude to divorce is very bad. I see no reason why this idea of collusion should be maintained, and agree that it does more harm than good. Of course I am in profound sympathy with the suggestions that have been made regarding reconciliation."

"And you would allow divorce in certain cases?" Dr. Minor enquired.

"Certainly. Though I regard divorce as a confession of failure and a departure from the ideal of marriage, I would rather see a couple divorced and re-married than living in disharmony."

"But would you re-marry them?" Dr. Minor demanded. "Doesn't the Church of England forbid the re-marriage of the guilty party in church?"

"Yes, I am afraid it does."

"And you agree with that?"

"I'm afraid I don't," Canon Heathcott said quietly.

"Then you are a much more enlightened parson than I took you for," Dr. Minor said warmly. "I don't think there are many of your brethren who agree with you."

"More than you suspect, possibly," the Canon said. "I must add, however, that I think some social stigma must remain. After all, vows have been taken and broken; that is not right, and society should not condone such behaviour."

"But society permitted the original marriage, which, in all probability, should never have occurred," Dr. Minor said.

"True. Nevertheless——"

"It seems to me," Lady Burr said, breaking into the discussion, "that if people are going to be encouraged to seek help towards reconciliation from such organisations as the Marriage Guidance Council, only two things can happen.

Either they will be reconciled, in which case all will be well, or they and their advisers will come to the conclusion that they are irreconcilable. What will then happen? Won't the Committee or organisation have to report that it can do nothing with the couple, and recommend divorce, in which case, if the couple agree, they are surely acting in collusion? What will the divorce court say when it hears the whole story? Tell them to go away and commit adultery, as Dr. Minor suggests? I hardly think so. Thus it seems to me that the very fact of introducing conciliatory machinery into the whole marriage situation will eventually bring about the abolition of collusion?"

"That is an interesting possibility, Madam Chairman," Dr. Hansell said. "I am afraid I am not sufficiently knowledgeable about the law to know whether you are right or wrong, but I imagine something like that will occur and the matter will be legalised."

Turning to the Canon he continued:

"Would you agree with me, Canon, that it would be much more satisfactory to make marriage more difficult and divorce more easy?"

"Yes, I think I would."

"In making marriage more difficult, I really mean that it should be recognised as a social function involving considerable responsibility, and should be carefully thought about and prepared for. That, in itself, might help to reduce the incidence of divorce."

"I quite agree."

"We must get away from the necessity of marrying in order to save face or put oneself right with society. No one should have a baby unless it is wanted and intentionally created and has a father and mother and a good home."

"I couldn't agree more."

"But you must allow that the Church makes all this very difficult. She does practically nothing to prepare young people for marriage—at least, she didn't until a very few years ago—and, once having married them, she says that marriage is a sacrament and cannot be broken. But if this is so, why doesn't the Church refuse to marry people until they have given some proof of their ability to fulfil the ideals the Church demands? Should they not be trained in some way before taking their final vows, much in the same way as a monk or a nun passes through a stage of initiation?"

"You are getting very near your betrothal idea if you demand all that, aren't you?" Canon Heathcott said.

"Not necessarily. I didn't suggest pre-marital intercourse, but proper preparation. Surely both Church and State should require some evidence of suitability before allowing people to embark on such a responsible adventure as that of marriage?"

"Yes, I agree."

"Would not the case be met if people attended certain courses on marriage and presented certificates to say they had received marriage guidance and preparation from doctor, priest or counsellor?" Dr. Minor inquired.

"Perhaps so; but we must avoid all idea of compulsion," Dr. Hansell said.

"Oh yes, I quite agree. All this will have to be brought about by careful education and encouragement. There are far too many people about who still think that they should never go near a doctor unless they are ill. The idea of doctors doing preventive work is quite new to them, and as for interfering in their personal lives, that is quite impossible," Dr. Minor said.

"Whilst you have concentrated on the Church," Canon Heathcott said, "you mustn't forget the State. It certainly doesn't bother its head about marriage preparation, whereas you must admit that some of the parsons do give great attention to the matter."

"Oh yes, I do," Dr. Hansell said. "And I agree that the attitude of the State is very bad."

"You might go farther than that," Dr. Minor added. "Apart from seeing that the couple produce the necessary certificates, sign a few forms and shake the registrar by the hand—carefully leaving the fee on the table meanwhile—the State doesn't concern itself with the matter at all. The whole procedure takes only about five minutes, then the couple are bustled away because the next lot are waiting. Before they have had time to realise what has happened to them, they are hurried into an enormous car decked out in white ribbon and driven to some hotel where they receive numerous guests, most of whom they have never seen before and, in all probability, will never see again. The cake having been cut and a few speeches made, drinks are passed round ad lib., and everyone takes a little too much and feels very jolly. Finally the happy couple are once more bundled into the car, to which various old boots have been tied by younger members of the party; confetti is thrown all over the place, making a horrid mess and sticking in everyone's hair; all the friends and relatives stand around wishing the happy couple God Speed with tears in their eyes, and embracing everyone they can see, and finally the newly married pair are whisked away to a life of unending bliss."

"And that isn't all," Dr. Hansell said, continuing the tale. "The 'happy couple' usually go away in complete ignorance of their anatomy, physiology and emotional make up. As a result, the honeymoon becomes a fiasco, the effects of which are to be seen weeks and months later in the disharmony cases we who are engaged on this sort of work see every day of our lives. The tragedy is that almost all these people started out with the highest hopes and ideals. I venture to say in all seriousness that these conditions arise to a greater or lesser degree in three-quarters of the marriages which occur in this country. And yet a little elementary teaching, a visit to a competent doctor and, let me add, an intelligent use of properly provided contraceptives, would have made all the difference to those marriages and, whilst by no means ensuring that everything would be satisfactory, would at least have prevented a good many of the pitfalls, broken marriages, divorces, unhappy homes and maladjusted children that we see around us to-day. Even the most primitive races make some attempt to prepare their young people for home and family life. We do next to nothing."

"And we parsons," the Canon said, "are often prevented from doing anything constructive because the couple come to us just before the wedding, their minds being already made up, and in no condition to think clearly anyway."

"I know," Dr. Hansell said. "Your hands are tied, too. I would stress, however, that there are certain things which you cannot do, with all the will in the world, and only the doctor can do."

"I am not at all surprised that the Church is losing her grip on our young people, both single and married," Dr. Minor said, "whilst she continues her policy of sitting on the fence in regard to some of the matters we have been talking about this evening. Whilst these people may not always know what it is that makes them feel the Church is out of touch with reality, they do feel in their innermost hearts that she is letting them down over these matters. Most of them have high ideals about home and companionship and love and passion which they do not feel the parson really accepts or deals with adequately. When they do have the luck to find a parson who is at one with them, they flock to his church and listen to his teaching. Although you may think I am critical of the Church, I can assure you that I know of many parsons who are doing a wonderful work in this respect. But I have talked too long. I apologise!"

"No! You have not talked too long," the Chairman said. "You and Dr. Hansell have painted a somewhat depressing picture between you, I think, and have not taken into account the numberless marriages which do work satisfactorily and in which the couples are happily adjusted. Like all enthusiasts, you tend to be a bit one-sided. I'm not at all sure that you don't make too much of the sex factor, in spite of all you say to the contrary. Not all people are so concerned or wrought up over the matter as you would have us believe. I agree with you, however, that if the Church is going to do its job properly, and demand the high standards of love and fidelity that she does, she should pay more attention to the matters we have been discussing this evening."

"I'm sure that neither Dr. Minor nor myself wishes to appear one-sided," Dr. Hansell said. "We are well aware that people vary—it is a physiological fact—and that many marriages work very well. But there is room for improvement even here. All we are concerned about is to help people avoid unnecessary unhappiness."

"There are some other points I would like to make," Dr. Minor said, "if you can still bear with me. Over half the marriages in this country are made every year in Register Offices, and not in church. Why is this? Out of many possible reasons I would suggest three:

" 1. A certain proportion of people do not believe in the idea of life-long union as preached by the Church and cannot put up with what they call the ' mumbo-jumbo ' of the marriage service.

" 2. Many people have been divorced and have to re-marry in Register Offices whether they like it or not.

" 3. It is easier to arrange and much simpler.

" It has been pointed out recently by the Archbishop of Canterbury in the House of Lords that many people civilly married are unaware that they are entering upon a lifelong contract. The words they use do not convey that meaning to them. ' " Lawfully wedded wife," ' he said, ' means to them simply " legally registered and therefore mine ". But " lawful," ' he continued, ' does in fact mean in this context " lifelong ". In Halsbury's ' Laws of England ' it is stated :—

" ' " The only kind of marriage which the English Law recognises is one which is essentially the voluntary union for life of one man with one woman to the exclusion of all others."

" ' " Lawful " means that in the English Law, and nothing else, although that lifelong union may be put an end to for some misdemeanour which cancels it. If the State does not mean that, and if the State attaches to the word " lawful " any other meaning than that of " lifelong ", then it must say so. It seems to me quite intolerable that we should allow the use of a form of words to go on which admittedly vast numbers of people misunderstand '.[1]

" Whilst we may agree that a proportion of those marrying in Register Offices do not realise the ' lifelong ' nature of the contract, I should say that the majority of people who marry either in church or Register Offices do visualise the idea of the relationship being ' lifelong '. That is what they hope for, but they also make a kind of mental reservation that if things go wrong they can get out of the contract. For that reason many prefer the Register Office, where the idea of committing some sin against God or the Church if the

[1] Hansard, House of Lords, Vol. 144, No. 8, November 28th, 1946.

marriage is terminated does not arise. It is only the minority of people marrying in church who really hold with the idea of 'lifelong' in the sense that the Church teaches; the majority are quite willing to forget their vows if the situation becomes intolerable. Similarly, at the other end of the scale it is only the minority who are so ignorant or callous that they marry with the avowed intention of getting out of the relationship directly anything goes wrong. The great difference between being lawfully wedded by the State and lawfully wedded by the Church is that whereas in the State marriage it is perfectly possible to terminate it without committing sin or being socially ostracised, the Church's interpretation of marriage is that the person must take vows of lifelong fidelity before God. Thus the marriage has a sacramental meaning. If these vows are broken, someone must be 'guilty', and the guilty party is then officially ostracised and cannot be re-married in church. I hope I don't exaggerate the case, Canon?"

" No, I think you state it very fairly, but you must remember that the Church has certain standards which she expects people to observe. Even so there are variations in procedure between the various Churches; the Roman Catholic Church permitting neither divorce nor re-marriage (although it has a wonderful machinery for effecting annulment in suitable cases); the Church of Scotland permitting the re-marriage of the 'innocent' party and the Church of England saying that 'no person who has a married partner still living may be married a second time in church, and with the use of the marriage service.' " [1]

" Exactly ! " Dr. Minor said. " Those people are automatically debarred from being married in church whether guilty or innocent—a very wrong attitude, in my opinion. It seems that there is confusion of thought and practice on all sides."

" The Church of England is in a somewhat invidious position," the Canon said. " Her priests are compelled by law to marry anyone, however unsuitable they may be, and however ignorant, provided they have fulfilled the necessary legal qualifications."

[1] *The Christian News Letter*, February 1947, p. 9.

"And, having done so," Dr. Minor said, "we are expected to believe that the marriage is a true marriage in the sight of God and is therefore indissoluble—an assumption which appears to many people quite ridiculous. You surely don't suggest that many of the recent war marriages were true Christian marriages or fulfilled the Christian conception of marriage?"

"No, of course not, but the Church can do nothing about it because she has no legal powers. These were taken out of the hands of ecclesiastical courts in 1857, and passed to the civil divorce courts. Whether this arrangement is a good one or not is a moot point. If the Church demands so much from those who marry under her auspices, it seems only reasonable to suggest that she should be allowed to manage her own affairs in her own way. If she says that marriage is 'life-long' and indissoluble and that to be married in church means that the couple must under all circumstances fulfil the teaching of the Church about marriage, then she should have power to refuse marriage to those whom she does not think reach her standard. Those who do not believe in the Church's teaching and don't like her vows should get married elsewhere. Similarly, it is only reasonable to suggest that the Church should have power to decide whether a particular church marriage was a true marriage, and of dealing with the various complications and difficulties that must inevitably arise. If she wants to allow divorce on certain grounds, she should be allowed to have her own legal system for dealing with the matter. If, as the Archbishop says, it is wrong for those who are married by the State not to be informed about the permanence of the relationship, it is equally wrong for people to marry in church who do not agree with the Church's teaching, and only do so to satisfy parental pressure or social convention."

"I quite agree," Dr. Minor said; "but all this presupposes that the Church takes far more care over marriage preparation on the one hand and establishes effective reconciliation machinery on the other. Similarly, the State ought to take more trouble over the whole matter. It is ridiculous to expect that marriages will just 'work'. They won't. Marriage is but a preliminary to family life, and is an art which has to be practised and learnt about. Marriage preparation is just as important for the civil as for the church marriage—more so, in fact. To my mind it is most essential to distinguish between Church and State when discussing marriage problems. Although all marriages, to be lawful, involve the principle of ' the voluntary union for life of one man with one woman ', and whilst this should be made abundantly clear to every couple who get married, it is obvious that the interpretation put upon the marriage contract by the two bodies varies considerably."

" I'm sure we are all in agreement with that," Canon Heathcott said, as Dr. Minor sat down.

" Thank you, Dr. Minor," the Chairman said. " As time is getting on, and I know he has some further things to say, I will ask Dr. Hansell to sum up."

" The discussion has been most interesting and has covered a good deal of ground," Dr. Hansell said. " There are, however, some further matters to which I should like to refer."

" The Guilty Party.

" Dr. Minor has mentioned the guilty party. Except in the rarest instances, there are faults on both sides in all cases of matrimonial discord, and the sooner we abolish the idea of there being a ' guilty party ', the better. There are, of course, cases of gross cruelty, various psychological abnormalities of a severe kind, and irresponsible behaviour, in which the fault is obviously on one side. Even so, the law is so arranged that many a woman who leaves her husband because he is a sexual pervert, for instance, puts herself in the wrong simply because she leaves his house, such an act often being sufficient to allow the husband to retain the custody of the children. All this is dreadfully unfair, and should be altered. It should be possible for a person to appeal to the courts, and for the courts to deal with the case without being in any way influenced or bound by the previous behaviour of either party. And I agree that except in the rarest instances no stigma should be attached to either party.

" It has been suggested that the sex element is often a

symptom of underlying psychological disharmony which makes it more or less impossible for the couple to live in harmony. Psychologically speaking, sex union between man and woman involves, not only an acceptance of heterosexuality, but a willingness and desire to put it into practice. That means that each partner is willing to leave home and parents and accept the new relationship. Inability to do this—parental fixation—is one of the chief causes of matrimonial discord. Christ's teaching in this respect is so absolutely right. Even so, a certain degree of 'fixation' may persist, but will ultimately have little significance provided the marriage is emotionally fulfilling not only in physical love and creative activity, but in mutual trust and companionship, the building of the home and the acceptance of children. Should these fulfilments not be achieved, and in particular should there be no adequate emotional release and mutual orgasm, there will be a holding up of development and a fixation at some immature level. There will be a desire to return to mother, for instance, and seek her help in every crisis. Whilst it will be more difficult for the woman who still retains some degree of mother-fixation to attain a good orgasm, it is by no means impossible provided she understands the position and the couple are technically proficient. Should the latter be lacking, the situation will become even more unsatisfactory because the inability to achieve anything will accentuate the resultant frustration and drive the individual back to mother so as to escape an intolerable situation. The outside influences brought to bear on the individual will have a much more serious effect in this type of case than the same influences brought to bear on one who is not deviated in this way. Everything should be done to remove the inhibiting causes before the marriage takes place. If nothing is done, and the situation develops as I have suggested, a woman might refuse union, leave home or remain so frigid that the husband would seek consolation elsewhere. Should this occur, the woman might be able to divorce him for a sexual offence—adultery—thereby placing him in the wrong as the guilty party, whereas in actual fact the cause would be on her side. If he defended the case, it might be very difficult for him to prove that she refused intercourse, and indeed many such women allow intercourse but remain frigid. To fight such a case would be very difficult, and a great many people would prefer to let the matter go by default. I saw a case recently where a woman strongly fixated to her mother had married twice, and in each case the marriage had been terminated on account of the husband's inability to consummate the marriage, whereas in my opinion the real difficulty lay with the woman, who was so unwilling for sex union that she frightened any sensitive man by her attitude. I'm not at all sure that in such a case she should not be prevented from further marriage until she produced evidence of cure. You will gather from this that I agree with Dr. Minor that more attention should be paid to the psychological element in divorce cases, and the matter becomes of even greater importance when we come to consider the meaning of consummation later on. I am not at all sure that we cannot draw an analogy in this type of case from the judgement given by Mr. Justice Macnaghten in the Bourne case in 1938. In that case, you will remember, a surgeon, Mr. Alec Bourne, performed an abortion on a young girl who had been raped, and in acquitting him the Judge said that, ' If the doctor is of the opinion on reasonable grounds and on adequate knowledge that the continuance of her pregnancy would probably make the woman a physical wreck or a mental wreck, the act is lawful.' [1]

"Why cannot the same principle be applied to matrimonial cases if the doctor and the court are agreed that the continuance of the marriage would probably make one of the partners a physical or *mental wreck*? The important words there are ' mental wreck ', because by accepting the fact that certain conditions can have a psychological effect on an individual, the law is broadening its attitude. There can be no doubt, for instance, that for a man to be married to a woman who is strongly fixated to her mother and unable to co-operate with him in any way is dangerous, not only for his mental health, but for hers as well. If the situation has persisted too long the resistances set up between the couple will be so strong that it will be impossible to break them down or make the marriage work in so far as they are con-

[1] *Lancet*, July 23rd, 1938.

cerned. If they tackle the matter early something may be done. That is not to say that each may not, after treatment and help, make a satisfactory adjustment with someone else.

"*The Re-Marriage of the Innocent Party.*

"Dr. Minor has already drawn attention to the unsatisfactory position of the innocent party. Let me give you an example. A charming but extremely ignorant girl of nineteen fell in love with, and married, a rich young man who appeared to have all the social attributes that anyone could desire. But his charm was superficial; his attitude to sex was quite abnormal, and his treatment of his wife was too disgusting to be talked about. Imagine that girl's situation—being bound to a man of that nature. At first, knowing practically nothing about sex, she supposed his extraordinary behaviour to be a natural part of marriage, but luckily she had the sense to talk to a friend, who soon put her wise, her parents, as is so common, having told her nothing. By the time she had found this out, however, she was pregnant, and had to put up with her intolerable husband until several months after the birth of the baby. At last, after about three years, she managed to get a divorce on grounds of cruelty, she being the innocent party. She had been married in church, and, her religion meaning a good deal to her, she was prepared to accept the Church's teaching about the permanence of the marriage relationship. But she couldn't live with a man like that. No one could. And now she wants to re-marry. What will happen? Will any priest have the courage to marry her, as her 'husband' is still alive? Such cases could be multiplied a hundred times, and should be dealt with by specially appointed courts. Some cases are irreconcilable. Must all these people be regarded as so sinful and misguided that they cannot be allowed a second chance? Is the Church so sure of herself that she can afford to pass these drastic judgments? Has she any right to do so without knowing all the facts of the case?— very often she certainly doesn't know them, and indeed I doubt whether she bothers to enquire into them. 'You are divorced,' she says, 'and so you are outside the pale, and that is all there is to it.' I do not wish to imply that this is the attitude of many of her priests, because I know it isn't, but it appears to be the official attitude. It isn't altogether surprising that people prefer to get married in the Register Office when they come up against this intolerant attitude. Dare anyone say that Christ would have dealt with these cases in such a manner? If the State has to put her house in order, so has the Church, and not until she does so can she expect intelligently minded people to subscribe to her laws. Indeed, I am inclined to think that the majority of church people pay only lip service to these ideas even now.

" *Collusion and Condonation.*

"According to the Denning Committee the law as to collusion does not need amendment, but better understanding. This is very true. The majority of people in this country have no idea of what the words imply. They think that if a man and wife discuss their marriage difficulties and agree to part and have a divorce, they are practising collusion and endangering any chance of obtaining a divorce. Whatever the law may be, the fact remains that in practically every case of marital disharmony there is considerable discussion between the parties, a good deal of letter-writing, and, worst of all, the interference of relatives and friends. Finally the couple agree to ' separate and get a divorce '. This means that someone leaves the home and sets up a separate establishment, even if that establishment is only one room. The presumption is, of course, that someone is innocent and someone guilty, which, to quote the article in the *New Statesman* to which Dr. Minor referred, is an ' antique conception of marriage as a contract '.[1] According to the Denning Committee, the law as to collusion does not forbid discussion with a view to reconciliation. If reconciliation is impossible, the law does not forbid discussions as to the future of the children, the house and the furniture, the provision of maintenance and necessaries for the wife, or costs. It only forbids the partners to concoct a false case in order that it may appear as genuine, or to create by arrangement between themselves the grounds for divorce, or to bribe one or the

[1] *The New Statesman and Nation*, February 15th, 1947, p. 126.

other in order to get a divorce.[1] As such it presents no bar to attempts at reconciliation. The Committee points out that the important thing is that lawyers should cease to advise their clients to have nothing to do with one another, but should point out that the law favours reconciliation. It seems, therefore, that collusion comes into action after a couple have decided to have a divorce, and not whilst they are contemplating divorce proceedings. The ambiguous words (in so far as the layman is concerned) are ' to create by arrangement between themselves the grounds for divorce '. If a couple agree to divorce, and the husband says he will send his wife evidence of infidelity, is that collusion ? If it is, a large number of people must be acting illegally. One would have thought that the wish to concoct a false case or bribe one another would disappear if there were no law forbidding collusion, and that in any case the judge would soon find out if people were trying to concoct false cases. Anyway, the marriage must be a pretty poor kind of marriage if the couple have to create a false case or are driven to bribery. I should imagine that most of these latter cases are concerned with money; ' I'll divorce you if you'll give me so much money '. Why should the rich partner be bribed? Why can't he go to the court and get a divorce because his partner is such a little beast that she stoops to bribery? All this sort of thing makes a travesty of marriage, and the sooner it is brought to an end the better it will be for everyone concerned.

" Then, again, many partners are so possessive that they will not agree to the divorce or take the necessary steps unless they can get something out of the other partner. In all such cases it should be possible for the aggrieved or distressed partner to bring the case to the courts and have the matter settled.

" There is a difference between collusion and condonation that has not yet been mentioned.

" *Condonation.*

" The law as to condonation is that ' if, after an offence has been committed, the injured party with full knowledge

[1] Final Report of the Committee on Procedure in Matrimonial Causes, H.M. Stationery Office, February 1947, p. 16.

forgives and re-instates the offending party, the offence is condoned '.[1] This means that if a man goes abroad for a year or more, as has happened during the war, and his wife has a child by another man whilst he is away, and he on his return, having heard all about the matter, forgives his wife and has one act of sex intercourse with her, the offence is condoned. But a recent decision of the Court of Appeal in Beard v. Beard 1946 has ' made it clear that the condonation is conditional on the offending party behaving in such a way as the Court can accept as consistent with matrimonial duty and if he or she does not do so, the original offence is revived '.[2]

" That is to say that if the couple cannot make the relationship work and the wife won't pull her weight, the husband's act of taking her back and forgiving her will not prevent him from obtaining an eventual divorce. If that is so, there seems very little reason in keeping the law as to condonation at all, and even the Denning Committee say that in some respects it is a hindrance to reconciliation. Another rule is that contained in the Statute which provides that desertion, in order to be a ground of divorce, must last for three years *immediately preceding* the presentation of the petition. If, therefore, desertion for three years is condoned by reconciliation, and the guilty party shortly afterwards again deserts, the injured spouse will have to wait for another three years before presenting a petition. This prospect may deter an injured party from attempting reconciliation, and is very unfair. It is obviously unfair to say that a man has condoned his wife's offence by one act of sexual intercourse with her, and not to say that the same applies to the woman who allows her husband to have one act of sexual intercourse with her, but such was the case until recently.[3] And who is to decide that the woman ' has really forgiven and re-instated him as her husband ' ? I have known women allow their husbands to have sex union with them for years after one single sexual lapse on the part of the man, and yet they have never forgiven him and never intend to forgive him.

[1] Final Report of the Committee on Procedure in Matrimonial Causes, H.M. Stationery Office, February 1947, p. 16.
[2] *Ibid.*, p. 16.
[3] Henderson v. Henderson, 1944, A.C. 49.

And very often they both know it, and yet connection continues. In my opinion the husband has just as much right to get a divorce from a wife who behaves like that as she has to get one on account of his one unfaithful act.

No, there is nothing much to be said either for the law of collusion or condonation, and it seems that the Denning Committee feel this, too, because they state it in at least two different places,[1] although they point out that it is not within the terms of reference to make recommendations in this respect.

" *The King's Proctor.*

" The office of the King's Proctor seems to be necessary to bolster up the law as to collusion and condonation. If the law were amended the office might well be abolished, because its functions appear to be undesirable in a well-organised society. It is a relic of some by-gone age, and is, in fact, little better than a large snooping organisation. According to the Denning Committee, the office is ' the only sanction which exists to ensure that petitioners who have themselves been guilty of adultery disclose the fact to the Court in a discretion statement, and it is the only sanction which exists to deter parties from collusion. So long as these statutory bars to divorce exist, it seems necessary to retain a period during which investigation can be made.' [2] This latter sentence refers to the retention of the decree absolute, which has now been reduced from six months to six weeks and allows the King's Proctor time to make these enquiries. It would be interesting to know how many cases he can investigate in six weeks, or, for that matter, in six months, and, further, whether he is impartial in his selection of cases, or merely looks into those which show some likelihood of being able to pay in the event of his intervention being successful, because I am given to understand that he works on the principle of payment by results—a most iniquitous system. If this is an inaccurate statement, I am willing to withdraw it, and I hope you will realise that I am not criticising any individual person, but rather a social system.

[1] On p. 11 (vii), on p. 16 (xii), of the Report.
[2] *Ibid.*, p. 27.

"*Consummation.*

"This brings me to another aspect of the divorce problem which is most unsatisfactory, to which Dr. Minor has already drawn attention, and that is the over-emphasis of the sex factor not only in our divorce system, but in our whole approach to the marriage problem. One act of 'illicit' intercourse on the part of the husband is sufficient for the wife to say that her husband has been unfaithful to her; that she won't allow further intercourse, that her marriage is finished, her life ruined, and that divorce is the only solution. And the same attitude in a more concentrated form is often taken up by the man if his wife is in the wrong. To make matters worse, the divorce court procedure is really built up on the question of sexual intercourse. Has adultery occurred? Has the petitioner disclosed the fact of his adultery to the Court? Has intercourse really taken place, and if so has the marriage been consummated or not? The last question is particularly important. Is it really suggested that one or two acts of intercourse can 'consummate' a marriage? And what constitutes consummation, anyway? If a man places the penis in the vagina and leaves it there for half an hour without moving and then removes it; is that consummation? Or supposing he effects penetration, hardly moves at all, and then withdraws immediately; is that consummation? Alternatively, he makes only a partial penetration and then ejaculates. Is that consummation? Or let us imagine that he manages to penetrate only once a fortnight for six months, and fails to maintain an erection for more than a moment or two, but makes violent love to his wife at other times, so that she gets into such a nervous state that she could hit him over the head with a hammer. Is that consummation? Or consider another type of case in which the man penetrates but the woman fails to co-operate in any way whatsoever. Is that consummation? Personally, I should hesitate to say that the marriage had been consummated in any of these cases, except in so far as the erect or partially erect penis has passed in some degree into the vagina. But is that what is really meant by the consummation of the marriage? The matter has never really been settled, and therefore causes considerable difficulty in deciding some nullity suits. Before the Herbert Act of 1937 the only ground for nullity was that the individual was incapable of performing the sex act—not of refusing to do so. That is to say, he was willing to obtain erection and penetration (intromission), but was unable to do so, and was accordingly impotent. The Herbert Act made it possible to obtain a decree of nullity on the grounds of wilful refusal by one partner to allow the other to have coitus. I heard the difference between the two well expressed recently by an eminent K.C. as being that in the nullity suit the defendant, if there is one, says, ' I would but I can't ', whereas in the case of wilful refusal he says, ' I can but I won't '. From a medical point of view a woman might be so repelled by the act that although penetration might be possible she would be so passive and non-co-operative that, in fact, she would be unable to enter into the act with that man or any other man. She would really be impotent; ' she would but she couldn't '. She would not be able to complete the act with anyone, and her condition is similar to that of a true male impotence. One is at once in a difficulty when one uses the phrase ' complete the act '. Does penetration and ejaculation —which we will presume occurred in this case—mean that the marriage is consummated? In so far as the man is concerned, perhaps we can say yes, but surely not in the case of the woman. All she has done is to permit access to her body. In every other way she has held back and refrained from completing it; indeed, she is psychologically incapable of completing the act in the sense of co-operating with the man. Should such a condition persist she might develop a muscular spasm of the vaginal and thigh muscles (vaginismus) which would even prevent penetration occurring. It looks as though the old ecclesiastical laws regarded the matter more from the man's point of view than the woman's. In the famous case in which Dr. Lushington gave a nullity decree because the woman's vagina was an impervious cul-de-sac about two inches long, he said that there must be the power of sexual intercourse. ' Without that power, neither of two principal ends of marriage can be attained, namely, a lawful indulgence of the passions to prevent licentiousness, and the procreation of children.' Further, he said that sexual intercourse 'is ordinary and complete intercourse; it does not mean partial and imperfect intercourse. . . . If so imperfect as scarcely to be natural, I should not hesitate to say that, legally speaking, it is no intercourse at all. I can never think that the true interest of society would be advanced by retaining within the marriage bonds parties driven to such disgusting practices.'[1] Thus, as Mr. Latey, says, the 'true test of consummation was complete and unhindered penetration'. In Chitty's 'Treatise on Medical Jurisprudence' (1834) it is stated that there must be erection, penetration and ejaculation. This is all very well in so far as the man is concerned, but it really leaves the woman in a very unsatisfactory situation. From a medical point of view it would be ridiculous to say that a marriage had been consummated merely because the man had penetrated and had an ejaculation, and some recent decisions in the Courts seem to show that this is being recognised. In the case of Cowen v. Cowen (1946) the parties had been married for some years, and the man had always used a sheath or practised coitus interruptus because it was mutually agreed that they would not have any children to start off with. Later the wife, who wanted a child, begged her husband to discontinue these methods, but he refused. In 1944 the wife left the husband and brought proceedings for nullity on the ground of the husband's wilful refusal to consummate the marriage. Here, therefore, he could, but he wouldn't. The Judge said that intercourse was complete in the sense that there was complete penetration and 'only incomplete if it can be called incomplete, that inasmuch as a sheath was always used there was no possibility of pregnancy resulting provided there was no accident to the appliance employed'. The K.C. arguing the case suggested that as there was never any physical contact between the organs of the parties (owing, presumably, to the use of a sheath), they two were never one flesh, but the Judge held this argument

[1] Robertson's "Ecclesiastical Reports", 279, quoted by William Latey in a paper read before the Medico-Legal Society on April 25th, 1946, and reported in full in the *Medico-Legal Review*, Vol. XIV, January 1946, p. 50.

to be unsound.¹ One would have thought that from a medical point of view it was most unsound because, in fact, the occasional practice of coitus interruptus was admitted, which necessarily allowed the organs to come together in physical contact. One would be tempted to suggest that penetration had been complete according to the Judge's ruling, whenever coitus interruptus had been practised. Anyway, the Court of Appeal over-ruled the judgment, allowed the appeal and found the marriage had not been consummated, because one of the chief ends of marriage—the procreation of children—had been prevented. ' We are of opinion,' the Judge said, ' that sexual intercourse cannot be said to be complete when a husband deliberately discontinues the act of intercourse before it has reached its natural termination, or when he artificially prevents that natural termination which is the passage of the male seed into the body of the woman. To hold otherwise would be to affirm that a marriage is consummated by an act so performed that one of the principal ends, if not the principal end, of marriage is intentionally frustrated.' ²

" It seems to follow from this that a man who has consistently practised coitus interruptus has not consummated the marriage, which, from a medical point of view, is true because he has never ejaculated. In addition, the constant use of a sheath contrary to the will of the woman constitutes wilful refusal to consummate and, presumably, the constant wearing of a contraceptive device such as a diaphragm cap or the use of a chemical soluble by the woman contrary to the wish of the husband will constitute wilful refusal on the part of the woman. Finally, you will notice that the Court of Appeal ruled that the natural termination of the sex act is ' the passage of the male seed into the body of the woman '. Even here there is difficulty, because the fluid ejaculated is called semen, and is made up of two portions : seminal fluid, which has no value except as a nourishing fluid for the sperms, and the sperms. What would happen if the ' seed ' contained no sperms and was only seminal fluid, as in a case

¹ *Medico-Legal Review*, Vol. XIV, January 1946, p. 54.
² *Ibid.*, p. 55, and *Lancet*, 1945, II, p. 183 and March 15th, 1947, p. 342.

of complete sterility? At present sterility is not a ground for divorce. A man can ejaculate fluid into the woman's body which is nothing but seminal fluid and cannot medically speaking be called 'seed'. It looks as though a woman could have her marriage dissolved on the ground of non-consummation and nullity if there are no sperms present, and the judgment in Cowen v. Cowen stands, and is logically interpreted. Presumably the couple would have to have been ignorant of the fact of the sterility at the time of the marriage. If this is to be allowed, the legal battles will be long and difficult, because even now it is very difficult to determine what is sterility. From a medical point of view there must be no sperms in the fluid and no germ cells in the testicles as determined by testicular biopsy—that is to say, by taking a minute sample of the testicular contents and examining it under the microscope.

"But we must still ask ourselves if all this really defines consummation. Is it really suggested in this enlightened age, when everyone is so keen on social betterment and the establishment of mutual harmony in the home, that the sex act is complete when the man has placed his 'seed' in the woman's body? What about the woman? Has she nothing to say in the matter? Or are we to presume that the law regards her as a mere passive receptor of the male 'seed'? Such an attitude may have been all very well at the time of Moses, but can hardly be said to be in accordance with modern psychological knowledge or Christ's teaching about the relationship of men and women.

"In order that the sex relationship between man and woman may be properly consummated it is not only essential that the man should effect deep and full penetration, carry out and maintain movement sufficiently long to provide orgasm and end with an adequate ejaculation; but it is also essential that the woman should accept the man fully, contribute actively and achieve a satisfactory orgasm. That, to my mind, is consummation—erection, penetration, ejaculation and orgasm. In order to achieve it, however, the couple will need time and practice, and only in the rarest instances will that result be experienced after one act of intercourse, and practically never at the first time between two people who have never had sex experience before—which, be it remembered, is what both Church and State expect. To my mind, we shall have to move away from this insistence on the sex act as being the deciding factor in divorce and nullity suits, because the more we consider the matter the more difficult does it become. Whilst it is probable that in almost all divorce cases the sex relationship is unsatisfying, or no longer practised by the couple, it should be realised that this unsatisfactory state of affairs has come about for two main reasons.

" 1. First the couple were so badly instructed to begin with that they spoilt the sex relationship within the first few weeks or months of the marriage. As a result there developed frigidity, impotence, premature ejaculation, painful coitus and other similar difficulties. These could have been prevented had marriage preparation been given *by a doctor*; cured if the couple had sought expert advice within the first year or two of marriage or after the birth of the first baby—if that occurred within a reasonable time; not cured if the condition had persisted for several years and the secondary symptoms of frustration, irritation, intolerance and the like have become well established. It is the development of these secondary symptoms which cause the situation to become so intolerable that the couple cannot support further existence together, and it is these conditions which must be removed or prevented from developing if the marriage is to be saved. If this cannot be done reasonably early, there is little chance of doing it at all, and the sooner the marriage is brought to an end the better. It is only to be expected that in such circumstances one or other of the partners will look elsewhere for some emotional outlet, and start an affair with someone else. This, in nine cases out of ten, is of no serious import—provided it is brought to an end quickly and too much notice isn't taken of it. It should be regarded as an escape from an intolerable situation. It seems, therefore, that in so far as divorce is concerned, we put the cart before the horse, concentrating on the sexual factor rather than on the underlying causes which upset the sexual factor in the first place. There are, of course, exceptions, but my experience leads me to think that in the majority of divorce cases the sexual adventures of one or both of the parties concerned is the least important aspect of the problem.

" 2. The second reason for the sex factor going wrong has already been mentioned; the psychological pattern of the two persons is such that they were really maladjusted from the word ' go ', although they didn't realise it. Thus their marriage was foredoomed to failure, unless, of course, they did realise what was happening in time, and took steps to have the matter put right, if that were possible. The trouble is that this putting-right process so often makes one or both partners realise that they have married the wrong person, thus making the need for divorce more obvious. For instance, if a young man of twenty-five, who has been strongly attached to his mother, marries a woman of thirty-five who has the mothering instinct well developed, he is likely to find himself partially impotent, and certainly incapable of satisfying his wife sexually, although he may effect penetration occasionally. If the marriage goes wrong—as it is likely to do on account of the inadequate sexual relationship—the attempted reconciliation, if it is properly carried out, will make the man grow up emotionally, in which case he will, for the first time in his life, escape from his mother's apron-strings, and therefore from a wife who no longer satisfies his needs. What he then requires is a normal young woman of twenty-two. Thus the attempted reconciliation can only lead to an eventual divorce. In some cases, of course, the couple can learn to adjust to each other quite satisfactorily, but the danger—if it is a danger—is always there, and must be accepted.

" The moral to be drawn from such a case is that had the couple received adequate marriage preparation they would have either recognised the condition themselves, or have had it pointed out to them by the counsellor or consultant, in which case effective treatment could have been started. If medical certificates before marriage were the accepted thing, such a couple would not have been able to marry until they had received proper instruction and treatment.

Note—The House of Lords has now set aside the finding of the Court of Appeal in Cowen *v.* Cowen (*Times*, Dec. 10, 1947). Thus a man married to a woman who refuses to have children has no redress. It is interesting to note that the psychological causes of the matter are not even considered. We shall hear more of this case.

Divorce by Agreement.

"I read recently that 'if marriages can be broken by the consent of the partners and new alliances formed, then marriage as in institution becomes trial marriage'."[1] I should say that if marriages cannot be broken by the consent of the partners, marriage reconciliation will become a farce. I would go farther, and say that practically every couple who come to see me to discuss their matrimonial difficulties are either reconciled or agree to separate or divorce. In other words, there is 'consent'. In trial marriage the couple agree to live together unmarried until such time as they can satisfy themselves that they are suited to marry. In the marriages we are considering the couple have almost certainly had the intention of remaining together in a lifelong relationship, whether they were married in church or Register Office. That, I am sure, is the hope and intention of the majority of couples who marry in this country, and differs materially from trial marriage. To suggest that a couple who, after discussing their difficulties carefully, agree to part and allow each other to make a new start, are acting wrongly or contrary to the highest ethical principles, appears to me to be absurd.

"Of course, if we are going to adopt the attitude that all marriages are indissoluble we can't get anywhere, nor can we get very far if we believe that marriages are dissoluble only on grounds of adultery. I fail to see how the reconciliation machinery can possibly work unless we accept the fact of mutual discussion and agreement and, in certain cases, divorce. Some people seem to imagine that all reconciliation will be successful, whereas it often fails to bring the couple together, but makes them face up to the fact that they must start again. When reconciliation has failed the Court should have all the facts before it and, provided the Judge is satisfied, allow the divorce. It ought to be possible for people to present their cases to the court together if necessary. The solution of the divorce problem lies largely in effective education, especially in the sexual field, and marriage preparation in every department of life. Whilst

[1] *The Christian News Letter*, February 1947, p. 4.

I can see reasons why the Church might object to divorce by agreement, I fail to see why the State should do so. Nor does it seem reasonable that the Church should demand such lifelong fidelity unless she takes adequate steps to see that there is some chance of the conditions being fulfilled.

Nullity Suits and Medical Examination.

" I have already suggested that the procedure with regard to nullity suits is far from satisfactory, and do not wish to labour the point. I would suggest, however, that the medical examination of these cases needs some revision in the light of modern knowledge. Consider a defended impotence case, for instance. The wife says that the man is incapable of performing the sex act satisfactorily, and the man says he is not. It is probable that the woman has already been examined by several doctors; her own to start off with, and then one or two that may be appointed by the other side. She is then examined by the Court doctor, who makes a simple examination to determine whether or no the hymen is present and penetration has occurred. He may report that the woman is not a virgin, by which he means that something has passed into the vagina at some time or other, and there is no bar to consummation. He may be expected to express an opinion on the frequency of the penetration and whether it was 'successful'. With regard to the hymen, one cannot learn a great deal from its condition unless it is intact. It may be very tight or easily dilatable. It may have been broken in various ways, or the woman may never have had much of a hymen at all. Then, again, she may have dilated her own hymen, or been to a doctor who dilated it for her and perhaps fitted her with a suitable contraceptive. She may have used some sanitary device such as Tampax. All this may have occurred without connection occurring. Thus, with certain exceptions, the state of the hymen is of little help. What is of much more importance is the state of the vaginal entrance. Are the muscles tight or easily dilatable? How many fingers can be admitted to the passage and for what distance? But even the fact that the passage is dilatable does not necessarily mean that penetration has occurred. Occasionally the state of the vaginal lining may help one to come to a decision. Its appearance differs in those who have never had connection and those who have, but even here one has to be careful, because a woman might have had half a dozen connections and yet show no signs of change in the vaginal lining. Of course if a woman has had a child, or frequent connection, or surgical interference, there are obvious indications. In the majority of cases, however, it is difficult to determine whether coitus has taken place, how often or how deeply, and quite impossible to say whether it was successful. In so far as the court doctor is concerned, he usually confines himself to a brief statement as to whether the hymen is present or not, its condition and the degree of vaginal dilatation he thinks is attainable.

" The examination of the man, however, is by no means so satisfactory. Apart from making sure that his sex organs are present and reasonably developed, there is little to be done. So far as I know, no attempt is made to find out whether erection is possible, and unless it occurs spontaneously during the examination the doctor has to rely on the man's word. Even if the man does get an erection, or says he can get an erection, it by no means follows that he can do so with the particular woman to whom he is married. In the majority of these cases the cause of the failure to obtain erection and penetration is psychological, and other means must be employed to determine the nature of the condition and whether or not penetration has or could occur. In an undefended suit these matters do not necessarily arise, but in a defended one I am of the opinion that the whole procedure should be revised. The couple should be examined by one or two doctors skilled in these matters and, in particular, in psychological medicine, who should be appointed by the Judge in consultation with both sides. Their findings should be accepted by the court, and the Judge should assess their value in relation to the whole case. The system of bringing various doctors to the court to give evidence for and against the defendant is, in this type of sex case, as objectionable as it is useless.

Partners Who Refuse to Co-operate.

"Whilst I recognise that the liberty of the individual must not be infringed—although in this age of Government restrictions and regulations the individual appears to have very few rights remaining to him—I cannot help feeling that something should be done about the partner who refuses to co-operate. He won't do anything about reconciliation; he won't go to the doctor; he won't take advice, and very often he won't allow his wife sufficient to live on. Neither will he give her evidence for divorce, although he is quite likely to be having sex relationships elsewhere. Very often, of course, he is just a mother's darling, and is having a fit of the sulks. But that doesn't make it any better for the wife, who may have one or two children to look after.

"If, on the other hand, the woman is the offender, she may be equally unpleasant, and refuse to take any steps towards a divorce, although the man is willing to provide the evidence, because she doesn't approve of divorce or thinks it wrong or horrid. Such people are a menace to society. They encourage immorality rather than prevent it, and are often psychologically warped and inhibited, and largely to blame for the situation which has arisen, and yet they adopt a self-righteous air, and pretend they are the injured party. It should be possible to devise machinery by which such people are compelled to come before some court at least once, so that the position can be put before them by the Judge, who should be assisted by a trained psychologist. It is occasionally possible to make such people see reason and become co-operative. If the individual persists in his refusal, the marriage should be terminated. Many people are prevented from marrying again because of this dog-in-a-mangerish attitude of the 'injured' party. Who is to blame the other partner if he or she forms a liaison elsewhere?

"Similarly, in some sterility cases the man often refuses to visit the doctor or have any investigations made even after the wife has done everything to persuade him and had all possible investigations made on herself. In such cases it ought to be possible to bring such a man before a court which could point out to him the error of his ways. If he still persisted in his refusal to co-operate, the woman ought to be able to have the marriage annulled.

Children.

" One of the major problems of divorce is centred round the children. Who is to look after them—the father or the mother ? The fights and arguments that go on in the courts over these poor children have to be seen to be believed. Much of the bribing to which I have referred is due to the desire of one partner to have the children. It by no means follows that the ' guilty ' party is unsuited to look after the children. I have known instances in which the man has become the guilty party out of consideration for the woman, who, in my opinion, was just as guilty as the man, if not more so, and was a most unsuitable person to look after the children. And yet she was given the custody of the children. One of the commonest Court decisions is that A shall have the custody of the children, but that B shall have free access to them ; that they shall go and stay with B during the holidays, and so on. The result is that the children never know to whom they belong, and in many cases are told by A how awful B really is or, when they go to stay with B, how frightful A is. They live in an atmosphere of hostility and insecurity. It would be far better for them to be brought up by the most suitable parent when they are young, and then, later on, when they have found their feet in the world, and are capable of more mature judgement, they should be allowed to contact the other parent, in which case they may possibly make a satisfactory adjustment to that parent. In the former situation they are unlikely to make a good adjustment to either.

" Divorce is one of those problems about which people never seem to be able to reach agreement, and I dare say they never will. Nevertheless, we shall have to make up our minds, because we shall never make much progress towards marriage reconciliation and a stable family life until we clear up some of the unsatisfactory features of the present situation."

" Thank you, Dr. Hansell," Lady Burr said, as the doctor sat down. " As usual, you and Dr. Minor have given us much to think about."

CHAPTER VII
GETTING MARRIED

IT is usual for the speakers to meet occasionally at most large conferences to discuss the progress of the conference, alter the programme if necessary, and deal with any problems that may arise. Such was the procedure at this conference, Lady Burr insisting on a short meeting of all the officers and speakers after the evening coffee and bun. After one such meeting, held two or three days after the Canon's visit to the clinic, Lady Burr detained him and Dr. Hansell.

" How did you two get on ? " she inquired.

" Very well," Dr. Hansell replied. " We have had some interesting discussions and cleared the air quite a lot."

" Have you come to any definite conclusions ? " the Chairman persisted. " The reason I ask is that there has been a good deal of discussion since your speech, Canon, not all of it by any means complimentary, and I think it would be wise to allow time for further discussion at one of the main sessions, so as to try and clear up some of the points that I know are still worrying a good many people. I would not like to do this, however, unless you agree and are prepared to put up with some further questioning."

" I have been thinking a good deal about the matter myself," Canon Heathcott said. " My views have altered in some respect since I visited the clinic and talked with the doctor, and I think it only right and proper that I should say so publicly at some convenient moment. In order to do this as simply as possible, I have made a note of the main points of our joint discussion, and tried to indicate those items on which we seem to have reached agreement. I have them here," he continued, producing a piece of paper, " and should like to discuss them with Dr. Hansell, and then, if you agree, make a short statement about the whole matter before one of the meetings."

" That would be excellent," Lady Burr said. " And I

should think the best time will be before the meeting on 'Preparation for Marriage'. You will both be on the platform, and can deal with any questions that may arise. What do you think, doctor?"

"An admirable decision, which should enable us to tidy up loose ends," Dr. Hansell said.

"In that case I will leave you two alone so that you can get the matter settled," Lady Burr said, going out of the room.

Half an hour later David Kerrans put his head in at the door. "Oh! I'm sorry to interrupt; they told me Wendy was here," he said.

"No, she isn't here; but come right in, my dear chap, and make yourself comfortable," Dr. Hansell said. "The Canon and I have just finished, and as I want to talk to you before you go, we may as well seize this opportunity."

"And I shall go to bed," Canon Heathcott exclaimed. "I think we have completed that quite successfully, don't you, doctor?"

"Certainly. I think you have made a very good job of it."

"In that case I will bid you good night. But don't let him stay up too late, young man: he is a demon for late hours."

"I'll do my best, sir," David Kerrans said, smiling broadly.

"When do you and Wendy sail for America?" the doctor inquired after the Canon had gone.

"About ten days after the wedding, unless the powers that be cancel our passages," David replied. "I have my job waiting for me, and want to get started as soon as possible."

"Good! I have been wanting to see you for some time, to clear up one or two points and tell you about Wendy. She is a typical example of the value of premarital examination. She had quite a tight hymen, and no doubt told you that she had some difficulty over the dilatation. However, that is all over now, and I have given her a perfectly adequate contraceptive method. Should she need any advice whilst in America I have given her the name of a doctor friend of mine in New York, or, should she not be there, she can write to the Planned Parenthood Federation, 501 Madison Avenue, New York 22, who will put her in touch with a good doctor in whatever town she happens to be."

"Don't all doctors do this sort of thing, then?"

"Unfortunately, no; although there are more in America than over here. It is important to make sure that the doctor you choose knows about contraception. The interesting point about Wendy is that had she not had this preliminary help, you would have had considerable difficulty in effecting penetration without hurting her; indeed, I am afraid you would have hurt her a good deal, and probably set up a whole host of unsatisfactory feelings and repressions. That is all avoided now. Wendy is a perfectly healthy young woman, and, so far as I can see, there is no reason why you should have any trouble. But you must go slowly, and not expect perfection to start off with."

"I know. We are both very grateful to you. Women must be stupid who don't get fixed up beforehand."

"The number of those who do is still comparatively small, I'm afraid," Dr. Hansell said. "It will take a long time before we can persuade the mass of young people that the physical side of marriage is something which has to be thought about and learnt about reasonably and dispassionately."

"Do all women have the sort of difficulty Wendy had?"

"Not necessarily. Women's bodies vary to an extraordinary degree, just as does our eyesight. It is impossible to tell the condition of the hymen without examination. In some women it is practically non-existent; in others it is so tight that it has to be removed by a simple surgical operation, and yet in none of these cases will coitus have occurred."

"I see."

"It is important that you both realise that no matter how well you two know each other now, the physical expression of marriage will show you a different side of each other. The achievement of perfection—of the total union of body, mind and spirit—will take time, and you mustn't try to rush it, or be disappointed if everything doesn't go according to plan to start off with. I should say, for instance, that in spite of all the help and teaching I have given you both, it may take Wendy anything from a week to six months before she gets a really satisfactory orgasm."

"How often should we have intercourse?"

"People vary; some couples, being more highly sexed than others, need to give expression to this side of their natures pretty frequently. I should say that twice a week is about the average. You must remember that some women seem to experience a definite rhythm of desire which is much more marked than in men. Most women find that they are more ready for coitus, and derive more benefit from it, just before or just after a period. In the majority of cases the ten days after a period has finished seems to be the most satisfactory time, and this, of course, coincides with the time of ovulation.[1] The more satisfactory the union, the less likely are a couple to wish to repeat it immediately. They will have been so satisfied and refreshed that several days may elapse before the natural rhythm demands a renewal of the experience. This fact is frequently overlooked by the opponents of contraception, who seem to think that if one provides people with the ability to ' indulge ', as they call it, whenever they want to, the result is one long orgy. Nothing could be farther from the truth; it is precisely in those couples who do not experience any real satisfaction, or who are abstaining from the act for a long time, and therefore are always thinking about it, that one finds a constant desire for repetition."

"I see. I've noticed already that Wendy likes me to make love to her more at some times than at others, and never quite understood the reason."

"Well, it's simply a physiological condition, and shouldn't worry you at all. You'll find, however, when you've become more proficient, that you can make love at almost any time. If you find that there are days when she is disinclined for the relationship you shouldn't force it on her. The woman should always have the deciding vote in these matters. This brings me to another point which deserves attention. I've known many people who have been married for months, or even years, and have never really ' let themselves go '.

[1] v.p. 197.

Some men seem to think that it is wrong to express real emotion to their wives; they seem to be possessed with the idea that passion in itself is something to be ashamed of, that it is quite all right to exhibit it with some woman for whom they haven't much respect, such as a prostitute, but that it is quite wrong to show it to a woman whom they really love."

"What a funny idea! I should have thought women liked men to be passionate."

"So they do. It is the men who are at fault. They have yet to learn that a woman can enjoy the sex relationship as much as, or even more than they do themselves.

"You two are young and very much in love, and delightfully free from foolish inhibitions. These factors, combined with the teaching and instruction you have received, are precisely the factors which make for permanent happiness. You will have your ups and downs, of course—you must expect them. No marriage rides permanently on the crest of the wave. You are embarking on a mutual voyage of discovery which may last a lifetime. You mustn't be in too great a hurry to experience everything at once, and always bear in mind that the basis of your married life is thought for each other. This is particularly important for the man to realise in regard to the woman. Marriage does not imply licence or selfish gratification. Rather does it demand thought, control, mutual respect and sacrifice. Your whole endeavour must be to co-operate; to believe in the other—to think for the other."

"In other words, to cultivate the habit of give and take."

"Precisely. And there is another important point to be made here. The sex act must never become stereotyped, or it will soon degenerate into a mere physical exercise. Many men fail to appreciate the fact that a woman needs arousing, and that it is their business to do this tactfully and skilfully. When a woman tells me that she derives no satisfaction from the sex act, I often find that this is due to the man's inability to make love properly, and in many cases he fails over the preliminary love-play. So many men seem to think that courtship ends with the wedding bells, instead of only just beginning with them. Some men think that once a woman has had some feeling—one could hardly call it an orgasm—the business is over as far as she is concerned. This means that if the woman is easily aroused, the whole act is completed in about two minutes, in which case neither can be really satisfied. Other men fail to make the second stage—the stage of penetration to ejaculation—last long enough and, being fearful, often prolong the love-making stage indefinitely, in the hope that the woman will be satisfied, which doesn't often happen. No woman can be really satisfied unless the second stage is satisfactory, and this is a matter for mutual practice."

" Do all women obtain an orgasm in the vagina ? "

" Not necessarily. Some women obtain sensation in the clitoris more easily than in the vagina, and vice versa ; some obtain sensation in both. The vaginal orgasm is usually more satisfying. An expert lover can occasionally provide his wife with several orgasms before the final one, which should coincide with his ejaculation. The timing of this takes practice. There is nothing so satisfying for both as a mutual orgasm, and it must be your constant aim to achieve this and, in particular, to understand the varying moods of your partner."

" You mean that women like the stage to be set correctly."

" Quite so. Men tend to let it pass as unnecessary, although, in reality, they will find that a correct setting enhances the pleasure for both. It is strange, when you come to think of it, that most people make love at night, when they are tired after a long day ; and often without any preparation at all worth speaking of."

" But I should have thought the need for preparation was obvious. After all, if two people are going out together for the evening, they usually make some sort of preparation," David said.

" You would think so, but I can assure you that it isn't a common attitude. Far too many people perform the affair hurriedly, in the dark, and very often in a cold, bleak bedroom. It isn't surprising that the woman derives so little pleasure. All the romance and tenderness disappear very quickly from such a relationship. And it is not only among thoughtless people that this state of affairs exists, but among many highly intelligent couples, who are really fond of one another and would never dream of hurting each other in the ordinary way. The sex act, if properly performed, should last at least half an hour, should be mutually satisfying and lead to a refreshing sleep. Some couples, as I have already said, find that there is no desire for further coitus for several days, although others may wish to renew the relationship the following night, and then wait several days. I'm sure that if only people would try and have coitus less frequently, and make it more satisfying when they do experience it, they would derive far greater benefit. Many men seem to think they are fine fellows if they can have coitus every night, or even twice in a night; but in reality their performance lacks finesse and is probably quickly over. You must guard against that."

" I certainly will."

" There is another point which I should like to make," Dr. Hansell said. " A little attention to one's toilet doesn't come amiss at this time. A bath and a shave are both refreshing and cleanly; a scrubby chin has put off many a woman. Clothes, too, are important. A dowdy nightdress or a pair of ancient pyjamas are by no means the best articles of attire. Again, please remember that all our senses can, and must, be employed. By this I mean touch, smell, sight, and hearing. Some women are aroused more quickly than others, and all are aroused quicker at certain times than others. It is for the man to sense the situation. It is up to the man to think out new methods of love-making, to spring little surprises on his wife. An intelligent couple will find that they are always making new discoveries about each other. The final stage is equally important. There is a positive delight in the close companionship which can be experienced at this time. A few words of love and appreciation; a kiss, or a touch, may be the prelude to a short sleep which is delightfully intimate and satisfying. Have I made this clear to you?"

" Yes, perfectly. With regard to the contraceptive side of the business, I imagine that the particular method you have given Wendy is the closest approach to nature that has been devised so far, isn't it?"

"Yes, it is. Of course the use of a single chemical soluble would be even more satisfactory, if only we had one, but unfortunately there isn't one on the market at present."

"Are they all useless?"

"Not useless, but certainly not safe. None of them provides such a high percentage of safety as the cap and chemical."

"Is there anything else that you want to tell me?"

"Just one or two more points. .You may think that I've paid too much attention to detail, but I can assure you that I haven't. To you, the things that I've said may be commonplace, but to the majority of people they seem to come as a kind of revelation."

"I've learned a lot myself."

"Good! Well, now, I hope you'll bear in mind that the procedure I've outlined must form the background of your married life, and must not end with your honeymoon. To make this possible in the ordinary humdrum of existence takes some doing; but it is possible. By such means your wife will be enabled to develop her own personality, and this you must always foster. Encourage her to make her own friends, to have her own occupations; and give her her own money to spend in her own way. Enjoy her independence, but let her feel that you are always there beside her, to help her in difficulties. Above all, avoid jealousy. True love is based on mutual confidence; jealousy has its roots in selfishness and fear. A jealous man is one who is afraid of losing his wife to a man who is bigger, or better looking, or more attractive than he is. He has forgotten, or never realised, that his wife has chosen him in spite of his snub nose or his stutter or his thin legs, or even his fat tummy; and that she loves him for himself. If she is wise, she will make allowances for his shortcomings, and he must do the same. None of us is perfect. So let her live her own life, but don't forget to live some of your life with her. Go out with her occasionally and enjoy things together, and don't always come home and say that you are so tired that all you want is your bedroom slippers and a book. And remember that looking after the home and children is just as fatiguing for her as managing your business is for you, and not half so interesting."

"Talking of children, is there any reason why Wendy shouldn't have them, because we want to start a family fairly soon?"

"No reason whatsoever. She is perfectly healthy, and appears to have perfectly normal sex organs. So far as you are concerned, the semen test shows that you have a very high degree of fertility. At the same time you must bear in mind that I cannot guarantee anything. I don't know whether Wendy may not have some condition such as a blocked tube which might reduce her fertility. I cannot go into all that now, nor is there any need. If you are interested you can come to the lecture Dr. Minor is giving on the subject in a day or two.[1] The main point to remember is that if, after trying to have a baby for six months, nothing has happened, you should both go to a specialist in sterility and have the matter looked into."

"Yes, I understand all that."

"And don't forget that after your wife has had a baby it is inadvisable to renew sexual intercourse for two months, and certainly not before she has been to a doctor to see that her contraceptive method is all right. And there should be an interval of two years between the birth of each child."

"It looks as though we shall be pretty busy during the next ten years," David said laughingly, "because Wendy says that she must have at least five children."

Dr. Hansell joined in the laughter.

"Well," he said, after a moment, "whilst you are engaged on all these important tasks, don't forget to allow your wife a little privacy now and then. Let her bedroom be her own, and don't look upon it as a room which you can enter at any time of the day or night, without even knocking."

"But that goes without saying."

"It may with you, but it doesn't with a lot of men. Some women never have a moment to themselves. They have to dress and undress, wash and clean their teeth with their husbands hanging about the room all the time, and in all probability doing the same thing. No matter how small

[1] v.p. 195.

your house, it is always possible to dress and undress in privacy. If I were a woman, I'd never let a man see me unless I was ready and willing to be seen. I'd cling to my personal privacy like grim death, because by that means I would invariably be nice and attractive. If you want to use the bathroom together, do so by all means, but do it because you want to, and not because you're in a hurry to get dressed and go out."

David laughed. " You hit the nail on the head there all right."

" And this is really my last word," Dr. Hansell said. " All that I've said will be useless unless you two adopt the right attitude to each other. The physical will mean nothing unless there is mental and spiritual harmony. Sex love is an unselfish communion between two free personalities, and lives in a spirit of mutual co-operation. It isn't the performance of a physical exercise, but an art, the technique of which requires care and forethought to acquire. It is a relationship in which the self is completely subordinated to the well-being of the other. It can only operate in a spirit of mutual understanding and complete emotional surrender."

The door opened and Wendy came into the room.

" Oh, there you are," she said, going up to David and taking his arm. " What on earth have you two been doing? I've been looking for you all over the place."

" We've been talking about you," David said.

" I hope you found me interesting," Wendy said, squeezing his arm. " Do you think he will be a nice husband to me, Dr. Hansell, and won't beat me or be horrid to me? "

" I think I can at least guarantee that, Wendy," the doctor said with a smile.

CHAPTER VIII
EXTRA-MARITAL RELATIONSHIPS

FOR those who are students of human nature, conferences are both interesting and amusing, because the people who come to them are as varied as a plate of pre-war hors d'oeuvres. Those attending this particular Conference were no exception to the rule; indeed in some ways they were more interesting than usual, because not only were the sexes well mixed, but ages varied enormously, those under forty showing as wide and accurate a knowledge of the subjects under discussion as those of riper years. Even the youngest —and there was a fair sprinkling of the twenties present— showed by their interest and knowledge that their time in the Forces had not been spent in mental blinkers. Only occasionally did Dr. Hansell come across someone who seemed to find the atmosphere of friendly and frank discussion strange or embarrassing. One such man had attracted his attention during the meeting on the previous evening. Tall and handsome, with greying hair and clear-cut features, he had sat alone and somewhat aloof from the others, but followed the lecture so closely that the doctor had become vividly conscious of his presence.

"Worried!" Dr. Hansell said to himself as he climbed the stairs to bed that night, an opinion fully confirmed by an incident that occurred the following morning whilst he was getting up. A hasty rap on the door scarcely preceded the man in question.

"I'm sorry to bother you," he said hurriedly, "but I wonder if you could possibly lend me a razor. I have stupidly left mine behind."

"Of course; I'm always doing that sort of thing myself," Dr. Hansell said, going over to his suit-case. "So I make a practice of carrying two. Now where——? Ah!" He straightened up and held out the razor. "There," he said, smiling at his visitor. " I thought for a moment that I had left it behind, too. Please keep it for as long as you like."

"Thanks," the man replied, ignoring the smile, but taking the razor and disappearing through the door as quickly as he had come.

"Dear me!" said the doctor, throwing off his dressing-gown. "He is upset." He wasn't altogether surprised, therefore, when the man buttonholed him after lunch.

"I wonder if I could talk to you, Dr. Hansell. Walker's my name—Andrew Walker. I'm worried. I think you might be able to help me. Of course if you would rather I made a proper appointment——"

"My dear chap. Please don't let that disturb you. I have nothing to do this afternoon, and shall be only too pleased to be of assistance to you. Indeed, that is one of the reasons why I am here. If one is prepared to air one's views in public, one must be equally prepared to defend them. Let us go to my room and make ourselves comfortable in front of the fire."

"I'm an engineer by profession," Mr. Walker said, when they had settled down. "Partner in a pretty big firm in London; married fifteen years; two children, twelve and fourteen; house in the country; no financial worries, and have spent the last five years in a hush-hush job in the Navy. Never went to sea, as a matter of fact. It is only within the last year that I have been able to get back to civvy street and return to the old firm. And now, being in a spot of bother, and having heard of this conference from a pal of mine, I thought I would pop down and see if I could get a wrinkle or two, and I must say I've been impressed. Although I've knocked around the world a good deal, I've never heard sex matters discussed so openly and sensibly as I have down here. I was particularly interested in what you said last night about love affairs—extra-marital relationships, I think you called them."

"Yes. I'm afraid I didn't say as much as I would have liked."

"Quite enough for me. I saw a lot of that sort of thing during the war, and I think everything you said was quite right."

"Thank you. I'm glad."

Mr. Walker shifted his position and looked at the doctor's impassive face. This was getting a bit difficult. Had he made a mistake? Why didn't the fellow help a bit more? Like having a tooth out. He plunged again.

"I——!"

"Yes?"

He pulled out his pipe and began to stuff it hurriedly with tobacco.

"Damn it!" he said suddenly, getting out of his chair. "I find this infernally difficult. You must think me an awful fool."

"On the contrary, I see that you are very worried about something, but I cannot help you unless you give me some idea of what the trouble is, can I? Why don't you sit down quietly and take things more calmly? Start anywhere you like."

"Thanks; I will," Mr. Walker said, taking up a commanding position in front of the fire, and lighting his pipe very carefully, looking at the doctor meanwhile through a haze of smoke.

At last, having got the pipe going to his satisfaction, he began to walk up and down the room, puffing furiously the while.

"You remember that I borrowed your razor this morning?"

"Yes, of course. What of it?"

"Well, I've never forgotten my razor during the whole of the last five years. I always carry it about in one of those leather cases that hold everything from a nail-file to a bottle of iodine. You know them, no doubt."

"Certainly; I have one myself: the iodine leaks out!" Dr. Hansell's smile was still ignored.

"When I came down here I packed the case, but left the razor out. Funny, wasn't it?"

"Oh, I don't know. We often do things like that when we are overworked or worried. It's like forgetting the names of people we know perfectly well."

Mr. Walker took his pipe out of his mouth and pointed it at the doctor. "Worried! Yes. That's it. I was. Damnably."

"Well, what was the worry?"

The pipe was replaced in its proper place as its owner began walking about again. "Damn it!" he thought. "Here we are, back again where we started." More puffs, more rapid glances, more haze, whilst the doctor continued to sit quietly in his chair. "I'll tell you," the man said suddenly. "I'll tell you if I die in the attempt; but it's a long story, and I don't feel too good about it."

"Sit down," Dr. Hansell said quietly. "You'll feel better sitting down."

"I prefer to walk, thank you."

"All right: as you please. Throw the fire-irons about if you think it helps, but do try and come to the point."

Mr. Walker glared at the doctor and continued his perambulations.

"Well," he said at last, "as I have said, I'm married. Been married for fifteen years, in fact. Although I was nearly thirty at the time, and my wife only a year or two younger, we were both incredibly ignorant about the so-called facts of life. The first baby came nine months to a day after the wedding, and, apart from a few times after that one, and a few times before the birth of the next one two years later, we haven't lived together as man and wife since. Needless to say we quarrelled a good deal, and generally made a little hell on earth for ourselves. After the second kid was born we considered a divorce, but decided to stick together because of the children, each going his own way as regards other affairs. Life went fairly smoothly for about ten years, during which time we each had one or two affairs, but nothing serious. Then, when the war came, I joined up, and I can't say that I was altogether sorry. The strain of keeping up appearances was getting me down. My wife continued to live in or near London during the whole of the war, but I was drafted all over the country; first to Plymouth, then to Scotland, and then to some filthy place in the depths of Wales. My work was hard and intensive, and I didn't get too much time at home. Indeed, I often went for several months without going near the place.

"After I had been on the job for about a year I met a girl considerably younger than myself, with whom I fell madly in love. She was a Wren, doing the same kind of work as myself—often in the same office. She was jolly and attractive, and extremely pretty, and got on very well with everyone in the place. Men buzzed round her like wasps round a jam-pot. In spite of my being older and in some ways more staid than the usual run of officer, something drew us together, and we clicked from the moment we first met, and never turned back. I discovered later that she had had an affair with some fellow which hadn't gone too well, so I suppose each sensed the loneliness in the other. Anyway, so far as I was concerned, my whole life was changed. For six months we remained together on the same ship, and then I was drafted."

"I thought you said you didn't go to sea," Dr. Hansell interposed.

"All naval stations are known as 'ships', whether they are on dry land or not," Mr. Walker replied, smiling for the first time.

"Of course. How stupid of me!"

"Well, the new arrangement didn't make much difference; indeed, in many ways it made things easier and brought us closer together, because we were not always having to be careful about our behaviour, and managed to meet fairly frequently for leaves and so on. As a matter of fact we were incredibly lucky, and there was scarcely a month in the next three years that we didn't manage to get at least one week-end together, and sometimes more. Occasionally we managed a week or ten days. They were wonderful."

"Yes."

"We had started living together by this time, and everything was really marvellous. We seemed to suit each other in every possible way—at least, I thought we did; and so, I think, did she. For the first time in my life I found a woman who was really responsive and understanding. No! That isn't quite true. I had had affairs with other women which had been pretty satisfactory whilst they lasted, but this, somehow, was quite different. Never have I known such happiness and contentment as I experienced with this girl. Such peace and quietness—such fun—such unity.

Never were two people so well suited to each other, each providing and fulfilling something that the other lacked. And now, for some incredible reason, it has all come to an end. She has just walked out on me. Like that." And Mr. Walker waved his arm dramatically over the doctor's head.

" When did this happen ? "

" Three or four days ago—I've lost count of time."

" Then you have been seeing each other since you were demobilised ? "

" Of course! I got her a job with my firm; she is very useful to them."

" I see. Does she give you any reason for walking out on you, as you call it ? "

" Yes and no. We have talked it over for hours. She says she is very fond of me, and couldn't bear not to see me again and all that, but she has found someone else who seems to attract her irresistibly."

" In the same way as you were attracted to each other originally ? "

" I suppose so. I don't know. I don't see how she can say that, because she has only known the fellow a short while. It can't mean the same thing."

" Women are funny creatures where love is concerned," murmured Dr. Hansell.

" So it seems. Anyway, she says she is very sorry to have hurt me so much, but she cannot help herself. When she feels that way she must act that way."

" In spite of her obligations to you ? "

" She says she is made that way."

" I see. Has she had other affairs, then, besides the one you mentioned ? "

" Oh yes, I think so; but I don't know much about them. I never bothered to ask. What was past was past. All I knew was that I loved her intensely, and she, I thought, loved me. But now—after this—I don't know. I can't understand how anyone can just walk out on a chap quite suddenly like that. One minute you are together and happy, and the next minute there is nothing left."

" But I thought you said that she was still fond of you ? "

"So she is; but that isn't the same thing. She can't love me—not like I love her. And all the things she said to me seem meaningless now. All the lovely letters she wrote, and the presents we gave each other, and the photos I have of her. They mean nothing. I sent them all back."

"What! All of them?"

"Well, most of them."

"But not the leather travelling-case."

"No! But how——?"

"It is obvious, my dear man. The razor perhaps, just to show your annoyance. You could leave that behind, but the case—No! And I daresay you have some photographs tucked away somewhere. Yes, I thought so. All that kind of behaviour is natural, but very childish. Why spoil your memories? Why hurt her more than you have done already? You said a minute ago that the past is past. Well, why not accept it and keep it so?"

"But I don't understand why this should happen. There was nothing wrong between us; we never quarrelled; we were blissfully happy. I know we were. I felt it. One always knows these things."

"And you never noticed anything."

"Well, I must admit that things didn't go quite so well after she was demobbed. I think she found it difficult to settle down in her new life; sharing a flat with two other girls—bothering about rations and so on—on top of her ordinary work. Circumstances were such that we couldn't be together very much by ourselves."

"Were you always by yourselves before?"

"Yes and no. We liked being alone, but we used to go out a good deal with other people—parties and so on. Oh yes, we had a jolly time. But underneath it all we liked being together. We would spend whole days together in the car—when we had any petrol—trotting around; walking in the country; or going to the cinema. She loved the cinema. We were happy in whatever we did and felt at one with each other. It's difficult to explain, and no doubt sounds silly when one puts it like that, but we meant a terrific lot to one another, I assure you."

"Of course. You aren't the first couple to have felt that way."

Mr. Walker looked at the doctor, laughed, and sat down.

"I know," he said. "I'm sorry, but I still don't understand, and it hurts horribly. Everywhere I go I think of her—every street or place I visit reminds me of her—every night I think of her—in another man's arms. That's what gets my goat: I see it all. I know her moods and ways, her intimacies, her love. It meant so much to me, and now it's all gone. Off she goes with somebody else. And yet she's not like that at all, really. She is true and loyal, sensitive and particular. I know. I know her very well. You probably think her a bit brazen to go on like that, but I assure you——!"

"I don't; but I think you are rather a fool—if I may say so without offence."

"Me! Why?"

"You don't understand much about women, I'm afraid."

"Perhaps not, but I understand about her."

"I wonder. Tell me, Mr. Walker, how old is the girl?"

"About twenty-six."

"And you?"

"Forty-seven. Oh, I know what you are going to say—too old and all that sort of thing—but believe me we talked all that out."

"I didn't say too old, Mr. Walker. Were you worried about the difference in age?"

"No, but——!"

"Anyway, what does age matter? You were not going to marry the girl, were you?"

"No, of course not. She knew that my wife and I had decided to stay together on account of the children."

"But you haven't seen very much of them recently, have you?"

"Well, no, I can't say I have; but now that I am home, things are easier that way; I see them in the holidays."

"Yes. And your wife? Does she know of this affair?"

"Oh yes, of course; I told her all about it."

"And what does she say?"

"She keeps to the bargain, but personally I'm not so sure."

"How do you mean?"

"Now that this has happened I find that I love Dorothy—that's the girl—so much that I don't think I can live without her."

"You want to marry her?"

"Yes."

"Have you told your wife of this new development?"

"Not that I want to marry Dorothy."

"I see. But what about Dorothy? She doesn't seem to want you now that she has found another man."

"I think that is just a passing phase."

"But she must have given you some definite reason for her changed attitude."

"I told you; she says she feels constricted with me—'tied' was the word she used. She says that this new affair may be the real thing and that she must find out. But find out what? That's what I can't understand. We were so happy, and now it's all over—gone. Oh God!" Mr. Walker leaned forward suddenly and rapped his pipe on the grate.

"I think you have been living in a fool's paradise, my dear fellow. Women don't just change all of a sudden, as you suggest—at least, not the nice type of sensitive young woman that your Dorothy seems to be. This has been coming on for some time, I expect, and either you didn't see it or you shut your eyes to it."

"You may be right. Now that I come to think of it, I did notice a few things, but I didn't pay much attention to them. She is a self-contained little person, and one never knows just exactly what she is thinking about. Introspective, I suppose."

"You mean that she lives in a world of her own."

"Oh yes. Very much so. It is very difficult to get inside the shell of reserve with which she surrounds herself."

"I see. But you didn't take that too seriously?"

"No, I was used to it and liked it."

"Perhaps she had met the other man by that time."

"I daresay she had. There were always men in her life,

but that never worried me. We understood each other so perfectly—at least, I thought we did—and trusted each other implicitly. But now I'm not at all sure that there weren't two sides to her life. I satisfied one aspect, and they satisfied another. She used to say that I did her good and kept her straight."

" Yes, I can understand that."

" Do you ? I'm damned if I do. To me the thing's an incredible mystery. All my faith in women has gone. I loved that girl to distraction, and would have done anything for her, and now she's walked out on me."

" Would you ? I wonder."

" What do you mean ? Would I ? I tell you I would go anywhere and do anything for her—give her anything——!"

" I don't know about that."

" How do you mean ? I assure you——"

" Come, Mr. Walker. Let us try to get some shape into this problem. So far as I can see, the position is as follows. Here we have a married man of middle age with two children, falling madly in love with a girl twenty years younger than himself. The war and mutual interests throw you together. Each is lonely; neither is inexperienced. The man's marriage has gone on the rocks ; the girl finds him attractive and is flattered by his attentions. The inevitable happens. It was all so easy—so pleasant for both of you. For three years you lived in a fool's paradise and let life drift."

" Oh, I say. I don't think either of us felt that we were living in a fool's paradise. We meant a great deal to each other, and had a great deal in common ; books—music—work——"

" I know. I know all that. But nevertheless if you are honest you will admit that that is what happened. Any chance of putting your own marriage right went by the board as soon as you met that girl."

" That isn't fair either. My wife and I had talked the whole thing over years before : we had discussed it from every possible angle."

" Exactly, but you didn't get any expert help or advice. You say things went wrong physically to start off with, by which I suppose you mean that your wife got no orgasm ;

that you were clumsy or inexpert in some way; that the honeymoon was a failure, and that any contraceptive methods you used were useless. And so the physical situation was allowed to drift, and no attempt was made to put it right, either then or after the birth of the first baby."

"That's true, but we had no one to help us. I agree that had all this happened now things might have been different. It wasn't that we didn't want help, or indeed seek it. We did, but we got none."

"I know. I fully realise your difficulties. It was much more difficult to get help then than now. Nevertheless there were times in your life when you could have made a further effort had you been inclined; but you didn't. You were always tying yourself up in some new adventure."

"Perhaps so. But things had gone on too long to be put right. Sex is a very tricky business, and when it once goes wrong it goes wrong, and don't I know it."

"No doubt, but there were other factors as well. Sex wasn't the only one. The children, for instance. What of them? You say that you decided to stay together because of them. I wonder how far that decision was a mere escape mechanism to avoid the unpleasantness of admitting both to yourselves and to the world in general that you had made a mess of your marriage and would have been better apart."

"Oh, I don't know. We were very fond of the children and, incidentally, of each other. We should have hated to part, and thought it much better for the children to have a proper home with a mother and a father."

"You don't seem to have put your principles into practice very well."

"Not during the war—no; but before that, yes. My wife and I were together a great deal and did everything we could for the children. I admit that I was remiss during the war, but my affection for the children has always been very strong, and we all get on very well together. Indeed, everyone gets on well provided the whole family isn't together!"

"Yes, many families are like that. It by no means follows that all the members of a family can get on together. But in your case there was a fundamental flaw."

" What was that ? "
" That each of you had agreed to allow the other partner to have other affairs. That would make for instability."
" Not necessarily. It wasn't ideal certainly, but we thought it was the best of two evils, and we knew other people who made it work."
" You cannot say that without knowing all the circumstances of each case. Those ideas were all the rage after the last war; they are now known to be unsound. Only very occasionally have I known such an arrangement work satisfactorily."
" They work quite well abroad—in France, for instance."
" Perhaps, and perhaps not. However, we are not French: we have a different temperament. Sexual adventures are not regarded with the same horror abroad. Nevertheless, they have a very strict code—stricter than ours in some respects. Besides, there is usually some emotional relationship between husband and wife. But in your case there was none; there was no positive relationship between you and your wife on the physical sphere; on the contrary, there was nothing but remorse and antagonism. Thus, in my opinion, you would have been wiser to have accepted the situation and divorced each other whilst the children were still too young to notice. Indeed, your wife would probably have found a new husband and made a new life, and the children would have had a new father who would have provided them with a security which you do not seem to have given them—not recently, at any rate."
" I'm afraid I can't agree to that. We didn't want to separate."
" Well, you may have been right; it is quite impossible for an outsider to say," Dr. Hansell replied, " but there can be no doubt that your relationship was most unstable."
" Oh yes, we knew that, and accepted it."
" You must have been very unhappy."
" We were—at times—very unhappy. At others, life was quite tolerable."
" Prolonging the agony," Dr. Hansell said with a smile. " However, don't let us spend more time considering that aspect of the situation. You decided on a certain course of

action and pursued it to the best of your abilities. Then the war came, and the whole situation changed. Not only were you called up, but you went away from home. Obviously, with nothing much to hold you to your wife, and under the emotional stress and strain of war, you quickly made a new relationship. It was only to be expected. It was only natural that the girl should be attracted to you : she must have been flattered by your attentions. After all, you were older and more stable. In all probability you had more money than the others and could take her around and give her a good time. That you liked the same things merely strengthened your hold over her. And she, being young and attractive, and, perhaps, feeling uncertain of herself—insecure, if you like, in her emotional life—found greater comfort in the security you offered her. At least, it seemed like security to her in the midst of the insecurity of war. Responsibilities, such as they were, remained in the background. Had the girl no home ?"

"Her people lived abroad, and she hadn't seen them for years, and never talked about them very much. She had various relations round the country, whom she visited occasionally. Yes, I think you have summed up the situation very well."

"It was really very unstable, you know, when you come to look at it dispassionately. It isn't surprising it came to an end."

"How so ? We had everything we wanted."

"Oh come, Mr. Walker, I can't really accept that. You had everything you wanted, certainly : a charming and attractive girl to take about and interest herself in your affairs—very pleasing to your vanity, no doubt—but I doubt whether she had everything that she wanted."

"I admit that she didn't have a home, if that is what you mean, but she wouldn't have had that anyway during the war ! "

"Why not ? She could have married you had you been free, or someone else."

"Certainly, but she always declared that she was very happy as she was, and she certainly didn't have a bad time."

"No! I think she had a very good time; the best of both worlds, in fact. Plenty of fun in her job with plenty of men around her all the time, and plenty of fun at your expense when she went on leave. Oh yes! She certainly had a very good time!"

"I don't think you are fair. I'm sure she never thought like that at all; it isn't in her make-up to do so."

"Perhaps not. You know her, and I don't; but as an ordinary man of the world that is how I should sum up the situation. I don't say she consciously thought that way, but that was her pattern of behaviour."

"We did discuss marriage once or twice in a perfunctory sort of way, but she always turned it down. Why, I could never make out."

"Did you discuss it after she came out of the Forces?"

"Yes."

"And she still turned it down."

"That's right."

"I'm not surprised."

"Why not? On account of my age?"

"Not necessarily, although I should imagine a girl would think twice before marrying a man so much older than herself."

"But many people do make that kind of marriage."

"I know, but they are usually older people. If she married you she would only be about forty-five by the time you were sixty-five. However, had she been head over ears in love with you I don't expect that age would have stood in her way."

"But she was head over ears in love with me. We got on splendidly together."

"No doubt. But I think she recognised, sub-consciously perhaps, that her relationship with you, whilst being admirable in many ways, was really a sterile one; it had no possibility of development. Whenever you spoke of marriage you implied that although it would be very nice to marry her, you had responsibilities at home which could not be broken. No nice girl would want to smash up that relationship, and Dorothy, on your own showing, is a very nice girl."

"She certainly is."

"Very well, then. In so far as she was concerned, there was no possibility of her entering into a more permanent relationship with you unless you divorced your wife, which would invalidate the agreement you had made. Thus, after she got out of the Forces and had time to look around and readjust herself to society, she realised that she could never get home or children from you without causing a great deal of unhappiness all round. She probably decided that it was time she settled down. After all, girls of twenty-six or so usually begin to take life a bit more seriously, you know. She met plenty of men whilst in the Forces, and probably knew very well what she wanted, or at any rate what she didn't want, and one of the things she didn't want was a continuation of a relationship which was, or would soon become, emotionally sterile. And what did you offer her? Yourself certainly and your friendship and love and protection, such as it was; and a flat, I suppose, if she wanted it. But to what end? None that she could see except the doubtful pleasure of being your mistress; working in your office; of sharing some parts of your life and concealing the whole affair from her friends. In addition, you demanded so much of her time that—to use your own words—you made her feel tied and frustrated. No wonder she hesitated, and longed for the good old times when she was free."

"But she always said she wasn't interested in the men she met in the Forces; that she liked me much better."

"Of course! She liked you very much indeed, and still does. You were different; more stable, more mature. But she liked them, too; she liked having them around—feeling their presence and their admiration—sensing her power over them—and, for that matter, over you. Yes, she was very favourably placed. You surely aren't going to tell me that she didn't go out with other men when you weren't there."

"Oh no! Of course she did. I encouraged it. After all, life in the Services can be pretty dreary at times; but she always assured me that they meant nothing to her in comparison with me."

"Nevertheless she was having the best of both worlds,

and when she left it she came down to earth with a bump. Who is the young man this time?"

"Some officer fellow she met somewhere."

"Well, there you are. The thing is as plain as a pikestaff."

Mr. Walker laughed mirthlessly. "It may be to you," he said, getting up and beginning to prowl about the room again, "but I'm damned if it is to me."

"You say that her parents are abroad and that she hasn't seen them for years. How does she get on with them?"

"Not very well, I gather. She had a lonely life as a child."

"Precisely."

"What do you mean?"

"Let me see if I can put the matter to you quite simply. Dorothy is a girl who, in spite of her comparative youth, has had a good many men friends and a considerable experience of life. You say that she was in love with some other man before she met you, and that the affair went wrong for some reason or other. It is very probable that she is still hankering after him, and that this new man is of his type. In that case she is really projecting her unfulfilled wishes and desires on to the new man, who in some way represents the old unrequited love, or exhibits traits and tendencies which she found delightful in the old love and has never had an opportunity of expressing. I expect this new man differs from you as does chalk from cheese."

"He certainly does."

"There you are, then. I don't see what you can do but allow her to work the situation out for herself. She must find out what she really needs."

"But surely she needn't go to bed with him?"

"It would have been better if she could have based the friendship on a firmer level to start with, but she is not made that way. She is not an unawakened girl, and so her needs are different; you cannot compare the two situations. That is one of the troubles that arise in women when they are both awakened and disillusioned; they are unlikely to exclude the physical. All very unsatisfactory, no doubt, but there you are. She should have thought of all that years ago, before she ever embarked on the original relationship. You must remember that you are not the first man with whom she has had a sex relationship. Having conditioned herself to that pattern of behaviour, she no doubt gets a thrill out of it, just as you do when you make a new conquest. Whether or no she intends to pursue that course remains to be seen. What she is seeking, however, is a relationship which will give her a greater sense of security and emotional stability than you can offer. That doesn't prevent her being fond of you, who are older and steadier than some of her other friends. In other words, you are really a father substitute, and I imagine that is how she wants to regard you."

"Good God! I never thought of that. But what about the sex side? What I cannot understand is her sudden switch over from me to him—just like that—in a flash——" and again Mr. Walker waved his arm over the doctor's head. "One night she is in my bed, and the next in his. That galls me."

"Yes, I expect it does; it hurts damnably. The essential instability of these affairs will always lead to pain in the long run. That is what young people cannot and will not see. I expect that if the truth were known Dorothy was conscious of her altered feelings for some time, but didn't know what to do because she didn't want to hurt, and yet had to bring the affair to an end somehow. Not being honest with herself, she couldn't be honest with you."

"I can hardly believe that; it seems double-faced to me. You mean to say that whilst she was going to bed with me and telling me how nice I was, she was really sick of the whole affair and thinking of someone else?"

"Oh no! It was a gradual process of realisation."

"It sounds quite incredible, but I daresay you are right. She might have told me, though. I'm not insensitive, and would have taken it better that way."

"I agree. She shouldn't have kept you in suspense like that. But women are funny over these matters."

"Funny! I should say they were," Mr. Walker said, shrugging his shoulders. "Well, what's to be done? Is everything lost?"

"It all depends upon the interpretation you give to the word 'lost'. Your attitude to her has been somewhat selfish, don't you think?"

"Selfish? Good God, no! I was always thinking of her and trying to give her things she wanted."

"Except marriage."

"But she won't have that."

"She might have, eighteen months ago. Now you must give her time to make up her mind between the two of you. The danger is that she may make another mistake. Here is your chance. You can save something from the wreck by standing by her as a steadfast friend, and not playing the role of outraged lover. You have been far too self-interested in the past, and have tried to possess her for herself. Now you have the chance of rising above the self, and learning the meaning of real love."

"But I have loved her; I wouldn't hurt a hair of her head. You make something idyllic a mere selfish adventure."

"No. I try to make you see what the relationship really was for both of you—a selfish escape from reality, a refusal to face up to life or grow up emotionally. And so in the process you have hurt each other unmercifully. Your 'love' was based on self-interest. Now I suggest that you think again. In the past neither of you have been willing to face facts; you would not face up to the unsatisfactory nature of your own marriage, and she didn't or wouldn't see the emotional quagmire into which she was drifting and in which, for that matter, she still remains. Her only chance is to make the break, and your greatest fulfilment lies in accepting it and helping her to learn to understand herself. If you can do that you can build a finer and more lovely relationship between you that nothing can break because it will be based on mutual respect and sympathy. If you cannot do that, or don't think her worth the trouble, you have the other alternative, which is to walk out on her and let her fend for herself, damning all women in the process and persuading yourself that you are a highly injured person. The fact that the affair has made you so very unhappy will be all to the good if it jolts you out of yourselves and makes you try and decide where you are going and what you are doing before you damage more people. Up to the present neither of you has understood much about the meaning of love."

"What? Good God! man, I've been madly in love with Dorothy for months—years, in fact—and so has she with me."

"So you said before, but I don't agree with you," Dr. Hansell said.

"You don't understand at all. You make the whole affair seem shoddy and petty. You——!"

Mr. Walker paused, exasperation expressed in every inch of his body. Sitting down suddenly in his chair, he gazed into the fire, his face drawn and unhappy, his fingers drumming on the side of his chair. "A selfish escape from reality." Was the doctor right? His eyes sought the clock, and his stomach twisted as he saw the time—eleven o'clock, and Saturday night. Where was she now? What was she doing? Out with that fellow; enjoying his company, laughing at him with her deep, flashing eyes; holding his hand, going to bed with him. Oh God! Was there nothing left? No outings, no letters, no thrill of her touch, no light in her eyes. Bah! The best thing he could do would be to forget her as quickly as possible; to go out of her life, as the doctor said, and let her get on with it. Selfish, indeed; he had done everything for her, given her everything. If that wasn't love, he would like to know what was. Oh God! He could almost hear himself groan as he stood up and went over to the mirror.

"What are you doing?" Dr. Hansell demanded.

"Just looking to see how old I have got in the last few days. But I can't see any change. Funny how things can hurt abominably inside and yet there is nothing to show for it on the outside. I would like my hair to go grey in the night."

"And wallow in an orgy of self-pity. My dear fellow, you really must pull yourself together."

Mr. Walker returned dejectedly to his chair. "I can't. I don't know what to do."

"Well, let us leave that aspect of the problem for a moment and consider your relationship with your wife."

Mr. Walker stirred uneasily. "I feel completely bogged there," he said slowly.

" Why ? "

" The situation has become much worse recently. We don't see eye to eye about anything these days. As a matter of fact, I only go home because of the children."

" But they must be conscious that something is wrong, surely! Children are very sensitive to the atmosphere created by parents."

" We get along well enough together. I don't think they suspect much."

" I can't agree with you. If you and your wife are quarrelling all the time, they will know all about it, and will draw their own conclusions."

" But you surely don't suggest that we should tell them ? "

" I don't see how you can tell them anything definite at the moment; neither you nor your wife know your own minds. But I do think that they should be told that you are going through a sticky patch and are trying to work it out intelligently. They will then realise that you are being honest with them, and will respect you for it. If damage has been done, it can only be rectified by frankness. The truth is that you are allowing this situation to drift just as much as you allowed it to drift with Dorothy. In neither case have you faced facts or made adequate decisions."

" What do you advise ? "

" There are various alternatives."

" Such as ? "

Dr. Hansell paused for a moment to collect his thoughts.

" You must first of all try and clarify your relationship with Dorothy," he said at length. " As it seems unlikely that she will marry you, you must either accept the paternal role or cut her out. You should then talk to your wife and try to decide what you will do. You can divorce ; try to make a go of it, or, of course, carry on as you are."

" But we are sexually quite unsuited to each other."

" That remains to be seen. You were unsuited, but you haven't really given your minds to the matter for years ; you have always been adventuring elsewhere. There is no knowing what you can do till you try. If you could get together on that side, although it might not be entirely satisfactory, it might enable you to become adjusted to one another on a more mature level. That would be the ideal. If you can't do that you would then have to consider a divorce, so as to free you both to start again."

"There isn't much point in our getting a divorce if neither of us wants to marry any one else, is there?"

"Not unless you find it impossible to form a relationship which has some stability and is not a constant emotional strain. I don't think you can settle all that now. The main thing is to do something constructive. The very fact of facing up to the situation will make it easier."

"You think I had better give up Dorothy?"

"That is for you to decide. The only possibility of you retaining her friendship is to cut her out emotionally so that you no longer get twisting sensations in your tummy when you see her."

"You know the symptoms quite well, I see," Mr. Walker said, with a laugh.

"My dear fellow, you seem to think that you are the only person who has ever been affected in this way," Dr. Hansell said quietly.

The two men looked at each other for a moment and smiled.

"I don't like any of your suggestions," Mr. Walker said at last.

"No, I don't suppose you do. The best thing you can do is to go home and have a straight talk with your wife. After all, there must be something valuable in your relationship, or you wouldn't have stuck together so long."

"Yes, there is; we are very fond of each other."

"Well then, go and find out what she thinks. Women are very sensible over these affairs if you only give them a chance to help. After all, you don't even know if she is happy or not."

"She always seems to have plenty to do."

"That doesn't mean that she is happy."

"No, I suppose not."

"It is essential for you to sort your mind out; you are making everyone profoundly unhappy at present. If you are as fond of your wife as you say you are, you really ought to try and effect a positive reconciliation with her. If you both discuss the situation frankly and honestly you ought to get somewhere. After all, you did marry each other, and have grave responsibilities to each other, to say nothing of the children. Besides, neither of you is as young as you were: you will think and act differently in the next ten years than you have in the past ten. You can't go on being a gay spark for ever."

" I don't want to be a gay spark," Mr. Walker said rather gloomily. " I just want to settle down and be happy."

" You will have to work for it, then. Marriage is like that, you know; it is something you just have to make work. So many people refuse to try. When anything goes wrong they fly off in a tantrum, or rush to the divorce courts. No human relationship can possibly work unless there is a profound willingness to give and take—to think about the other person and make sacrifices. That is one of the reasons why your affair didn't work with Dorothy; you were both too selfish. Indeed, the same can be said of your marriage; you have never tried to make it work."

" No, perhaps not. Tell me, doctor, do you really think it would be possible to make my friendship with Dorothy work along the lines you suggest? Have you known other cases in which it has worked? "

" Oh yes. But you would both have to put your backs into it. I can visualise a very firm relationship growing up between the two of you which would not violate any other relationship that either of you might have. You might come to love each other very dearly."

" You always harp on this word love, as though we hadn't loved each other, but we did."

" Only in a self-seeking sort of way. True love must throw out the self and pay due regard to the other. Comradeship perhaps explains my meaning. Love is an overrated word."

" Comradeship ! Yes, I like that."

" But your relationship together must be such that it doesn't prevent either of you from putting all your energies into other creative activities—you with your wife—if you can—and Dorothy with her future friendship; you must each allow the other to have perfect freedom of choice, and still retain much which is personal to you both. You have much between you which need never be forgotten. If you can't both do that, you had better cut the whole thing out."

"I don't want to do that."

"Well, it's up to you. I think Dorothy needs your friendship and stability."

"Perhaps, but it seems to me that I get nothing and she gets everything—a new man and an old flame—a hanger-on. Won't she despise me?"

"Only if you cheapen yourself. She will respect you and value your friendship if you manage to weather a dangerous storm."

"I still don't see why the physical has cracked up."

"For the reasons I have already given you: disparity of age, possibly; no future to the relationship; other and more exciting attractions. We have been into all that. I think she is looking for something she hasn't found. You might have given it to her two years ago; now it is too late. All you can do is to stand by her."

"And watch her enjoying herself with someone else? No, thank you. I may be a fool, but I'm not quite such a fool as that."

"If you only could realise that sex can never be truly expressed when it is possessive you might get somewhere," Dr. Hansell said. "So long as we regard the other person as our personal property—our possession over whom we have rights—we get nowhere. Only when we begin to realise that sex can be lifted on to a higher level, can be translated into something which is finer and deeper do we begin to grow up. If you can reach that level you will be a better and happier man and she, incidentally, will be a nicer and more understanding woman. If you cannot rise above the self, then I am afraid you must accept the inevitable. Come, let's go to bed; it's very late, and I think we have talked enough."

"Thank you, doctor. I'm sorry if I have appeared difficult; I am really very grateful."

Later they met again. Mr. Walker looked happier. " I've seen my wife," he said, " and we have decided to make a go of it."

" I'm glad to hear that," Dr. Hansell said. " What exactly do you propose to do ? "

" We had a rotten time," Mr. Walker replied, going off at a tangent—" the worst time either of us have ever had. We hurt each other abominably—just as Dorothy and I hurt each other—only this was worse because it meant the break up of everything we had meant to each other for fifteen years. A long time, fifteen years, and roots grow deeper than one realises until one starts pulling them up, and then— phew! We pulled all right. So much so that there was very little left to say—we said it all, stripped ourselves of cant and humbug. We talked half the night ; agreed to part—to divorce—to get away from each other for good and all, and went to bed. But not to sleep. I read, and Sally— that's my wife, you know—went downstairs and did the household mending. Never mended so many socks before, she said later. And I daresay she cried. Her eyes were blurred when she came to see me in the morning. So drawn and unhappy she looked. Then, for the first time, we realised how silly we both were.

" ' What is the use of parting if neither of us wants to marry again ? ' she said. ' What is to become of me ? Where am I to go ? How can I start life afresh at my age ? I realise now that the way we have been living is ridiculous— I pulling one way, and you another.' "

" ' Yes," I said, ' so do I, and I think we ought to try and make a go of it.' ' Do you ? ' she said. We smiled—took hands again, and made it up ; but with a difference. Each is now on his mettle ; each will do his part in the reconstruction. Habit is everything, Sally says. Let's get into a different habit of life, and then things will be easier."

" A wise woman, your wife," Dr. Hansell commented.

" Yes, I think you're right. I'm going to live at home for a bit and get this straightened out, if it's at all possible. If not, then I think we are both agreed that it will be wiser to separate. Meanwhile we will do our damnedest to make it work."

" Good ! I'm glad."

" I saw Dorothy, too."

" Why ? "

I wanted to ask her one or two questions ; to prove or disprove your theory, in fact."

" My theory ? I don't understand."

" You suggested that Dorothy might have known for a long time that the sex side wasn't working right."

" Yes ? "

" You were quite right."

" Oh ! I'm sorry," Dr. Hansell said quietly.

" Yes. It was a bit of a shock. I felt as though I had been led up the garden path."

" What did you do then ? "

" Having told her what I thought about it, I put my hat on."

" And walked out full of righteous indignation, I suppose."

" I felt awful, but I didn't see why she should have it all her own way."

" And so you left her feeling profoundly unhappy, I suppose."

" I'm afraid so : she was crying as I shut the front door."

" What did you do then ? "

" I banged on the door and went in again."

The doctor smiled. " Of course," he said.

" I think I realised then that it was no good kicking against the pricks, and that I had messed up my life pretty well, to say nothing of the effect on other people. I would like to remain friends with Dorothy and give her the kind of love you talk about, but I have been so hurt that I doubt if it will ever be possible. I must think that out quietly. Of one thing I am quite sure, and that is that I will never give myself body and soul to anyone again."

" Except your wife."

" Possibly ! I feel numb at the moment. We all seem to have made a pretty good mess of things."

" You can't behave like that without hurting people. You have all sinned."

" Sinned ? "

" Of course. That is what that kind of behaviour used

to be called in the good old days—hurting others, being selfish, having no moral principles."

"Oh! I hadn't thought of it quite like that."

"These kind of relationships never really work; they are based on false principles; makeshifts condoned by a society which is morally sick. You will have to do a lot of rethinking before you get yourself straight."

"I know, but I shall try."

"The initial difficulty started with the maladjusted relationship of your early marriage, due largely to ignorance and lack of marriage preparation. In addition, your early upbringing developed a particular life-pattern. Both you and your wife have a certain temperament, and tend to react to a given situation in a particular way because of that pattern. If you could understand that pattern better—if you could analyse it out a bit more and learn to understand yourself better—you might become a more adjusted person. At the moment you are mal-adjusted. I doubt if you will be able to reach adjustment without the help and guidance of someone skilled in this type of work. I would suggest that you consider seriously whether you should not obtain this assistance. You appear to me to be a man who tends to skate over the surface of life, taking what comes easily and avoiding difficulties wherever possible. You imagine that marriage is a kind of clock which, once started, works automatically, not realising that it is a contract willingly entered into by two understanding and responsible people. It must be constantly tended and encouraged to grow by mutual co-operation. This you have failed to do; indeed, your marriage has been nothing better than cohabitation. Any real attempt at mutual understanding, any real effort to expand the relationship creatively disappeared in the first year of your marriage. Whilst you are by no means selfish, you are far too self-sufficient; too satisfied with yourself and too much the centre of your own picture. That is an infantile state very proper in the first year or two of life, but very unsatisfactory in the adult, who should concern himself with creative activities which take him outside himself and away from the centre of the picture. Never having established your physical relationship on a firm and creative basis, you have spent the rest of your life over-emphasising the physical. Whether or no you can, at this late stage, save anything from the wreck is impossible to say. The fact that you are both willing to try is, however, of supreme importance. Indeed, I would go so far as to say that no effective reconciliation is possible unless both partners are willing to try and make the situation work. If you can't do this you must make a new start with someone else equally mature as yourself.

"In so far as Dorothy is concerned, the picture is clearer. Here you have a young woman whose home background has been negative and unstable, who has had to make her own way in the world, and has done so by embarking on a variety of emotional affairs, which, whilst no doubt proving temporarily satisfactory, have in reality deprived her of the ability to accept a mature and stable relationship. Her attitude to life is that of the adolescent who is always flitting from flower to flower in order to find the perfect bloom, and the more often she changes, the more difficult will it be for her to find perfection. Indeed, she cannot find perfection; she has to learn to manufacture it out of her own life. The reason for your inability to suit each other physically lies in the fact that she has always accepted you with reservations, some of which, such as your age or your marriage, are valid, and some, such as her own self-centredness and refusal to give or accept responsibility, are open to criticism. That she is aware of the unsatisfactory nature of her relationship with you is good. Her change-over to a new partner may be a mere continuation of her former life-pattern, in which case it is an escape from reality and bad or it may be, as she herself says, the 'real thing'. As it is most important for her to find adequate adjustment in a creative relationship, we must hope that she is right.

"An analysis of your physical relationship is really very interesting because, although you both derived considerable benefit from it and obtained a mutual orgasm, it finally broke down because she was really holding herself back.[1] Only because you were practised lovers were you able to continue as long as you did. Had neither of you had

[1] See pp. 183 and 220.

previous experience, she would have remained cold and frigid, and you, no doubt, would have developed evidence of premature ejaculation. Had she really endeavoured to let herself go and put her mind into the relationship, the picture would have been quite different. As it was, most of the giving was on your side; the taking on hers—a most unsatisfactory state of affairs."

"Yes, I believe you are right. I felt for a long time that she was holding something back, but I was too foolish or too infatuated to understand or face up to the real reason. When you put it like that it hardly seems worth while trying to save anything from the wreck."

"On the contrary, it is because of what remains that I think it well worth your while to turn the relationship into a lasting friendship. But you must not be in too much of a hurry. If you cannot rise to the heights, you had better give over. If you do you will, I think, be avoiding your responsibilities to each other once again. You have loved, hurt and suffered pain. From such ingredients can come a really satisfactory friendship."

"Well, we can but see. It all sounds a bit up in the air to me. It's a funny thing how love always seems to hurt, isn't it?"

Dr. Hansell laughed. "Do you know that nice little poem about love? How does it go?"

> "If love should count you worthy, and should deign
> One day to seek your door and be your guest,
> Pause! 'ere you draw the bolt and bid him rest,
> If in your old content you would remain;
> For not alone he enters; in his train
> Are angels of the mist, the lonely guest
> Dreams of the unfulfilled and unpossessed.
> And sorrow, and Life's immortal pain.
> He wakes desires you never may forget,
> He shows you stars you never saw before,
> He makes you share with him, for evermore,
> The burden of the world's divine regret,
> How wise you were to open not, and yet,
> How poor if you should turn him from the door!"

"I like that. Who wrote it?"

"A man named Lysaght. You will find it in a book called 'Poems of the Unknown Way', published I think, by Macmillan."[1]

"Well, thank you very much, Dr. Hansell. I am really most grateful."

[1] "Poems of the Unknown Way", S. R. Lysaght, to whom I am indebted for permission to publish.

CHAPTER IX

HOMOSEXUALITY

GEORGE RANKIN sat stiffly on the edge of a chair in Dr. Hansell's consulting-room. " I hope you won't think I've come on a foolish errand, Doctor," he said. " My friend Audrey Kitchen advised me to come; she says you'll be able to help me."

" Audrey Kitchen? I'm afraid——"

" She knows Lady Burr, whom I think you know."

" Of course. She is chairing a conference which I'm attending at the moment. What can I do for you? "

" I'm thirty-two, and on the Stock Exchange. My elder brother was killed in the war. Though I come up to town every day, what I really enjoy most is a country life, walking, fishing, riding and helping my father with our property; we have several hundred acres which we farm. Besides that, I take an interest in the local affairs and run the Scouts."

He paused, doubtfully.

" I don't make friends very easily, though I get on quite well with most people, in a casual sort of way. I suppose that Audrey knows me better than anyone else. She lives near us, and we were more or less brought up together. We're both very fond of music."

He leaned forward. " Now, the trouble is, Doctor, that my family want me to marry. Father says it's ridiculous for a man of my age not to be married. He married when he was twenty-five. You see, I'm the last of my line, bar a cousin or two, and he says it's my duty to see that the family doesn't die out. We get on very well, except over this question of marriage. I'm not particularly keen."

" Perhaps you haven't met the right girl, Mr. Rankin."

" I like Audrey as well as anyone I've met."

" Have you discussed the matter with her? "

" Yes, frequently. My father is always telling her that

he's looking forward to the day when she is his daughter-in-law. He looks upon the matter as more or less settled; but Audrey and I never seem to come to any definite conclusion."

"But why not?"

"I don't know."

"You have common interests?"

"Well, we like walking and going to concerts together, and reading the same kind of books. Of course she's more energetic than I am, but I don't think that's a bad thing. I think people who marry should have their own interests."

"What's stopping you, then? Money?"

"Oh dear no! I have ample means, and there's a delightful cottage on our property which my father will put in order for us. Oh no, it isn't money." He paused for a moment, as if he were choosing his words very carefully. "I've been making some enquiries lately in sex matters, Dr. Hansell, and I'm not sure that I ought to marry. You see—er—girls don't attract me like that."

"You mean physically?"

"Yes, they mean nothing to me really. I like being with them but that's all. Audrey says it will all come right when we are married. But I'm not so certain."

Dr. Hansell leaned forward. "Let us get this quite straight, Mr. Rankin," he said. "Have you *never* been attracted by any woman?"

"Not that I can remember."

"Don't you like kissing them?"

"Not particularly. I don't seem to get the same thrill out of it that my friends do."

"Doesn't the sight of an attractive female figure interest you at all?"

"Not in the least."

"Have you ever felt any sexual emotion for anyone?"

"Yes, I've occasionally noticed it when I've been camping with the boys; but I've always managed to suppress it. As a matter of fact I had some advice from a doctor a couple of years ago, but we did not discuss the question of marriage. Perhaps you would like to see his report."

"That is very interesting," Dr. Hansell said, after

reading the report. "I think that it was very wise of you to come and talk to me."

"Do you? I'm glad. I have had a feeling for some time that I'm not made like other people, and it has worried me. I doubt very much whether marriage with Audrey would be a success."

"I'm quite sure it wouldn't. You see, you have a particular type of make-up which is not uncommon and perfectly understandable. This doctor suggests—and I am inclined to agree with him—that you are what is known as homosexual; that is to say, you are emotionally attracted to people of your own sex, and not to people of the opposite sex."

"Yes, I gathered that. Is that a bad thing? Should I endeavour to overcome it."

"I don't think you could, even if you wished to. You would only complicate matters for yourself. True homosexuality, such as you have, is probably a biological condition; it's born in you. It may be that there is an actual defect in the germ plasm, or it may be that the early influence of the internal secretions from the sex glands, which assist in our early differentiation into male or female, has failed in some respect. The exact cause is a little obscure, but the result is that a true physiological homosexual is normally interested in his own sex only. Some people are 'intermediate' in character, in which case they have leanings to both male and female. The cause is probably lack of complete psychological development; the individual has not progressed from the ordinary homosexual stage to that of heterosexuality, or interest in the opposite sex. In some cases of true homosexuality there is reason to believe that there may be an hereditary tendency."

"It's funny that you should say that, because my father had several brothers and only one of them married. His only child, my cousin, is very like me in many respects and has never married either."

"That's very interesting. It would be even more interesting if you could work out your family history in detail. What about your mother's side?"

"As far as I know she was an only child, but I've never

bothered to enquire very carefully. I will do so if you like."

"Yes, please do."

"What would you advise me to do about Audrey?"

"I think it would be very unwise for you to marry her. Such a relationship would lead to endless trouble and difficulty if, as I presume, she is a normally sexed woman. I'm afraid we must consider you an abnormal man, or rather a deviation from the strictly normal, which, however, is an entirely different thing from a pervert. Yours is a true homosexuality. Some homosexuals are far more troubled emotionally than you are. They feel drawn towards people of their own sex in just as overpowering a way as the average man is drawn towards women. The problem for these people is profoundly difficult, because any relationship they may have is contrary to the law, in so far as men are concerned, at any rate. Quite apart from that, however, they tend to teach their practices to presumably normal people and thus upset the normal psychological development of those people."

"Yes, I understand that. Then I may think myself lucky not to have stronger feelings?"

"Yes, indeed! You are like the man who has a very slight sex feeling towards women; it hardly bothers him at all. Were he to marry a passionate woman with a high degree of sex feeling, the marriage would be doomed to failure from the very start. In any case, I think your marriage with Miss Kitchen would be unsatisfactory, even if you felt capable of having a sex relationship with her; because you're the type of man whose interests are mainly centred in himself. I don't mean that you're selfish, but you're normally self-sufficient; whereas Miss Kitchen, judging by my own observations and what you have told me, is the exact opposite. She's fairly highly sexed and is immensely interested in outside activities. Of course if the physical were right between you, the other matters would probably be capable of adjustment. As it is, I'm afraid you would be making a serious mistake."

Mr. Rankin sighed audibly. "I must say that your information is a great relief; but what shall I say to my father?"

"I doubt if it would be much use trying to explain the situation to him; he would probably refuse to believe you. I'm afraid that the only thing for you to do is to tell him that you don't feel like marrying, and that Miss Kitchen won't have you. She might tell him herself."

"I suppose you wouldn't like to explain the business to her, would you, Doctor? She is downstairs waiting for me, and I think it would come better from you. Besides, I'd like to keep our friendship, if that is at all possible."

Dr. Hansell glanced at his watch. "Yes, I'll certainly do that. I'll get her up when we have finished."

"Thank you. What about the Scouts? Would you advise me to give them up? I'll willingly do so if you think I could possibly harm the boys?"

"Not at all. I should carry on. You understand the position and can manage yourself perfectly well. I should say your influence would be wholly beneficial. It might be advisable for you to do a little more reading, however. There is a small book called 'The Invert,' written by a homosexual, which you might read, and there are of course the 'Studies in the Psychology of Sex', by Havelock Ellis. You might also get some help from a book called 'Motives and Mechanisms of the Mind', by Graham Howe."

"Thank you; I'll read them, because I'd like to understand the matter more fully. Is it true that homosexuality is on the increase?"

"It's difficult to say. We know much more about the subject than we did, but I don't know if there is any evidence that real homosexuality is on the increase. There is a tendency, however, to laud sexual abnormalities at the present time, of which acquired homosexuality is certainly one. There are some people who maintain that the only 'interesting' people, the only 'cultured' people, the only people who are really 'worth knowing', are homosexual; if you're concerned with the arts you must be homosexual. This attitude is the inevitable result of the reaction towards a proper appreciation of 'true' homosexuality, and will no doubt pass. Its existence should by no means be overlooked, because the danger of the situation lies in the fact that homosexuality can be taught to others, and acquired homosexuality means an unbalanced person. There are some who are bi-sexual and can 'love' both man and woman. You will find that such people have their emotions fixed at an immature level and find it very difficult to maintain a satisfactory relationship with anyone for long. Their only chance is to develop a strong heterosexual relationship which has real meaning. I've the greatest respect for the true homosexual, but he's a rarity. The majority of homosexuals exhibit abnormal sexual propensities; their sex development has not progressed along proper lines. They have left the main road and are wandering down a side turning. When they attempt to initiate others, and usually younger people, into their practices, they commit an offence against true morality."

" Then most homosexuals are of the acquired type?"

" Yes, I think they are. It's not really necessary to be a homosexual to be a fine artist or an accomplished actor."

" No, I suppose not."

" Acquired homosexuality is an easy way out of an *impasse*. It's an escape from reality, and is frequently caused by a mixture of psychological and economic conditions. One need not have any 'responsibilities' towards the other individual if one is 'homosexual'. There is no need to provide a home or education, such as is necessary if one marries and starts a family. It's not so limiting. Neither does it produce a fully developed personality. It's high time society recognised acquired homosexuality for what it is, and ceased to admire it. It's a deviation from normal sexual feeling, and owes its vogue to the foolish way in which society deals with the whole sex problem. Acquired homosexuality is a perverted sexuality, because the people who practise it have repressed the natural feelings they should have for the opposite sex."

" Yes, I see. I'm really grateful to you for your help. Tell me one thing more. What about the legal aspects of homosexuality?"

" That, unfortunately, is very complicated. The law doesn't recognise male homosexuality as a medical condition and winks its eye at female homosexuality. If a man is caught by the police soliciting another man he can be put

HOMOSEXUALITY

in prison. This is a most unsatisfactory state of affairs and should be altered. Homosexuality should be regarded as a medical matter and those who come in contact with the law should be properly treated."

"Yes, I quite agree. Well, thanks very much. It doesn't look as though things will be improved till public opinion demands a change, does it?"

"No, I'm afraid not. We should take a leaf out of Sweden's book."

"Why? Do they deal with the matter more sensibly?"

"Much more sensibly. They have a whole series of laws safeguarding the homosexual and providing for his efficient treatment. However, I mustn't start telling you about all that or I won't have time to talk to Miss Kitchen. I will see her at once, if you don't mind waiting in the other room."

. . . . .

"It would be unwise for you to marry a man like that," Dr. Hansell said to Audrey Kitchen when he had enquired into her own history, and outlined the whole case to her. "You'd be unlikely to experience normal physical satisfaction, and that would be a source of great unhappiness to you, because you're a normal woman with normal feelings."

"Yes, I understand that. I often wondered if George was really all right, because he never seemed to be particularly anxious to kiss me or make love to me in any way, which seemed odd. I've never found other men particularly backward in that respect, but, funnily enough, they didn't attract me much."

"Don't you think that the reason may be that you didn't really wish them to do so? Isn't it possible that you see in George Rankin a person who appeals to your mothering instinct rather than to your sex instinct? Perhaps you're a bit frightened of the others, and afraid of losing your independence and 'power' over people, because you have a strong personality which you probably find very difficult to surrender to anyone else. Haven't you a feeling, deep down inside you, that marriage means loss of this freedom and power? I doubt whether you have really grown up emotionally; whether you realise that the power a woman has over a man is derived from the feminine side of her character. Don't you like to be top dog?"

Audrey laughed. "Yes, I do rather, I'm afraid."

"Now if you could visualise marriage as a co-operative relationship in which each keeps and develops his or her own personality and neither is 'top dog', you might see these other men in a slightly different light."

"Perhaps I might. I must think about it. But tell me something, Dr. Hansell. I thought male homosexuals were namby-pamby sort of people, with silly, simpering ways, but George isn't a bit like that. How do you account for that?"

"We can take George Rankin as an example of a mild type of true physiological homosexuality," Dr. Hansell said. "In a more advanced degree you'd find a man with a highly feminine nature; with a tendency towards a female figure and exaggerated mannerisms. Such people are comparatively rare. When it comes to psychological homosexuality, however, matters are different. Homosexuality is a normal stage of psychological development through which we all pass in adolescence. It's during this time that the boy is interested in games and pursuits that are followed with other boys, and girls are more concerned with their own sex. The stage is accompanied by great emotional development, and if the sexual tension becomes very strong, it may show itself in definite sexual practices. A bigger boy may be attracted by the feminine side of a younger and less fully developed boy. This state should normally end in attraction towards the opposite sex (the heterosexual stage), but it may persist until the boy is twenty or more. The change-over largely depends upon the attitude of the boy to his own emotional development, and the way in which the problem is handled by those who are responsible for his upbringing—both parents and teachers."

"But I suppose we all retain some feeling towards people of our own sex in later life, don't we? Otherwise I don't see how we can form friendships with people of our own sex."

"That's quite true, but these friendships must never

dissolve into real physical expression. I heard of a case quite recently, in which a young man of twenty-three or so was convinced that he was a homosexual because he had had emotional feelings towards his own sex, both masters and boys, when he was at school: this idea was accentuated in his mind by reading some books about abnormal sexuality, most of which he obviously didn't understand. The result was that he grew up feeling that he was 'tainted' and different from other men, and therefore not a suitable person for women to know. So he kept himself to himself and projected his sex life on to people of his own sex. He even went so far as to try to repress the occasional sex feelings that he had towards women. In spite of his twenty-three years his emotional development had remained stationary. He was afraid to launch out on his heterosexual adventures, and he didn't understand that his liking for men was something which could persist throughout life as a normal friendship."

"Yes, I see all that. But you've been referring to men most of the time. What about women?"

"The same applies to them, especially when you're dealing with young girls who are flattered and fascinated by the attentions of older women. Many parents even now teach their daughters that normal sex relationships are disgusting and unmentionable, and that it's only the man who derives any sex pleasure in marriage. Such being the case, it is not to be wondered at that girls sheer off from men and are drawn to their own sex. Then again, many girls have little chance, even in these days, of meeting men; and spend a lot of their time herded together with other women. It isn't surprising if they too seek relief for their pent-up emotions in some violent affection for another girl, as a result of which they drift into unwise practices. Finally, there is the woman who has reached early middle age without having had any normal sex experience and sees little chance of marriage; and who won't, or can't, enter into an 'irregular' relationship. Such women have a very difficult problem to face, and many of them acquire homosexual tendencies merely by force of circumstances, but they are not really homosexuals either physiologically or psychologically."

"How would you advise such people to deal with themselves?"

"That is a big question, and would require a book to answer fully. The first point worth noting, however, is that the problem can only really be solved by some change in our economic conditions. This will allow more sensible relationships between the sexes, and will permit the development of real companionship between men and women. The second point concerns the transference of sex energy. People have yet to appreciate the creative purpose of sex in their lives; to realise that only by a true understanding of sex will they be able to develop their personalities properly. They think that sex is solely concerned with reproduction and self-gratification; that life is individual rather than collective; that self is the most important thing in the world. They look upon the old idea of 'loving their neighbour' as a religious truism, which has no meaning in present day life, nor any scientific backing."

"But that isn't true, is it?"

"No, of course not. Our personality can only be developed by projecting our energies towards unselfish ends. This is a process that has to be attempted by us all, whether we are married or single; celibate by intention or merely by necessity. We mustn't be frightened of sex, nor put it away from us as something horrid or unclean. Rather must we realise that it embraces other things besides the physical, though I admit that it is more difficult to lead a life in which the physical finds no place. Only certain people are fitted for a truly celibate life, but those people often have a great understanding of sex. We must change our attitude, therefore, and realise the essential truth and beauty and power which can be drawn from the sex urge. Sex embodies the whole personality and, rightly used, develops and ennobles life. It embraces heredity, evolution and knowledge. It is constructive and unselfish, always demanding thought and care for the other. We must recognise the motives behind our actions; the primary impelling motive which is born in us and the end motive which must be used for the welfare of other people. As such it must be satisfying to us. Thus the quality of the action must be right, and we must find joy in our action."

" Yes, I see all that; but it's going to be rather difficult, isn't it? "

" Yes, I'm afraid it is. It means that we must use our intelligence, our will and our imagination."

" I should have thought that we used our imagination too much nowadays and are always stimulating our emotions."

" That's true, but it's no use denying the existence of factors which do stimulate our emotions. There's no sin in experiencing the stimulus; sin can only enter in when we dwell on the emotion and do not use it constructively —when we are beset by guilt feelings. We must always be trying to direct it on to a higher plane. Young men are more emotionally immature than young women. They are always falling in and out of love, and haven't a mature judgment where sex is concerned. They like to have transitory affairs. Girls who pander to this side of their nature do no good either to themselves or to the men. I think it is Jung who points out that constant flirting makes the deeper emotion of love more difficult to achieve. Girls tend to take men too seriously and fail to recognise this unbalanced trait in their character. They should be prepared for it, and not become broken-hearted if they find the young man's affection cooling. We have to grow and develop all the time, endeavouring to co-ordinate sex with the other functions of life."

" That means that we've got to learn something about the working of the mind, doesn't it? "

" Yes, we may look upon the mind as consisting of three layers; the conscious, the sub-conscious and the unconscious. The conscious mind deals with all those activities and thoughts with which we're concerned at the moment. The sub-conscious contains the memories and impressions which are not needed at that moment, but which can be recalled into the conscious mind at will. The unconscious mind holds all the feelings, memories and experiences that we've ever had, some of them so deeply buried that they can only be brought up into the conscious mind by careful psychological treatment. An instinctive emotion can rise up in the unconscious and pass into the conscious mind, where it is dealt with in several ways. It can be given normal expression, or it can be displaced by another emotion if the original one is likely to cause damage to the personality. It may be pushed back into the unconscious, in which case it may show itself in some strange way quite unlike the original emotion. Finally, it may be sublimated or transferred. It's this process of transference that we're concerned with at the moment. I've already told you that for this we need to make a conscious act of will, so as to direct the emotion on to a higher level than that concerned with the self. This process is difficult but quite possible, provided we have a definite intention; that we make a conscious act of will, and take appropriate action. We have, as it were, to climb a ladder, but the ladder must be a suitable one and must not be directed to selfish ends nor must it conflict with society."

"That might mean the re-organisation of the whole of a person's life, I should imagine."

"Yes, that's very often necessary. There must be a willingness to cultivate a more serious and responsible outlook. People must stop stirring the emotional pot quite so actively."

"But that's very difficult to do at present, because we're always having our emotions aroused one way or another, and it's frequently impossible to obtain relief."

"That's perfectly true. The only thing to do is for each one of us to think out a plan of campaign. Some people can concern themselves with public affairs or educational projects, others with the social services, or with creative occupations such as writing and painting which provide a definite outlet. In addition, we can see to it that our physical life is not neglected and that we maintain our bodies as near a state of perfection as possible. Transference will only be brought about by a process of mental reshuffling that will cause a change of outlook as to the purpose of our existence. In other words, we must make life a vocation and realise that the sex instinct is given us for a creative purpose, which is in harmony with the evolutionary idea of life."

" I see. I'm afraid I've been drifting along rather complacently," Audrey said. " I shall have to think things out. Could you tell me some good books to read ? "

" Yes, certainly. I'll give you a list." [1]

" Thanks very much. But you wouldn't condemn my activities, would you ? My interest in physical culture, for instance ? "

" Of course not. They are admirable social activities into which you are putting an enormous amount of valuable energy, and are thus able to lead a life that is useful to yourself and to society. But I wouldn't make such activities the mainspring of your life. I'd admit that actual sex experience has its place, if the opportunity arises, and that the expression of that side of your nature need not necessarily conflict with your other activities."

" But I should love to be married and have children."

" Of course you would, provided you could continue to exercise complete authority over your husband and your occupation ! You must learn to reconcile the two and not be afraid of your emotional life swamping the rest of your personality. You are a little afraid of your own femininity, I think, and, rather like a man I heard of recently who was engaged to a girl and wished to marry her, but was so interested in his friends and his religious activities that he wanted her to change her whole life for his benefit ; to give up her own occupations and friends and submerge herself entirely in his scheme of life. He was unable to realise that his love for her should be the main concern of his life, that he could not change her, but should encourage her to lead her own life, in which case all the other activities would fit into that scheme in their true proportion. He was really very self-centred and had failed to grow out of his homosexual phase, and she, very stupidly, surrendered more and more of her individuality to him in a desire to please him and, unconsciously, to possess him entirely. She was obsessed by the fear of losing him, and so, on the one hand there was an excessive desire to dominate, and on the other

[1] *Psychology of Sex*, Havelock Ellis. *Sex and Citizenship*, Edward Griffith.

too great a feeling of possessiveness. Neither could really live for the other. A marriage like that will never work satisfactorily. Both partners must be able to develop and express their own individualities. Sex relationships should be a source of strength to both partners, not weakness."

"What happened to them?"

"Life became so intolerable that they broke off the engagement, which was the best thing that could happen under the circumstances. Unfortunately, they had done each other considerable psychological damage before this happened."

"Yes, I see. We're very complicated beings, aren't we?"

Dr. Hansell got up. "The marvel is that so many of us manage to function in a comparatively normal manner," he said, laughing.

"What would you advise two people to do who were having an affair—two women, for instance?"

"It depends on the circumstances. I know of a few cases—very few, mind you—in which the relationship works well, but I should say that in the majority of cases there is always trouble and sorrow and friction. Indeed, you can't expect anything else because the very nature of the relationship is sterile and immature and can only lead to frustration. One at least of the two partners is too possessive—too jealous. The thing to do, of course, is for the couple to realise that the situation is unsatisfactory; that each is misusing her sex power over the other and that one at least, being really heterosexual, is being psychologically warped. The trouble is that until something happens neither will get expert help, either because they are frightened or because they don't know to whom to go. The situation is always difficult, and is not improved by the attitude of society, which holds up its hands in horror one minute and encourages the couple to carry on the next minute."

"Well, thank you very much, Dr. Hansell," Audrey said, shaking his hand. "I've learned a great deal, and feel sure I shall be able to help George a good deal. I think we will be able to understand each other much better now."

[1] v. p. 290.

CHAPTER X

FRIGIDITY AND IMPOTENCE

DR. HANSELL'S next patient was an old friend, Monica Rich, who had been married for some time. Although he had not met her very much recently, he had had a feeling that all was not well, and wasn't altogether surprised when he found her name in his engagement book.

"Well, Monica," he said when she had settled down. "What brings you here?"

"Peter and I have been married for about two years, but I'm afraid it's a hopeless failure," she said quietly.

"Why do you say that?"

"So far as I can see, sex is just a nuisance from which we can't escape. Unfortunately, neither of us knew much about the physical side of things before we were married, although Peter had read a bit. We were frightfully in love, and thought that everything would be all right. Everybody tells you how lucky you are when you get married, but as a matter of fact you can't tell about that side of things till you try, and we didn't try—at least, not properly."

"And now you are disappointed?"

"Very."

"Tell me! How did you learn about the sex side of life?"

"From my friends, and one or two books, and talking to Peter. We used to make love a good deal before we were married."

"How much?"

"We held hands, and kissed, and so on. We were always out a lot."

"Nothing more?"

"No. At least, we used to get a bit excited, one way and another. I mean, Peter did."

"Didn't you?"

"I enjoyed it, too. Why shouldn't I? There's nothing wrong about that, is there?"

"It rather depends upon the amount of love-making that you indulged in. Men and women differ considerably in their reactions. Sex is usually more on the surface in men. They are more easily aroused and more quickly satisfied. Women, on the other hand, are less easily aroused, more deeply stirred and take longer to settle down afterwards. If the love-making during an engagement is rather violent, it is likely to cause dissatisfaction to both partners for different reasons. To start off with, any satisfaction that is obtained is not the result of a complete sex act, and cannot be compared with the normal act. If the couple are constantly arousing their emotions and not getting proper relief, this is bound to have a bad effect on them, and make them irritable and over-wrought. The reason for this is that part of you is driving you on and part holding you back, so that you are always in a stage of emotional tension. When the couple eventually do marry, they often find it difficult to make the necessary adjustments. The man, through over-excitement, may suffer from premature ejaculation, and the woman may not have time to be properly aroused."

"I see. Probably that applies to us. We don't make very much more love now than we did then."

"But you have proper sex relationships, don't you?"

"Oh yes, but it's all over in two or three minutes. You see, we thought that the sensation in the man had to coincide with that of the woman."

"So it does."

"But the sensation I get comes very quickly, and then, just afterwards Peter has a sensation, but I feel nothing of it."

"Then you do get a sensation?"

"I suppose so, but it doesn't mean much."

"Let me get this straight. I'm not sure, from what you say, that you're getting any real sensation."

"How do you mean?"

"Well, sensation for the woman may be in two places—the clitoris or the vagina. Occasionally it's in both.

Ideally speaking the clitoral sensation should be transferred to the vagina. That causes a deeper and more satisfying feeling which amounts to an intensity of pleasure that is difficult to describe, but is easily recognisable once it's felt."

"I'm sure I never had that. We must have been very stupid. You see, I thought the clitoral sensation, as you call it, was all there was to it, and that as soon as it had come, the whole affair was over, and the man had to finish too."

"Oh dear no. You've got the business all wrong. The sensation in the vagina can only be produced by the rhythmical movements of the penis, and this cannot occur if the man has a premature ejaculation. It looks to me as though you two must start again. The whole sex relationship should be divided into three stages. The first stage of love play should be sufficiently long to arouse the couple, but not so long as to fatigue the man. It may last for five minutes or half-an-hour, depending upon the individual conditions at the time and the experience of the lovers, but on no account should it be omitted. The second stage also varies in length, but should last long enough for a mutual orgasm to be achieved."

"Did you say that the sensation in the vagina is produced by rhythmical movements of the penis?"

"Certainly."

"Well, I haven't ever felt any rhythmical movements, in fact I don't think Peter 'moves' at all."

Dr. Hansell stirred in his chair. "Look here, Monica," he said. "Let us get down to brass tacks. Either you are incredibly ignorant or you are hedging. Do you and Peter really have a proper sex relationship?"

"Well, I must admit I have been a bit doubtful for some time," Monica said.

"Perhaps we can get at the facts if I ask you a few questions," Dr. Hansell said kindly. "Does your husband get a proper erection?"

"Oh yes, I think so."

"Does he get penetration?"

"That's what I'm not really certain about. You see,

after we have been making love for some time I seem to get a sensation, but when he tries to have penetration I don't believe anything happens."

"You mean that the sensation you get is obtained by manual stimulation of the clitoris."

"Yes, that's it. We have always done that, even before we were married."

"I see. A very bad habit, I'm afraid."

"Yes. I realise that now."

"Well, anyway. What happens after that?"

"When Peter tries to penetrate he either doesn't succeed, or he only manages to get in a little way, and then it's all over."

"A sort of modified coitus interruptus, in fact."

"Yes, that's about it."

"Hasn't he ever effected full penetration?"

"Only about once, and then he came out before anything happened."

"What on earth for?"

"It was the early days of our marriage, and we didn't want a child, so he came out."

"I see. So it comes to this really," Dr. Hansell said. "Although you two have been married for two years, your husband has only effected penetration once or twice, and then he withdrew, and at other times he has either made a small penetration or none at all, either because he can't get a proper erection or suffers from premature ejaculation."

"Yes, that is right."

"And you have been sitting on this trouble all this time? Why didn't you come and talk to me?"

"I kept hoping it would get better, and Peter is so sensitive about the whole thing. Besides, we have only been home a year."

"But a year is a long time."

"I know. I did suggest coming to you once or twice, but Peter begged me not to. He doesn't know I am here now."

"My dear Monica, I am sorry," Dr. Hansell said, getting out of his chair and walking about the room. "I suppose you realise that your husband is suffering from some degree of impotence, and that you could have your marriage annulled for non-consummation if you wanted to?"

"Oh, but I don't; I'm very fond of Peter. Can't you do anything about it?"

"Perhaps, and perhaps not; it all depends on whether or not Peter will co-operate. If he will I may be able to help; if he won't you will have to consider having an annulment. You can't go on like this; having your emotions constantly roused without obtaining any effective outlet. It is very bad for you, and you must certainly stop all this love-making until we can see what to do."

"Yes, I understand that, and will have a talk to Peter. But I thought it would be impossible for me to have an annulment, because Peter had had penetration and the hymen is broken."

"Oh no. I don't think that is the position at all. There have been several cases in the courts recently where penetration has occurred and yet the marriage has been annulled. Every case has to be considered on its merits and differs in many respects, but one or two acts of penetration, especially where there has been no ejaculation, would not, I think, constitute a true fulfilment of the marriage from the legal point of view. The matter was dealt with pretty fully in 1945 in a case known as Cowen v. Cowen."

Having explained this case in detail, Dr. Hansell continued:[1]

"You see therefore that the wife got her annulment on the grounds of 'wilful refusal'. In your case your husband has not refused to consummate the marriage, but with one indifferent exception, which you say lasted no time at all, has been unable to effect penetration. I am quite sure that when all the facts were presented to the Court you would have no difficulty in obtaining an annulment on grounds of impotence."

"I see. That is a very interesting case you have just mentioned."

"Yes, it is. If you don't want to bring the marriage to an end—and I think you are right to say that at the moment because you don't know what the exact position is—we

[1] See Chapter VI.

should try and do something for your husband. Don't you think you had better tell him you have been here and I say there is a lot to be done to help him if only he will co-operate ? "

" Yes, I do, but I should like to know a bit more about the possibilities of cure first of all."

" I can't tell you a great deal until I have seen Peter," Dr. Hansell said, " because the causes are so numerous. It may be a true impotence due to some deep-seated psychological cause or to a physical dysfunction—some glandular disturbance possibly, or an anxiety state, or one of those cases that are so common just now in soldiers returning from abroad after a long absence."

" Well, Peter had a pretty bad time in the war, I believe, although he never talks about it very much. I have a sort of feeling that he isn't altogether keen on having a child now that things are not going very well between us."

" In fact he has got himself into a regular muddle, hasn't he ? If he is one of these quiet, introspective and self-reliant people who find it so difficult to talk about themselves, and if he had a lot of nasty experiences in the war and tried to put sex out of his mind, refusing to allow himself any emotional outlet at all, and if he then marries, it is not altogether surprising that he finds it difficult to adjust to the new situation. Part of him wants to enjoy life and ' let go ', and part of him holds back. If, in addition, he knows practically nothing about sex and thinks, as many men do, that a man ought to be able to perform the sex act perfectly from the word go, and at any time of the day or night, it will come as a terrific shock to find that he can't do either. Add to that the desire to avoid pregnancy, lack of love technique and contraceptive knowledge, and you have produced a very good example of a particular type of impotence case."

" Can you do anything about that kind of case ? "

" Of course. I should say that provided he will co-operate and the other partner will do likewise, there is every chance of effecting a cure pretty easily."

" That all sounds most encouraging," Monica said, getting up. " I shall go home and persuade Peter to come and see you at once. Dear me, how silly we are! Just to think that a simple little talk like that can do so much good. I feel an entirely different woman. And I have been trying to make up my mind to come and see you for the last year."

" I expect you were afraid I should tell you that there was nothing to be done for that condition."

" Yes, that's about it."

" Well, there is a lot to be done, so send your Peter along as soon as possible. Meanwhile, you might read the following books : ' The Sex Factor in Marriage ' and ' Sex Fulfilment in Marriage ', both by Helena Wright, and ' Modern Marriage ', by Edward Griffith."

" I will, and I'll help in every possible way."

CHAPTER XI

ABORTION

As soon as Monica Rich had gone a small, well-dressed woman of about thirty, with a rather drawn face, was shown into the consulting-room. Her large, appealing blue eyes appeared to the doctor to have an aggressive expression difficult to define, but almost diagnostic in itself.

" Dr. Hansell ? "

" Yes. I hope I haven't kept you waiting. I think you'll find this chair comfortable. Let me take your coat."

She allowed herself to be relieved of her coat and sat down.

After glancing at the name and address on the slip of paper prepared by his secretary, Dr. Hansell turned to his patient. " Well, Mrs. Gregory, what can I do for you ? "

Mrs. Gregory had been waiting impatiently for permission to start. She spoke rapidly and to the point.

" I am twenty-six years old, Dr. Hansell, and have two children aged four and two. I am afraid that I am going to have another baby, as my period, which is usually perfectly regular, is now ten days overdue. My husband is a professional man earning about £700 a year, and we cannot possibly afford another child. I've been told that you are knowledgeable about these matters and can no doubt help me, so I shall be obliged if you'll do so."

Dr. Hansell sighed quietly to himself. Another of these cases. He foresaw a difficult interview. " I'm afraid you have come a little late," he said quietly.

" Ten days ! I could hardly come earlier ! "

" You misunderstand me, Mrs. Gregory. If you are pregnant I can do nothing about it, unless there are medical indications for the removal of the pregnancy."

" But my husband says he is perfectly willing to pay anything within reason."

"It's not a question of payment, I'm afraid. Are there any medical reasons why you shouldn't have a baby?"

"Not so far as I know, but I was told——"

"I cannot help what you were told, Mrs. Gregory. Every case is different. There may be reasons in one case which justify a medical man in taking a certain course of action, whereas in the next case those reasons may be absent, in which event the whole affair has an entirely different complexion."

"But I'm perfectly willing to pay substantially."

"If you have sufficient money to pay for an abortion,[1] madam, I don't see why you shouldn't spend the money on having the baby."

"Has it never occurred to you that an extra baby is not only an extra mouth to feed, but an extra child to be educated. How do you suppose we can bring up three children on £700 a year?"

"I admit it's difficult, but it has been done before and can, no doubt, be done again. How do you know, for that matter, that the child will be alive when it is born, or won't be clever enough to pay for its own education by means of scholarships?"

"My good man, don't be absurd!"

"I'm no more absurd than you are, Mrs. Gregory. You come here and suggest that I should perform an illegal operation upon you, for which the penalty is a long term of imprisonment, and you get annoyed because I don't instantly agree. Except for the nature of your circumstances, you haven't advanced a single argument that carries any weight, and I am afraid that economic conditions cannot be taken into consideration. How do you know what is going to happen in the future? Your husband may get a rise, or possibly your relations might help you if things got bad."

"I wouldn't dream of asking them for help. And there is no chance of my husband obtaining any increase in salary for years, and then it'll only be a paltry £100 a year or so. I tell you we haven't got a bean."

Dr. Hansell allowed his gaze to travel towards the corner

[1] Another aspect of this matter is discussed in Chapter XV.

of the room, where an expensive fur coat was hanging on the door. It returned slowly to the well-dressed owner sitting truculently in front of him. "But if you didn't wish to have another child, Mrs. Gregory, I'm surprised that you didn't take suitable precautions."

"That's just the point. I went to a doctor and was fitted with one of those cap things, but it let me down."

"Are you certain you used it as directed?"

"Oh yes, but it was very uncomfortable. I've only used it twice."

"I see; but why didn't you return to the doctor? If a patient feels a cap, that is an indication that the cap is either the wrong size or has been incorrectly fitted."

"Well, to tell you the truth, the doctor asked me to return for a second visit, but I couldn't be bothered."

"Then you've no real certainty that you mastered the technique correctly, have you?"

"I suppose not, but I should have thought the doctor could have fitted it in one visit; it seemed to work all right when I was there."

"The reason for a second visit, Mrs. Gregory, is to ensure that the patient has mastered the technique. It looks as though you had failed to do this. Probably you placed the cap wrongly. Didn't the doctor explain to you how to satisfy yourself that it was always in the correct position?"

"You mean to feel that nobbly thing?"

"The cervix, yes. You should be able to feel it through the rubber."

"I'm afraid I couldn't."

"It doesn't look as though you can very well blame the method, then, does it?" Dr. Hansell remarked.

"I can't be bothered with all these things."

"But you take trouble with your personal appearance, your clothes and your make-up. Why shouldn't you take a little trouble to learn a method which is so simple and safe when once mastered? I'm afraid I can do nothing for you, Mrs. Gregory. If you're pregnant I should strongly advise you to have the baby and then return to the doctor who originally fitted you, and learn the technique properly."

"I couldn't do that; besides, the doctor lives miles away from here."

"Well then, find another one or come here; but whatever you do, make up your mind to learn the method properly and then you won't have any further cause for worry."

Mrs. Gregory shrugged her shoulders and looked out of the window, while Dr. Hansell fiddled with his pencil and looked surreptitiously at his watch.

"Then you can do nothing for me!"

Dr. Hansell jumped slightly. Was the woman going to start all over again? This was too much of a good thing. "No, madam, I can do nothing, and what's more I can see no valid reason why you shouldn't have your baby. The country needs babies nowadays, and although things may look black at the moment, I think you're foolish to adopt the attitude you do. You admit that you have plenty of money to pay for this particular operation, so you can easily put that towards the birth of the baby. You also say that your husband will get a rise in the future. Anything may happen in the meantime. You seem to be wholly ignorant of the dangers of the course you are suggesting. Don't you know that a very high percentage of the women who die every year through causes connected with childbirth do so as the result of illegal abortion? The operation itself is by no means devoid of risk and may involve a severe illness and chronic ill-health, to say nothing of the possible danger of sterility. You have a husband and two children who are dependent on your state of health. If you become ill you won't be acting fairly to them or, for that matter, to yourself. I advise you to return to your husband and talk the matter over again in the light of what I've told you. You must forgive a little plain speaking, but I think you need it."

A smile flickered across the doctor's face, and he was pleased to see an answering glimmer in the face of his companion.

"Thank you, Doctor," Mrs. Gregory said, getting up. "Perhaps I have been stupid, but I'm worried, and that's the truth."

"I fully realise that, but you must face facts, you know."

"Yes, I suppose so, but I dislike the process, especially as the facts are so unpleasant."

"They might be much more unpleasant if you adopted the line of conduct you suggest. Let me assure you that I sympathise with your difficulties, in spite of my inability to help. It's possible that you'll value this child more than either of the others when it comes. So think it over quietly before coming to any decision."

"I will. Thank you very much. Ah, my coat, I was nearly forgetting it. Rather nice, isn't it? I won it in a raffle at the church bazaar. Good-bye, Doctor, and thank you again."

Dr. Hansell returned to his chair and rang the telephone which connected him with his secretary's room. "Half fees for Mrs. Gregory," he murmured into the mouthpiece. "I'm going back to the conference now."

CHAPTER XII

STERILITY AND ARTIFICIAL INSEMINATION

"THE subject before us to-night," the Chairman said, " is one of considerable interest, about which far too little is known by the general public. There is evidence to show that at least one marriage in ten is sterile—that is to say, that if 350,000 couples marry every year in this country, 35,000 women cannot become pregnant for one reason or another. In five years the number would be 175,000. If we could help half of them to have children we should make a considerable contribution to the birth rate. Dr. Alice Minor, who is talking to us to-night, has had considerable experience in this particular subject and will, I feel sure, give us a most interesting address: Dr. Minor."

"Quite apart from the fact that the reduction of the annual percentage of childless marriages would, as our chairman has just said, make an appreciable addition to the population," Dr. Minor said, " childlessness appears to be a fruitful source of matrimonial discord, and often leads to the divorce court. It is a significant fact that about 40 per cent. of divorce cases occur in childless couples, although this does not imply that all these people are biologically sterile. Their childlessness may be intentional, and is often fundamentally selfish in origin."

"Inability to have children has always been regarded as a great misfortune amongst all civilisations. I only wish I had time to tell you something of the fascinating theories about its origin and methods of treatment that have been in existence for centuries. It is worth remembering, however, that until very recent times it was always presumed that the woman was at fault. Now we know better. The reason for this idea can be traced back to the old Jewish belief that the man's ' seed ', having been placed in the body of the woman, grew into the child. The semen was the seed.

The discovery by the Dutch scientist Leuwenhoeck in 1679 of the sperms in the semen upset this theory, and it took one hundred and fifty years before the scientists and the Church could adjust themselves to this new discovery. It is rare to find one partner at fault, unless, of course, two tubes are completely blocked or the man is completely sterile. It is far more common to find a variety of causes, which, added together, are sufficient to cause the condition.

"All those who have been trying to have a child for a year without success should seek medical aid. It is useless to go on hoping for the best when the matter can so often be put right quite easily. I shall confine myself this evening to a general outline of what may be done in a straightforward case. By this I mean a case in which there are no gross abnormalities in either partner and no inability to perform the sex act. This rules out such conditions as painful coitus, impotence, congenital abnormalities, psychological difficulties and so on. When present they must, of course, be dealt with by appropriate methods. It is impossible to understand the sterility problem, however, unless one has some knowledge of physiology, so you must forgive me if I spend a minute or two dealing with this aspect. You are all aware, no doubt, that the testicles possess two functions —the manufacture of sperms and the production of a chemical messenger or hormone which is responsible, not only for the sexual development of the individual, but for the manufacture of sperms as well. The matter is more complicated than this, however, because the regulator of the whole hormone system is the pituitary gland. It is this gland which initiates activity in the testicles and is largely responsible for sperm growth. It does this by means of its own particular hormone, which is therefore called a gonadotropic hormone, because it stimulates the gonads or sex glands to activity. The production of sperms starts when the child is about ten, but is not fully established until eighteen or so. The early sperms are immature. The mature man produces about three teaspoonfuls of semen during one act of ejaculation, and this may contain anything up to five hundred million sperms, which number is made up again by the testicles in about forty-eight hours. This process goes on until the man has reached an advanced age.

"The ovaries, on the other hand, whilst producing a similar ovarian hormone which is responsible for turning the girl into the woman and producing all her secondary sex characteristics, contains all the eggs that she is likely to want in her ovaries at the time of birth—between thirty and forty thousand immature eggs in each ovary. The onset of menstruation is an indication that the pituitary gland is not only stimulating the ovary to produce a mature egg every month, but encouraging the production of more ovarian hormone which, in its turn, prepares the lining of the womb to receive the egg if it is fertilised. If this does not occur the egg passes out of the body in the monthly period together with the lining of the womb. That, very briefly, is the physiology of an extremely complicated subject, but enough, I think, for our present purpose.

"You will appreciate that if these various hormones do not function adequately in either sex and are not up to full strength a variety of conditions of under-development or sub-fertility may occur. For instance, the sex organs of the woman may not be fully developed; the eggs may not be coming out of the ovary, sperm production may be poor or the sperms abnormally formed, and so on. We may summarise the situation by saying that the testicular hormone is partly or entirely concerned with the following matters:

" 1. The production of sperms and the development of the sex organs.

" 2. The growth of the secondary sex characteristics.

" 3. The maintenance of virility and sex drive.

" 4. The maintenance of all those energies which develop the personality and give the individual creative ability.

"The action of the ovarian hormone may be summarised as follows :—

" 1. Stimulation of the lining of the womb to prepare itself for the reception of the egg when fertilised.

" 2. The development of the uterus and tubes.

"3. The encouragement of egg production in conjunction with the pituitary.

"4. The development of the secondary sex characteristics in the female.

"Amongst others, the gonadotropic hormones from the pituitary are responsible for, or contribute towards, the following functions :—

"1. The early development of the immature eggs in the ovary (the follicles) and the growth of sperms in the testicle.

"2. The production of the sex hormones in the gonads, of which the female one is called oestrin and the male testosterone.

The causes of sterility, therefore, are numerous and varied. They may be summarised as follows :—

"1. Absence of under-development of the sex organs.

"2. Atrophy of the sex organs, as occurs at the change of life, for instance.

"3. Malformations in the man or woman.

"4. Difficulty in performing the sex act and bad technique.

"5. Illness and debility, especially in the male, who seems to be particularly susceptible in this respect.

"6. Hormone deficiency.

"7. Various psychological causes.

"8. Various medical conditions and diseases, such as deficient diet, mumps or venereal disease."

Dr. Minor paused for a moment and took a sip of water.

Male Infertility

"It is probable," she continued, "that the time will come when most men will have their semen investigated before marriage. It being so easy to obtain a specimen, it seems only reasonable for a man to determine the nature and degree of his fertility. This having been done, the following matters must be looked into at the laboratory before a report can be given.

STERILITY AND ARTIFICIAL INSEMINATION 199

Volume and Density.

"Sperm counts vary enormously, but a normal man should produce a volume of about three teaspoonfuls (4 c.c.), which should contain about four hundred million mobile sperms—that is to say, about a hundred million per c.c.

"Except in the case of the 'fertile' man, one specimen is not sufficient to give a definite opinion. Nor must it be thought that numbers by themselves are an indication of high or low fertility. Density is probably of greater importance, the presence of vast quantities of live sperm being essential if a man is to be considered fertile.[1] Sperm scarcity may be due to partial blocking of the testicular tubes or poor production from the germ cells. The fluid in which the sperms live whilst in the body of the male is alkaline, that of the vaginal fluid is acid. Thus when the sperms reach the female organs they may find an entirely different state of affairs, because the vaginal fluids are frequently excessively acid, in which case the sperms may not survive. If the seminal fluid is highly alkaline, the vaginal acidity may be overcome and the sperms may find their way safely into the mouth of the womb, where the fluids are normally alkaline. Thus you will appreciate the importance of estimating not only the degree of semen alkalinity, but, in certain cases, the degree of vaginal acidity. We term this the pH of the fluid.

Types of Sperms.

"Sperms consist of a head, body and tail. The tail is long and thin, and moves rapidly with a lashing kind of action which propels the sperm in a straight line. The egg cannot move by itself, but has to be pushed about. All normal semen contains some abnormal sperm forms, but this figure should not rise above 35 per cent. The determination of these various abnormalities is a complicated business, into which I need not go here. Suffice it to say that where abnormality occurs in excess it is usual to find

[1] Harvey and Jackson, "Assessment of Male Fertility", *Lancet*, July 28th, 1945, p. 100.

sterility. Cure the abnormality in the sperms, and the woman becomes pregnant.

Mobility and Viability.

Once they become mobile, the human sperms do not live long—probably only for about two hours in the vagina even under the most suitable conditions. If the vaginal acidity (pH) is very high this period of time will be greatly reduced. Once they have reached the neck of the womb or cervix, however, where the pH is alkaline, they can live for as long as two or three days. Sperms vary, however, in their capacity to survive difficult conditions, and no hard-and-fast rule can be laid down, although the degree of viability in any particular case can be determined in the laboratory.

Effects of Abstinence.

Some people think that they are more likely to conceive if they have connection very infrequently. They imagine that by this means the husband can ' build up his strength '. There is not a scrap of evidence to support this view; indeed, there is a much greater chance of conception occurring if couples have regular intercourse at not too infrequent intervals. It is wise to have several connections round about the time of ovulation—that is to say, about the fifteenth day of the cycle. Five connections between the tenth and twentieth days would be a reasonable amount.

Female Infertility

All possible impediments to fertility must be considered when investigating a case of sterility.

Retroversion.

Apart from various gross physical conditions in the female which may impair fertility, there is one common condition —namely, retroversion—which must be mentioned. In this condition the body of the womb points backwards instead of forwards, thus altering the position of the cervix and making conception more difficult. And, further, should pregnancy occur there is much greater chance of abortion occurring. It is advisable for a woman to have this matter looked into before she attempts pregnancy, because the condition can usually be corrected quite easily.

The Shape and Size of the Womb.

The normal womb consists of a body and neck or cervix, the body being two-thirds of the total length, and the cervix one-third. Should the womb be under-developed, due, let us say, to imperfect hormone action, these measurements will be reversed and the condition of infantile womb produced. This may vary in degree, and is one of the most fruitful causes of sterility. It can be cured by the administration of the appropriate hormone.

Cervical Erosion.

The neck of the womb is sometimes inflamed, and weeps somewhat in the same way as the mucous membrane of the nose weeps when we have a cold. This may, in certain cases, contribute to the sterility. Various conditions in the vagina may have a similar effect.

Psycho-physical Conditions.

Many conditions, partly physical and partly psychological, may contribute to or cause infertility. We call them psycho-physical conditions. I will mention them quite briefly. Dyspareunia or pain during connection is one. This may be due to a variety of causes, and if very severe may lead to a condition of spasm of all the vaginal and thigh muscles which prevents entry, and is termed vaginismus. Both these conditions are largely psychological in origin and are amenable to treatment. They are discussed at length in the literature.

Another trouble is that the semen may not be delivered to the right place—that is to say, on or near the cervix. This is often impossible in cases where the conditions I have just mentioned are present or when the man suffers from a severe degree of premature ejaculation. Whilst it is well known that healthy sperms can find their way to the egg even when the semen has been placed on the outside of the woman's sex organs, it must be obvious that in the majority of cases it must be more difficult for them to reach the cervix from outside the vagina, or from just inside the vaginal entrance, as occurs in premature ejaculation, than if they are placed deep in the vagina, and so nearer to the cervix. All these conditions are contributory factors in the sterility picture."

Once more Dr. Minor paused.

Orgasm.

"Whilst it is possible for a woman to have a dozen children without ever experiencing orgasm, there can be little doubt that the achievement of a good orgasm is likely to assist conception. Thus, quite apart from any other reason, the acquisition of a good love technique is an important matter. At the same time I would add this word of warning. Just as many women fail to achieve orgasm because they are over-anxious, so do many of them fail to become pregnant for a similar reason.

Abortion.

"One of the commonest causes of sterility and, in particular, of one-child sterility, in which the woman has one baby but fails to become pregnant again, is the occurrence of an abortion as a result of which the lining of the womb has not been properly removed. In such cases it may become infected and the entrance to the tubes blocked. This is a difficult condition to cure, but well worth attempting."

The Hormone Factor.

"I should not like you to think that the hormone factor is as simple as I have made it appear. On the contrary, it is extremely complicated, and much work has been done to determine the nature of these hormones and to discover how to manufacture them in the laboratory so that we can give them to patients. Luckily, some of them are excreted in the urine, and so there is an easy source of supply readily at hand for investigation and analysis. By this means we can determine the strength and effects of the hormones that are being made by the individual."

STERILITY AND ARTIFICIAL INSEMINATION

Tubes and Womb.

" Quite apart from all this, however, it is necessary to determine whether the womb is of the right size and whether the tubes are open to allow the egg to come down and the sperms to swim up. Sometimes the passage in the neck of the womb—the cervical canal—which is about an inch long, is so tight that it is necessary to enlarge it under an anæsthetic with special dilators.

The Fallopian Tubes.

" It is possible to discover not only if the tubes are blocked, but where the blockage occurs, by means of two tests. The first, known as Rubin's Test, is very simple. Some gas is forced into the womb under pressure and the strength of the pressure measured. If the tubes are not blocked, the gas can be heard bubbling out of the end of the tubes in the abdominal cavity by means of a stethoscope placed on the outside of the abdomen. No anæsthetic is required. If this is not satisfactory the doctor can inject some special oil, called lipiodol, into the cavity of the womb and watch its passage under the X-Rays, taking photographs whenever he wishes. In this way he can determine the size of the body of the womb and also see whether the lipiodol will pass through the tubes and 'spill' out at the end. It is also possible, whilst doing this simple operation, which also does not require an anæsthetic, to measure the relative size of the body and neck of the womb and take a minute scraping from the lining of the womb which, when examined under the microscope, will show whether or not the eggs are coming out of the ovary or, as we term it, whether or not the woman is ovulating."

Sterility and Contraceptives.

" One frequently comes across people who say that the practice of contraception causes sterility. It cannot be too clearly stated that there is absolutely no evidence that the use of proper contraceptive methods ever leads to sterility."

Dr. Minor paused for a moment and took a deep breath. " I hope I'm not boring you," she said, " but you have no idea how difficult it is to talk about this subject simply, and yet include all the relevant facts. However, if you can bear with me, I won't keep you much longer."

The audience having signified that they were not bored, the doctor proceeded.

What To Do.

" I want now to run over the chief steps that can be taken to deal with the matter. What should a couple do? I will be as brief as possible. Whilst the G.P. should be consulted in the first instance, it must be remembered that this is a matter for the specialist, and the majority of G.P.s either refer the patients directly to a specialist or to one of the sub-fertility clinics which are being established by many of the hospitals. Ideally speaking, both husband and wife should visit the specialist, but if this is impossible the woman can go to start off with. If the husband goes first, he must have a semen test.

Post-Coital Test.

" It is possible to avoid this, however, by carrying out a special test on the woman, known as a post-coital test. It can only be done if special laboratory facilities are available. The procedure is as follows. After a period of three to five days' continence the couple have normal intercourse at night, and the woman then visits the laboratory in the morning—eight to twelve hours after coitus. If necessary the sex relationship can take place in the morning, and the patient go to the laboratory in the afternoon. A small amount of cervical secretion is then removed by the doctor, together with the mucus plug which blocks the entrance to the cervical canal during ovulation. The whole business is quite painless, and takes about two minutes. If the sperms are healthy and have been delivered to the proper place they should be found alive and active in a clear mucus plug. If they are not there, or are dead or not very active, that indicates that the semen is unhealthy or the cervical secretions are unhealthy. It will be obvious, therefore, that this test gives us a great deal of information quickly and easily, and often avoids the necessity for any semen analysis. If the sperms are present and healthy and the cervix is healthy, an X-Ray examination or a Rubin's test is the next essential. That, combined with a measurement of the cavity of the womb and an examination of its lining, will give us about as much information as is necessary to make a diagnosis of where the fault lies. We can then formulate a scheme of treatment. That, briefly, is the essence of the sterility problem as it appears to-day. Our knowledge of the whole subject is advancing by leaps and bounds, as is our capacity to treat the cases effectively.

"In spite of the complexity of the subject, I hope you will see that in so far as the patient is concerned the necessary investigations, though taking time, are simple and easy to carry out, and you can take it from me that the treatment, though lasting some time—months occasionally—is not too troublesome, and is often most effective. I must apologise for keeping you so long, and if I have not made myself sufficiently clear, I hope you will ask me questions."

. . . . .

"I know you will agree with me when I say that we are fortunate in our lecturers," Lady Burr said. "They have all put their points clearly and succinctly up to the present, and Dr. Minor is no exception to the rule. Her lecture is so crammed with information that one feels one would like to read it all over again at one's leisure.[1] You have about twenty minutes left for questions, so hurry up."

"Can you tell us something about sex determination, please?" a man said. "Is it entirely brought about by genetic influences, or do the hormones you have been mentioning play any part in the process?"

"I doubt whether I am sufficiently expert to answer your question," Dr. Minor said. "You are aware, no doubt, that the male produces two types of sperms, known as X and Y, which determine the sex of the individual. If the egg, which is neuter, is fertilised by a female-determining sperm (X) the result is female; if by a male-determining

[1] See Griffith, Edward F., "The Childless Marriage", Methuen, from which most of the material for this lecture has been taken.

sperm (Y) the result is a male. Apart from this, however, there is some evidence to show that the hormones of the new individual do help to determine and maintain its sex during intra-uterine life."

" Do undescended testicles have any effect on sterility ? " a young man asked.

" Oh, certainly. If a testicle remains in the abdominal cavity it cannot produce sperms because the heat of the cavity is too great. It is for this reason that the testicles descend into the scrotum, which may be regarded as a heat-regulating mechanism bringing the testicles closer to or farther away from the body, as seems necessary. The fact of having only one testicle, however, does not necessarily alter hormone activity or impair fertility in any way."

" You said that there were only two ways of obtaining a specimen of semen—by coitus interruptus or by self-production. In the case of the unmarried man the first method is ruled out. Do you approve of the second ? Why is it not possible to use a sheath, because I take it that in the case of the married man practising coitus interruptus a sheath is essential ? "

" A sheath should never be used for obtaining seminal specimens for examination ; the rubber destroys the sperms very quickly. If coitus interruptus is practised, the specimen is collected in a small glass receptacle supplied by the laboratory. Your question about self-production of semen is more difficult to answer because ethical principles are involved, some people regarding it as being morally wrong. The Roman Catholic Church considers the act as sinful and contrary to nature, and so this method must be ruled out as far as that Church is concerned. Personally I see nothing wrong in the act if the motive is right. I should have thought that some distinction might be drawn between the self-production of semen for selfish reasons, as in masturbation, and that which is done for a scientific purpose, namely the production of children—a subject in which most people, in particular the Roman Catholics, are always profoundly interested. If a man feels it is wrong to produce a specimen in this way he should not be pushed to do so. If he is married, some other means can be devised, and if he isn't, he must wait until he is."

"We hear a great deal about artificial insemination in cattle," a woman said. "Can it be applied to human beings and, if so, do you approve of it?"

"This audience certainly knows how to pose difficult questions, madam chairman," Dr. Minor said, with a laugh, as she rose to reply.

"Artificial insemination can certainly be applied to humans, and a considerable amount of work has been done on the subject both here and in America.[1] It is necessary to distinguish between artificial insemination of the woman with the husband's semen, which is known as A.I.H., and artificial insemination of the woman by an unknown donor, which is known as A.I.D. Whilst few people, except the most bigoted, can object to A.I.H., there are many ethical and social problems raised by A.I.D., which make it a much more controversial issue. The procedure in both cases is the same, the sperms being placed in or about the entrance to the cervical canal by means of a small syringe.

"Indications for A.I.H. are:—

"1. Highly acid vaginal secretions which cannot be corrected.

"2. In the case of women with under-developed sex organs there comes a time in treatment when she does not appear to be able to become pregnant by ordinary means, but can, occasionally, by means of A.I.

"3. In certain cases of sub-fertility in both partners an A.I. will occasionally prove effective.

"4. In certain cases of paralysis or difficult psychological situations in which coitus is difficult, and yet there would be no bar to childbirth, and A.I. will often prove successful.

"5. In some men there are anatomical defects which prevent the semen from being delivered properly.

"6. Male sub-fertility.

"7. Complete impotence—that is to say, failure of the

[1] "Artificial Insemination", Barton, Walker and Wiesner, *Lancet*, January 13th, 1945.

husband to effect penetration. Many men who suffer from this condition have excellent sperm counts and can produce a satisfactory specimen although unable to effect penetration.

" 8. Partial impotence. In such cases coitus occurs very irregularly, or else there is premature ejaculation.

" In many of the discussions that take place about A.I.H. the position of the child that is to be born is frequently overlooked, attention being chiefly centred on the needs of the woman and her desire to have a child. No child should be brought into such a home unless there is good evidence that the husband and wife have discussed the problem from every angle and are agreed together and likely to prove good parents. There are often psychological conditions which may affect the relationship between the husband and wife and, of course, the new baby. For instance, it is no use a woman agreeing to have a baby from an impotent husband if the woman is not prepared to forego sexual intercourse and all that it means. Has she really faced up to that side of the problem ? "

A.I.D.

" The chief indication for A.I.D. is the complete sterility of the male. In such a case the couple have three courses open to them. They can go on as they are, they can adopt a child, or have one by A.I.D. In the latter case, in which, of course, the child is at least 50 per cent. theirs, certain rules are usually regarded as essential.

" 1. Defects in the wife must be attended to.
" 2. No one must know who the donor is except the doctor.
" 3. Care and time must be taken by the doctor in assessing the needs of the couple and determining the social group, interests, background and so on into which the new child will come. For instance, it is not a good idea to choose a donor who comes from a highly intellectual and cultural background for a couple in a different social

grade, the husband being one more accustomed to manual activities.

" 4. The donor's semen must pass some very drastic tests.

" 5. On no account must the donor be related to the husband, as this is likely to make for psychological difficulty later on.

" 6. The donor should have at least two legitimate children of his own.

" 7. The child must never know that its ' father ' is not its real biological father.

" 8. The doctor must be legally protected in so far as this is possible, because there seems to be some doubt as to the legality of the whole procedure of A.I.D. As a matter of fact there is little doubt that the child is legally illegitimate.

" Whilst there are certain advantages to the woman in having a child in this manner, it is by no means so certain that there are so many advantages to the child, who has to be lied to about its parentage from the time of its birth. This aspect of the matter does not seem to have received the consideration it deserves, most people accepting the dictum that the child should never be told anything about its origin, in the same way as some people never tell adopted children the truth about their adoption. There is, however, another side to the question, and that is whether a policy of complete honesty will not prove best in the long run. Whilst I have by no means discussed the matter fully, I hope I have said enough to give you some indication of the difficulties of A.I. I might add that in A.I.D. the ' father ' has to perjure himself by saying that he is the father of a child, when in fact he knows very well that he isn't. All these facts make people view A.I.D. with considerable suspicion." [1]

" What is the Rh factor ? "

" The Rh factor, or the Rhesus factor, is present in the

[1] For a full discussion see Griffith, Edward F., " The Childless Marriage ", Methuen. "Artificial Insemination ", Report of a Conference held by the Public Morality Council, Heinemann, 1947. Willink, The Rt. Hon. Henry, "Legal Aspects of Artificial Insemination ", *Practitioner*, April 1947.

blood of most adults. If the blood of a person who has the factor mingles with that of one who has not got the factor, antibodies are produced which cause the red cells to clump and join together instead of remaining separate. These antibodies, if produced in a baby by an Rh-negative mother, cause it to get diseases like jaundice and anæmia, which often lead to death. Such a baby can be saved by being injected with new and wholesome blood." [1]

A young woman got up at the back of the hall.

"I know a woman," she said, "who is married to a man who has a considerable amount of mental disease in his family. As it seems inadvisable for them to have children, do you think she would be justified in having an A.I.D.?"

"Perhaps so; but what are you going to tell the child? Supposing it should find out later on that its paternal forbears are so tainted that there is a chance of passing on mental instability, and the child, when grown up, decides that it won't have any children for that reason, it is rather hard luck on it, don't you think, considering that in fact it is not tainted in any way?"

"Well, if that isn't a good idea, why shouldn't the man be sterilised?"

"He could be, of course, but that opens up all sorts of other difficult questions. Personally I should teach the woman an efficient contraceptive method and leave the matter alone."

"And on that note I think we must finish," the Chairman said. "Thank you very much, Dr. Minor, for your most interesting address."

[1] See Roberts, G. Fulton, "The Rhesus Factor", Heinemann, 1947.

CHAPTER XIII

PREPARATION FOR MARRIAGE

" SOME of you will be surprised to see Canon Heathcott sitting here this evening," Lady Burr said; " but the truth is that although the meeting to-night is concerned with the important subject of Marriage Preparation, I have felt for some time that it would be a good idea to try and clear up some of the differences which seem to exist between the Canon and Dr. Hansell and have, I know, been worrying some of you quite a lot. It may surprise you to know that these two have been getting together behind the scenes. I am told that they have sat up talking half the night, and Dr. Hansell even went so far as to take the Canon to a birth-control clinic. As a result they have found themselves in a considerable measure of agreement, more so, indeed, than those of you who heard both their lectures would have expected. For this reason I have thought it wise to ask Canon Heathcott to summarise these findings, because the more we can reach a real measure of agreement, the better it will be for all of us.—Canon Heathcott."

" I do not wish to take up too much of your time this evening, because we have a most important subject to discuss," Canon Heathcott said, " but, as the chairman has just told you, it is perfectly true that Dr. Hansell and I have been trying to sort out some of our differences, and I think you will be glad to hear that, on the whole, we have reached some positive conclusions."

A murmur of appreciation came from the audience.

" I may as well say at once," the Canon continued, " that I have altered my views considerably in regard to contraception since visiting the clinic, and, having done so, I think it only right that I should say so. I can summarise the main points of agreement as follows.

" 1. We are agreed that for the majority of people it is only within the orbit of the family that they can find the fulfilment of their highest objectives, and it is to the stability of the family unit that society must give more adequate attention in the future.

" 2. The sex impulse, being a God-given activity of the human body, finds its highest expression within this framework.

" 3. Monogamy is the ultimate ideal of man and woman.

" 4. Sex has three equally important functions : the continuation of the race, the expression of mutual love and affection and the transference of energy into other channels. Each of these functions has to find expression in marriage at different times according to the circumstances. The latter is the means by which celibacy may be achieved.

" 5. Contraception, taught by competent doctors, has a positive part to play in the achievement of mental and physical health. I may say here that my visit to the clinic convinced me of the value of these institutions and of the importance of encouraging their extension throughout the country. I must therefore withdraw my statement that birth control is immoral, although it may, of course, be used for immoral ends.

" 6. We are agreed that whilst abstention may have its place in the married state, it is not a contraceptive method, and its practice may lead to the development of tensions and frustrations, which can do nothing but accentuate difficulties.

" 7. We are agreed that the state of celibacy is no higher or better than that of marriage. Each has its limitations and its rewards, but neither prevents the ultimate development of the full personality.

" 8. The term self-control can be misapplied, in which case it often means repression.

" 9. The use of adequate contraceptives permits the planning and spacing of children and, by relieving emotional tension through normal union, encourages stability and the exercise of proper self-control.

" 10. The indiscriminate sale of contraceptives is most unsatisfactory and, by giving people a feeling of security which is quite unwarranted, causes much unnecessary misery.

PREPARATION FOR MARRIAGE 213

"11. The true expression of the sexual urge is to be found in the love of man and woman when it is used for the fulfilment of all that is highest and best in both their personalities.

"12. Thus there should be no conflict between science and religion over the teaching of sex and the education of our young people for marriage and family life.

"Needless to say, these points do not cover the whole ground, but they do go a long way towards agreement."

"Thank you very much," the chairman said as Canon Heathcott sat down amidst much clapping. "You will all agree, I hope, that the statement has cleared the air enormously and shown how much closer we all are in regard to essentials than was at first apparent. Have any of you any questions you wish to put to the Canon?"

A rapid glance round the room being sufficient to satisfy the chairman that no one was burning with a desire to speak, she asked Dr. Hansell to address the meeting on the subject of Preparation for Marriage.

. . . . .

Having said a few words of appreciation and agreement with what Canon Heathcott had said, Dr. Hansell lost no time in getting under way.

"You will realise that marriage preparation has many facets to which a variety of people can contribute at different times throughout the early years of development. Of all the influences leading to final stability in marriage, that of the happy, well-adjusted home in which the child finds security and love is probably the most significant. It is here that the basic pattern is forged and, provided the raw material is sound, the final product—the young man or woman—should be well equipped in so far as his emotional life is concerned. Repressive parental influence shows itself in various ways. One type indulges in actual physical chastisement, in frequent naggings and interferences with reasonable freedom, and is a fruitful source of frustration and disharmony in adolescence which may persist into later life. Another type is even more insidious. The parents who never raise their voices, never get angry, never beat and never do anything to express emotional feeling, save by showing a pained expression implying that they have been grievously hurt or shamed or otherwise upset, are a menace to young people. Such passive domination, so common in some of the ' best ' homes, is a fruitful source of future unhappiness in marriage. And as for the possessive mother—well, I need not discuss her further because I gather that you have heard about her already from Dr. Minor.[1]

Other influences, such as school, friends and occupation, all have their effect on the growing individual, moulding his character and training him for the venture of life. Unless these influences are very bad or there is some flaw in the developmental pattern, the ultimate result will be good, and a person of integrity, balance and understanding will eventually emerge. Marriage preparation, therefore, as has been said repeatedly at this conference, starts in the cradle, and concerns itself with many matters which can only be mentioned to-night. Although we in this country are backward in marriage preparation, a considerable amount of experimental work has been done in America in order to devise courses of lectures which will be of value to young people who are engaged or thinking seriously of being engaged. More recently the Marriage Guidance Council in this country has drawn up a syllabus of lectures on Marriage Preparation which covers a variety of subjects related to sex and family life, and is broad enough to include matters like finance, homemaking and the spiritual aspects of marriage. My purpose this evening is to presume that all these various matters have been or are being tackled by the couple and to concentrate on the contribution that can be made by the doctor in what is now known as the pre-marital consultation. This is quite a new idea, the medical aspect of marriage preparation in the past being confined to the provision of health certificates stating that the individual is physically fit, free from venereal disease or the grosser forms of physical disability such as tuberculosis, mental deficiency and other hereditary conditions. The more positive idea of adequate pre-marital instruction and clinical assistance, in both the

[1] The subject is not considered in detail in this book.

physical and psychological spheres, is something quite new, and has been forced upon us both by increasing scientific knowledge of the human personality and by the distressing failure of the former policy of *laissez-faire*. I would go so far as to say that there is not a single couple marrying for the first time who would not benefit from a pre-marital consultation with a doctor, and in many cases an eventual breakdown in the marriage can be prevented by such a course. No matter how much preparation and advice are given to a couple by friends, parsons and counsellors, there are certain aspects which, if present, will wreck the marriage unless they are dealt with by a physician trained in marriage guidance work, no matter how much the couple think they know each other, are in love with each other and, as they say, ' have talked the matter out and have no false modesty '.

" Whilst the pre-marital consultation does not and cannot cover the whole ground, it is, in my opinion, an essential to marriage, and I hope the time is not far distant when the parson, at any rate, will refuse to marry a couple who do not give evidence of having had a pre-marital consultation with a recognised expert. Whether or no the State will ever bring itself to insist upon a similar certificate for those who marry in Register Offices is a question no one can answer at present. Some such procedure is, of course, the logical conclusion of the Denning Committee's recommendations, which state that : ' There should be a Marriage Welfare Service to afford help and guidance both in preparation for marriage and also in difficulties after marriage. - The principal aims of this service should be :

" ' First: to make available a sufficient number of suitable persons to give advice and to see that their availability is generally known.

" ' Second : To encourage young people to seek competent advice in preparation for marriage.

" ' Third : To encourage married couples to seek competent advice as soon as serious conflicts arise.

" ' Fourth : To attempt reconciliation whenever a break has occurred.' [1]

[1] " Final Report of the Committee on Procedure in Matrimonial Causes ", February 1947, p. 13.

"Whilst any form of compulsory examination or certification is not likely to prove successful in this country, I see no reason why it should not become customary for both parson and registrar to be encouraged to ask for one and thereby gradually building up a public opinion which considers it right and necessary for such a certificate to be produced. I am well aware, however, that this will take time."

Dr. Hansell paused, and poured himself out a glass of water, but omitted to drink it.

"Let us therefore consider," he went on quickly, "the pre-marital consultation in some detail. The matter is well put in a recent article in the *Lancet*. The writer stresses what has already been suggested to you in this conference—namely, that the sexual impulse has three complementary and mutually inclusive functions : the transference of sex energy into other creative channels, mating and reproduction. The first is the channel through which sexual energy can be released in activities of social value and is the basis of vocational celibacy and the safety-valve which should prevent distortion or deviation. The second is one of the chief ways in which the emotional needs of man and woman can be fulfilled, and is the more personal and intimate. The third, by creating children, is the fulfilment of the individual's biological and social needs and the way in which he perpetuates himself. All three must find expression, both separately and together, in the marriage relationship. There are times when sexual activity must be curtailed or foregone. There are times when the achievement of an emotional rhythm and orgasm is essential, and there are times when children must be brought into the world. Each has its own proper uses and provides its own rewards.[1] It is to enable the couple to fulfil these aims that is the main purpose of the pre-marital consultation.

Prediction Tests.

"Before proceeding to consider this matter in more detail I should like to mention quite briefly that there is considerable evidence from America to show that it is possible to

[1] Griffith, Edward F., "Medical Aspects of Marriage Guidance", *Lancet*, February 1st, 1947.

assess in some measure those qualities in a couple which will make for stability or the reverse in marriage. Various prediction tests have been devised to enable people to choose a satisfactory mate, and any of you who are interested should consult such authorities as Norman Himes, Burgess, Cottrell and Terman.[1]

" It is perhaps easier, however, to recognise those factors which make for unhappiness. Some authorities consider that an underlying collusion of wishes leads to much marital unhappiness, and whilst this may be true, I am inclined to think that it is more often a desire on the part of one partner to change the other partner and fit him or her into a preconceived pattern of what that partner should be which leads to so much trouble. The one is always striving, consciously or unconsciously, to dominate the other and prevent that freedom of growth and expression which is the essence of comradeship and love.

" Terman suggests eight points as being most productive of marital happiness. They are:

" 1. Superior happiness of parents.
" 2. Childhood happiness.
" 3. Lack of conflict with parents.
" 4. Home discipline that was firm, not harsh.
" 5. Strong attachment to parents.
" 6. Parental frankness about sex matters.
" 7. Infrequency and mildness of childhood punishment.
" 8. Pre-marital attitude to sex that was free from disgust or aversion.

" The subject who ' passes ' on all these items is a distinctly better-than-average marital risk. It is probable that the most important factors making for happiness in marriage are a happy parental background and childhood happiness, absence of conflict between the child and its mother and emotional stability. After marriage it is important to achieve adequate mutual orgasm and equality in the sex drive

[1] See Himes, N. E., "Happy Marriage", 1941, London, or Terman, L. M., "Psychological Factors in Marital Happiness", 1938, N.Y. and London.

between husband and wife. This is something which, though present in the make-up of the individual, can be developed and regulated to a large extent by mutual understanding, knowledge of technique and practice. The equality isn't just there and the orgasm doesn't just come; both have to be worked for. This is a most important point, which isn't recognised by a large majority of young people to-day. They seem to think that a night or a week-end will enable them to achieve perfection. This is a fallacy and, in my opinion, one of the strongest arguments against sex relationships before marriage. Unless the latter are carried on for some time, and in fact are akin to marriage in everything but the legal formality or religious service, they will be utterly useless to prove whether there is equality of sex drive or mutual orgasm. These matters can be assessed by other means, as I hope to show you to-night. Ideally speaking, prediction tests should be worked out before the couple reach the consulting-room for a pre-marital consultation, and there is no doubt that this will be done with increasing frequency as marriage preparation becomes more acceptable to society. There are, however, an increasing number of people who avail themselves of the opportunity of having a ' check up ' before engagement, and it is to these people that these tests can be of most value. Should the results be unsatisfactory, the couple can think again, whereas this is much more difficult when the wedding day is all but fixed. At present all that can be done is to make some kind of assessment of these factors during the pre-marital consultation and discuss any particular problem that may arise. Occasionally it is possible to persuade a couple to postpone their wedding date under these circumstances and obtain some simple psychological help. I need scarcely stress the importance of the individual having received adequate sex instruction as a child, having had no sex shocks during adolescence and not having indulged in excessive petting before marriage.

" There are many factors closely connected with the sexual function which have been ignored or glossed over in the past which are constantly arising as inhibiting factors to a healthy mental adjustment and if present must be dealt with."

The doctor paused for a moment, looked at his glass of water and drank a little.

. . . . .

"Let me now pass to the actual examination of the patient.

"Some couples come together, and some separately. Some come six months before the wedding date, others the day before. Some want advice about a particular aspect of marriage such as the genetic one or the state of their physical health. Some are timid, embarrassed and woefully ignorant, others have the whole matter taped, even to deciding the best day on which conception should take place. It is best for each partner to see the same doctor separately to start off with, and together later on if they so wish. The best time for the first visit is about a couple of months before the wedding. Before making any physical examination or doing anything, in fact, it is important to reassure the couple and obtain their confidence. It is often advisable to devote the whole of the first interview to discussion. Every case has to be handled differently, and it is inadvisable to have a set rule of procedure. Any of you who are interested in this aspect of the work, either as consultants or counsellors, must assure yourself that you have put the individual at ease. In no circumstances should matters be rushed, and above all it is important to encourage the couple to express their own views regarding their marriage.

"Beyond saying that unless a general physical overhaul has been done recently it is necessary to make one at some time during this preparation period, I will not consider the matter further. You will have gathered that two or more interviews are usually necessary, although this is by no means always the case. I have often completed the whole business most efficiently in three-quarters of an hour.

The Mating and Reproductive Functions.

"Both the mating and the reproductive functions must be expressed if the married life of the couple is to be fully integrated. The tendency in the past has been to concentrate on the reproductive and to presume that the mating aspect will function automatically. But this is not so. The achievement of an adequate orgasm is of prime importance in the development of marriage harmony and should be established before the reproductive function is expressed. This I believe to be of profound importance, and it is round this idea that much argument still persists. To many people the reproductive function is so important that they feel it must be fulfilled at once; nothing must interfere with the woman becoming pregnant. Everything must be subservient to that idea, because that is the true function of woman and the chief purpose of marriage. But people who talk like that forget or ignore the profound importance of the mating aspect, because it is through the proper achievement of this function that the couple express their mutual appreciation and release emotional tension. It is completely inaccurate to suggest, as do some people, that the mating aspect will come 'all in good time'. It won't and, what is more important still, if it is not achieved before the woman becomes pregnant it may not be achieved for months. You would be surprised at the number of ordinary normal women who come to the doctor, either privately or in the clinics, wanting contraceptive advice after the birth of their first child, who admit that they experienced practically no sensation before and during the pregnancy or after the birth of the child. There is evidence to show that it is still rare, both here and in America, to find the marriage in which adequate orgasm is achieved. Terman states that one woman in three rarely or never achieves an orgasm, and other workers are of the same opinion.[1]

"In order to achieve a satisfactory orgasm the following are essential.

"1. There must be no bar to effective penetration. Thus the hymen and vaginal orifice must be adequately dilated.

"2. The man must achieve full erection, effect deep penetration and maintain this state sufficiently long to enable the woman to achieve orgasm.

[1] See Himes, N. E., "Happy Marriage", 1941, London, or Terman, M. L., "Psychological Factors in Marital Happiness", 1938, N.Y. and London.

" 3. In order to do this, both couples must have a knowledge of technique.

" 4. None of the above will be of any use unless the woman gives herself freely and willingly to the man. This is a psychological process. She can't make herself do it; she can only do so because she loves him and, let it be added, because she is free from worry, anxiety and fear of interruption.

" The same can be said of the man. He cannot love his wife adequately unless he feels that she is understanding and co-operative and willing to give herself entirely to him without fear or reservation. She must realise that it takes time for the man to reach perfection in regard to the maintenance of erection and various other matters of technique. If he senses that she is anxious, critical, unresponsive or bored it is almost impossible for him to co-operate. Indeed, he may be unable to obtain an erection or, once it is obtained, he may have an ejaculation almost immediately. This is one of the reasons why a man may be more or less impotent with one woman and yet be able to make love for an hour or more with another. This attraction between the couple, this ability to sense the inner feelings of the other, is one of the most potent forces in regulating the strength and capacity of the sex urge. Once a man feels that the woman is no longer responsive to him, he becomes anxious and worried. It is in this way—non-co-operation on the part of the woman—that much so-called impotence develops in the man. I stress this point because I am constantly coming across cases in which the woman seems to think that once she has allowed penetration to occur she has no further contribution to make to the proceedings and that the husband, once having achieved an erection, can maintain it indefinitely whatever her state of mind may be. Nothing could be farther from the truth. If the woman is susceptible to atmosphere, the majority of men are doubly so. Many a man living in one or two rooms in his in-laws' house has told me that the very fact of there being no key to their room has prevented him from maintaining effective erection. Anxiety is a potent cause of sexual disharmony. You will see, therefore, that there must be no bar to penetration, and the doctor must ascertain the state of the hymen and, if necessary, either dilate it himself, remove it surgically if excessively tight or teach the patient to dilate it herself. This latter procedure is possible in about 80 per cent. of the cases; [1] is very simple and is completed in about a week or ten days.

"Having done this, the doctor must see that the couple understand something about technique. This may take a short or long time, according to their experience and knowledge. Books are particularly helpful in this respect. Three may be mentioned.[2]

"Finally, should the woman so desire, she should be taught a suitable contraceptive method. This takes about a quarter of an hour in the majority of cases, and, once learnt, is easy to apply and provides about a 98 per cent. safety margin.

"On no account should women obtain their contraceptives from shops, or through advertisements. They all have a considerable failure rate, and are nothing like as reliable as the methods taught in clinics or by private doctors who know their business. The male sheath is not to be recommended as a contraceptive method. Apart from the fact that its real purpose is to prevent venereal disease, it is unæsthetic and has quite a high failure rate in so far as pregnancy is concerned. Many men find it so troublesome that it leads to premature ejaculation or even to temporary impotence.

"In my opinion no marriage in the future can possibly be conducted adequately and allow for the expression of that mental and spiritual unity which we all regard as so essential unless the couple use an adequate contraceptive method and learn to space their children properly. That is the purpose of contraception; to enable women to space their children. There is ample evidence both here and in America that

[1] See "Modern Marriage", by Edward F. Griffith (Methuen), for directions as to how this can be done.
[2] "The Sex Factor in Marriage", Helena Wright. "Modern Marriage", Edward F. Griffith. "Ideal Marriage", Van de Velde. This latter is a bigger and more complicated book and should not be read till after the others. All these books can be obtained from the Marriage Guidance Book Room.

women who do so space their children have more and healthier children than those who do nothing. If you are interested in these matters I should advise you to apply to one of the societies who can give you adequate information.[1]

"I have endeavoured to give you a comprehensive survey of a subject which is both new and interesting.

"I would end by saying that when all this work has been done there is no guarantee that things will go right. It will take time and practice before perfection is achieved, and an intelligent couple must pay constant attention to this aspect of their life, making sure that they are maintaining the high standard with which they presumably started their marriage."

. . . . .

Nearly a minute passed before Lady Burr could obtain a hearing.

"Judging by the nature of your applause," she said, "I gather that you have enjoyed this address as much as I have. Dr. Hansell has given us a very clear explanation of the purpose of marriage preparation and what may be achieved. If, as I am, you are convinced of the importance of establishing some means whereby people can obtain this help for the asking, you will do all you can to further the cause he has at heart. Personally I am convinced of the great need for marriage preparation. My work takes me much amongst girls and young women, and I am quite appalled at the number who marry knowing practically nothing. I would stress, too, the importance of young people visiting the doctor. I notice a growing attitude on the part of the clergy and church people in general to consider that everything is satisfactory if the couple have received advice from the priest. This I feel to be a form of escapism, due to the fact that those who adopt this attitude will not face up to the two main points that Dr. Hansell has just made : the importance of establishing the mating factor in the marriage relationship and the insistence upon the positive role that contraception can, and indeed must, play in marriage in the future. It is not the

[1] The Family Planning Association, 69 Eccleston Sq., S.W.1. The Planned Parenthood Association (America) Federation, New York. The Marriage Guidance Council, 87 Duke St., Grosvenor Sq., London.

function of the chairman to make speeches, but rather to keep order and watch the time; but I must end by saying that I can underline every word that Dr. Hansell has said regarding the amount of preventable disharmony which develops from lack of knowledge—a conviction which, if allowed to persist unchecked, produces the maladjusted couple and the unhappy home. And now for questions. You still have a few minutes."

" You mentioned various inhibiting factors," someone said from the back of the hall, " but you did not enumerate them. Would it be possible for you to do so shortly ? "

" Yes, certainly. I did not do so because they are by way of being somewhat ' medical ' in nature, and I was not sure that in a mixed audience of this nature they would be altogether welcome. However, if you wish——"

He was interrupted by a chorus of people shouting " Go on."

" Very good. I will do as you wish," the doctor said, smiling broadly. " The following list is by no means complete, but is sufficient to show how easily the couple may set out on the wrong tack.

" 1. A negative approach to sex, often originating in early infancy, and usually due to parental mismanagement, which has produced a series of fears, inhibitions and misunderstandings. The passive domination already mentioned, and so often found in so many ' good ' homes in which sex is never mentioned, is as bad, or even worse than the type of family where sex is loosely discussed.

" 2. The presumption that the sex act is a mere copulatory activity, mainly concerned with self-amusement outside marriage and with reproduction inside marriage, is usually combined with a refusal or inability to realise its social and spiritual value.

" 3. ' Sex is a naughty mystery, both frightening and exciting.' Such an attitude has usually produced excessive sexual excitement during engagement without adequate release, self-stimulation (masturbation) and misguided sexual adventures. Having experienced excitement on the one hand, and lack of fulfilment on the other, the individual is always seeking new adventures in the hope of finding positive and satisfying adjustment. This situation often leads to pre-marital relationships, which usually prove unsatisfactory and, by prematurely awakening the emotional life, encourage other adventures or an acceptance of marriage as an escape from an intolerable situation.

"4. 'Sex activity is a fatiguing process leading to the loss of vital energy.' This idea, more prevalent in men than in women, is usually the result of foolish teaching about self-stimulation during adolescence.

"5. Many young people, particularly men, are firmly convinced that the practice of self-stimulation has led to permanent injury to their sex organs and mental lassitude. This situation is not improved either by the nonsense still widely disseminated by much 'sex literature' or by the admonitions of so-called moralists. The idea that sex is beautiful or refreshing and essentially positive is foreign to the minds of the great majority of the parent population.

"6. 'Man is capable of erection at any moment, and once this is established it can and should be maintained indefinitely.' Its temporary disappearance is viewed with the gravest concern, and is a fruitful cause of temporary impotence in the sensitive type of male.

"7. 'A man should be able to perform the sex act several times a night.' This is a foolish and misinformed opinion which prevails in every section of youthful society.

"8. 'Stimulation of the clitoris is an essential preliminary to coitus.' Many men spend a considerable time trying to rouse the woman, who is probably perfectly ready for coitus in a few minutes. Many women do not distinguish between orgasm of the clitoris and vaginal orgasm. The one is a precursor to the other, and may or may not be experienced. Petting, which usually includes stimulation of the clitoris, fixes the emotions at an immature level.

"9. 'The penis must not be withdrawn from the vagina once penetration has occurred, and little or no variation in position is either possible or advisable.' The use of a sheath encourages this idea, owing to difficulties arising over its management.

" 10. ' The whole sex act should be completed in about five minutes—delay leads to fatigue, and is therefore physically dangerous.'

" 11. ' The only time to carry out the sex act is at night, in the dark, and in the cold.' The æsthetics of sexual intimacy have still to be learnt by 90 per cent. of the population.

" 12. ' The man needs sexual activity more than the woman.' This I believe to be profoundly untrue.

" 13. ' A woman should pretend she gets an orgasm whether she does so or not.' This is the first step on the downward path to marital disharmony.

" 14. ' Sex and religion are antagonistic to one another ; hence sexual enjoyment is neither " right " or " nice ".' "

" Thank you, doctor ; that is most informative and makes the matter quite clear," the questioner said.

" Don't you think it would be wiser to allow people to try each other out physically before entering into the marriage bond ? " a young man asked.

" I see so many difficulties in the way that I think it would be much wiser to give a really good try to marriage preparation for a generation or two and then, if that is an obvious failure, to think again. Some people think that a form of betrothal permitting sex union should be sanctioned by society. Others, of whom I believe the Archbishop of York is one, think that there should be two forms of marriage, civil and religious, and that no one should be married in church until they have had a civil marriage. In any case, I am convinced that no sex union should occur between man and woman until they have received adequate preparation."

" I suppose I'm either very stupid or very ignorant," a young woman said, " but in all the discussions we have had this week, although the importance of an adequate sex relationship has been stressed over and over again, no one, so far as I am aware, has given us a satisfactory definition of ' adequate '. We are told that there are various stages ; that they should last a varying degree of time ; that mutual orgasm is essential, and many other things, but to me, at least, the picture of what is really essential is not clear. If I am alone in this attitude, then perhaps you will be good enough to tell me later on, but if others feel the same way as I do, perhaps you will kindly enlighten us."

"Well," said Dr. Hansell, looking at the audience. "What is it to be? Do any of you want further information?"

A number of people put up their hands.

"Very good, then," he said. "The task you give me is a difficult one, because every couple vary as to their needs and reactions, not only from year to year, but from week to week. There are so many unknown factors which impinge on the best-regulated households that it is impossible to be dogmatic. What suits one couple will be entirely unsatisfactory for another. I have patients who tell me they are perfectly happy if they make love about once a fortnight and make the whole relationship last about ten minutes. Indeed, I have many patients who tell me that they are perfectly satisfied with three minutes, but I am ready to pick holes in that story pretty quickly! And I have other patients who make love once or twice a week for an hour or two at a time. In between these two extremes you will find a variety of different experiences. Let me try and answer your question by mentioning some of the factors which seem to me to be important in this relationship."

Preparation.

"Love-making is an art, and should be prepared for in some measure. There is plenty of water and soap about even in these days, and people should use them. I admit that in many instances this is difficult if there is no bath in the house and every drop of water has to be boiled on a gas stove in an overcrowded kitchen. That is why I say that the sex habits of a large proportion of the population cannot be improved until the housing situation is improved. In some houses there is so little privacy that a woman even finds it difficult to manage her contraceptive technique. However, we are considering the ideal. As soon as love-making becomes a weekly habit, like the Saturday night bath, there is something wrong somewhere. Then, again, why make love last thing at night, when everyone is tired and wants to go to sleep ? And why, as I have already said, make love in the dark, in a cold room and under the bed-clothes ? It is no doubt possible to copulate under those conditions, but quite impossible to make love unless the couple are very well versed in sex technique."

Duration.

"This suggests another point—namely, the duration of the relationship. Owing to the fact that no man ever seemed to consider the feelings of women until a few years ago and thought that all that was necessary was to introduce the penis into the vagina as quickly as possible, writers on these matters have stressed, and possibly over-stressed, the importance of 'preparing' the woman for the relationship. I have come across men who tell me that they have spent as long as forty minutes trying to rouse their wives, and that because nothing much seems to happen they presume that either their own technique is bad or that their wives are cold. After a while they don't hesitate to tell their wives that they are cold, which doesn't improve matters one little bit. They are somewhat surprised when I tell them that they can make love in this fashion till they are blue in the face and get nowhere. It is impossible for this preliminary approach to do more than bring the couple together and make the woman responsive to the man ; so responsive, in fact, that she feels the need of the penis in the vagina. It is of course obvious that this 'need' will present itself more easily after some effective practice than the first time intercourse is attempted, although a great many women are very conscious of this need after a very small amount of love-play even before they are married. Every man has to learn to sense when this need is present, or of course the woman can indicate her readiness. Penetration should then occur, because no woman can advance beyond a certain distance until penetration has occurred unless she has become conditioned to some other and less valuable form of sex satisfaction."

The Second Stage.

"This first stage, therefore, should last for a few minutes—five to fifteen, perhaps. It must be remembered that man is not capable of continuous erection for an indefinite period. The whole object of the love relationship is to enjoy and prolong the second stage—from penetration to final ejaculation. This may be made to last for a long time, let us say from ten minutes to one hour, and during that time the following things must be aimed at:

(*a*) No ejaculation until mutual orgasm is possible.
(*b*) Change of position and occasional rest.
(*c*) Withdrawal and re-entry several times. This is difficult to achieve, but most satisfactory to both partners, and likely to encourage orgasm in the woman.

(*d*) Free and rhythmical movements of both man and woman, leading to deeper and most satisfying penetration and eventual ejaculation and mutual orgasm. The technique of this particular part of the sex act is complicated, and considerable practice is necessary before it becomes satisfactory. Even then it may vary according to the time of the woman's cycle, fatigue and worry and a host of other minor conditions."

The Third Stage.

"A mismanaged third stage—that is to say, after the act is completed—is often a cause of disharmony and worry, on the part of the woman in particular. There is no need to separate at once; indeed, it is inadvisable. It is possible to rest and sleep for a while or talk, but on no account should the man withdraw or turn over and go to sleep. This, in my opinion, is a gross insult to the woman who has just co-operated so satisfactorily in this supreme expression of mutual affection. Of course if she hasn't co-operated or has been difficult, or provoking, then I can well understand his desire to leave her and so, no doubt, can you."

Dr. Hansell paused for a moment, and looked in the direction of the questioner. "These few points will, I hope, be sufficient to indicate to you the nature of an adequate sex relationship," he said, after which he turned to his chair and sat down.

Realising that he was tired, Lady Burr came to his rescue. " I don't think we can well keep the speaker any longer this evening," she said. " He has given us a magnificent lecture and plenty to think about, so we will give him a good clap and let him go."

CHAPTER XIV
ADOLESCENT PROBLEMS

A YOUNG man buttonholed Dr. Hansell whilst he was drinking his coffee that evening and began talking rather rapidly.

"I don't think any of the lecturers realise the difficulties young people get themselves into over this pre-marital business," he said. "The problem of what to do with one's sex feelings before one is married is extremely difficult—to some people, at any rate. Providing us with opportunities for meeting people of the opposite sex and so on will not meet the case. It may do something for those people who are out at work all day and find little rest in the home for one reason or another, or are working on their own and are bored and lonely and want to meet people; but it won't do much for a fellow like me, who has a steady job and knows very well he can't afford to marry for years, and yet needs female companionship and love. To some people sex is so forceful that something has to be done about it; it gets in the way of one's work, and one becomes restless and irritable. Then, again, girls are different now-a-days; they seem to expect you to make love to them or, at any rate, are quite willing when you start to do so, and many of them are quite prepared to have intercourse—nice girls, too. It's not easy to steer a middle course, I assure you. We aren't indifferent to women."

"You would be strange beings if you were, Mr. ——?"

"Holmes is my name—Oliver Holmes. I'm an engineering student."

"Well, Mr. Holmes, I agree with you that life is very difficult for people of your age," Dr. Hansell said, sitting down on a sofa.

"The trouble is to know where to draw the line," Mr. Holmes said, pulling up a chair in front of the doctor. "You say that one's general attitude to women must be based upon the principle of never doing anything which will harm them or oneself, either mentally or physically."

" That's true."

" Well, I find it a difficult principle to live up to ; especially as half one's friends seem to think that sex experience is a necessity. A fellow the other day said that one's sex glands will go to seed, as he put it, if one doesn't use them. I told him he didn't know what he was talking about, and asked him if he thought every woman who didn't marry until she was thirty had lost her reproductive possibilities."

" Good for you. What did he say ? "

" That it merely proved his point ; because it was a well-known fact that many women of that age can't have children and that most of them were sexually inhibited by that time, anyway."

" What rot ! They're perfectly capable of marrying and leading normal sex lives."

" Yes, I know. I tried to explain this ductless gland business to him but I got a bit tied up, I'm afraid. I wish you'd go over it again for me so that I can get it clear in my mind."

" It's really very simple. The sex glands have a dual function, connected on the one hand with the production of eggs and sperms ; and on the other with the manufacture of an internal secretion, or hormone, which travels round in the bloodstream and influences our growth and development. It is possible for the first purpose—the reproductive purpose —to be blotted out for some reason or other, but for the other to continue functioning quite normally. This activity not only causes the egg to burst from the ovary every month, but enables us to develop our secondary sex characteristics and maintain our sexual power and energy throughout life. As a matter of fact, it acts from the very beginning of life, and determines in some respect the degree of maleness or femaleness that we all possess. A strong production of female hormone in a male (or, for that matter, a weak production of male hormone) in early embryonic life—that is to say, before birth—means that the individual, whilst remaining male, will possess many characteristics which are more definitely feminine. The hormone exercises its greatest activity at puberty, when not only do physical changes occur, but there is a widening of emotional ideals and an awakening of specific sex feeling. Subtle differences are developed between the sexes, which often cause much unnecessary trouble if they are not understood. It is here that your friend's argument falls to the ground."

" Why ? "

" Because the reproductive side of our nature can lie dormant for years and yet become active should necessity arise, in the same way that our sex instinct can get along quite happily without expression."

" You may be right about the reproductive side of the business, but I'm not so sure about the other. I should have thought that the sex instinct was pretty active in most men."

" Maybe, but it is possible to keep it under control."

" Yes, of course ; I don't suggest that we should all indulge in an orgy of licence, but I think people are becoming tired of this constant harping on ' control '. I've frequently heard fellows say that it is essential for them to give expression to their feelings, and I must say I am inclined to agree with them. I believe one would do better work if one had a girl to live with, or at any rate have an affair with occasionally."

" Maybe, but if the setting is all wrong you will soon find that love flies out of the window."

" Oh, I don't see why the setting should be so wrong as you suggest. Lots of men have small flats to which they can take their girls, and many girls who work on their own have their own places. I admit that these people often fall down on the contraceptive issue, at any rate from your point of view, but I'm bound to say that I don't find all the psychological difficulties developing about which you and others have spoken so frequently during this conference. I think young people to-day are more healthy minded and take all this in their stride. Lots of students have affairs of this kind, which are very often quite satisfactory while they last."

" Exactly ! While they last. And what happens after the affair has come to an end ? "

" They get fed up for a bit, of course, but they soon find

someone else. Oh, I know you think that is all wrong, but I should say that the majority of these affairs go on for quite a long time, and very often end in marriage. And if they don't it may be a very good thing for everyone concerned."

"I know all that. I see these cases every day of my life, and it is my considered opinion that in almost every case this kind of behaviour leads to eventual unhappiness and disillusionment for someone or other. Of course you may say that it is worth while and we all have to learn by experience, which is true up to a point, but I can hardly believe that you would suggest that all young people should behave in this way."

"Well, a large majority of them do."

"Precisely, and look at the mess we have got ourselves into. I do not suggest that we must all behave the same way. I know very well that there are individual variations and difficulties, but I do suggest that life must be conducted according to certain definite standards and values. If the student finds life boring in his digs, so does the young factory worker find life difficult in an overcrowded home in which there is no privacy and frequent quarrelling. But these people are in the minority; you can't have the whole of society behaving in this way."

"Why not, if they want to?"

"For the reasons I and others have tried to give you at this conference. If we haven't convinced you, then all I can say is that I am sorry. I am inclined to think that the real trouble with you is that you haven't sorted out your own particular problem, whatever that may be, and are trying to find social approval for your own inclinations."

"Perhaps. But I must say that I know lots of my friends who are having quite satisfactory affairs."

"From their point of view, perhaps; but you are not in a position to take the long view; you don't see the results as some of us do, and I can assure you that the results are not pretty. Someone is always hurt, sometimes pretty badly."

"And your solution is early marriage?"

"Properly prepared for," Dr. Hansell said, with a smile.

"And you would not allow any love-making before?"

"But of course, only it must be done reasonably and in accordance with positive standards."

"How do you mean?"

"The guiding rule must be one of motive. If two people are genuinely fond of each other, and the relationship is open and wholesome, and unaccompanied by any sense of shame or guilt, and at the same time intelligently restrained; then, as it is a natural part of courtship, it is all right. But it must not be prolonged indefinitely, and must always be conducted with forethought and a due sense of responsibility. If, on the other hand, a man is merely attracted physically by a pretty girl and wants to have some 'fun' and see how far he can go; then I think he is using his sex energy in the wrong way—in a selfish way—which will benefit neither himself nor the girl. If she has any sense she will stop him. Girls can make a man shut up quickly enough if they want to. The trouble is that they don't always want to. One thing leads to another; a touch leads to a kiss, and from kissing it is but a short step to fondling, and fondling quickly leads to coitus. In my opinion, petting is a disastrous pastime."

"Why?"

"It can be indulged in for quite a long time without the couple realising that they are stimulating their emotions without obtaining the proper relief of tension which should occur normally in coitus. This constant titillation of the senses leads to an unhealthy, emotional state which shows itself in nervousness, irritability and, later on, in an inability on the part of the girl to experience normal satisfaction in marriage without considerable re-adjusment."

"What's the effect on the man?"

"The same, in the long run."

"You may be right, but I think a couple like that would be much better off if they went to bed with each other properly."

"And jump out of the frying-pan into the fire? No! I am sure you are wrong. Is the whole of society to behave like this? Where are you going to draw the line? I think young people should be taught to remain continent until such time as they can marry, and be prepared for marriage along the lines I have suggested. That there are exceptions

I know, but that should be the general line. If, on the other hand, the couple decide that they must live together, then for goodness sake insist upon them getting proper advice. If you think I am avoiding the issue, I am equally convinced that you are doing likewise."

They both laughed.

"The kind of behaviour you seem to advocate," Dr. Hansell said, "over-emphasises the sexual element and takes it out of its proper context. Besides, the average woman is not content with a mere physical activity; it does not provide her with the fundamentals she needs—permanence, love, children, family—and if she doesn't get that she will suffer for it in some way eventually. Sex must be filled with love, rather than love be subservient to sex."

"You surely don't suggest that a fellow should go on for years without some relief," Mr. Holmes said.

"Of course not, but it all depends upon what you mean by relief. Continence is not incompatible with health."

"There you go again, doctor. Sublimation! I thought we had finished with that sort of thing years ago. It has worried moralists for years."

"How do you mean?" Dr. Hansell enquired.

"Well, they have always preached about it, but it has never worked satisfactorily for them or for the people they have preached to. All that they have done is to make people regard sex as base and animal and disgusting; as something to be sat upon, squashed or defeated in some way. But why should I be saying all this? I am really taking the words out of your own mouth."

"Quite true, but so far as I can make out you don't believe that a man can put his own house in order. You appear to be at the mercy of every wind that blows. I don't believe sublimation means repression. It is an unconscious state which happens to a man largely owing to his having a profound and valuable purpose in life. Having found this purpose, everything else has to fit into it. But the purpose must be creative and on a higher level of life, which means that it must be concerned with other people; with social welfare in some way. This means that the individual must re-arrange his life—give up his baser habits and his less reputable friends and so on. If he spends his evenings drinking and tale-telling or reading erotic literature, he will undo the good work that he has already done. He must consciously acquire different habits until he does it unconsciously. Habit of mind will produce habit of body and lead to discipline. Whilst I am not one of those who believe that the fetish of constant games will enable a man to manage his sex life, I think you will agree that the man who has learnt to discipline himself, whether it be by training for sport, walking or work, will find it easier to discipline his sexual thoughts and actions."

"Yes, I do, but I think that schoolmasters pay far too great attention to this aspect of the matter. I never found that the games I played at school helped me to sublimate my sex energy."

"Perhaps not, but they did enable you to take a more sensible attitude to life, surely. The very fact of being healthy and having plenty to do must have an effect, you know."

"Possibly, but to suggest that constant exercise and movement help boys to manage their sex lives is, in my opinion, an idea which is not borne out by facts."

"I agree with you. It by no means follows that the captain of Rugger or the best-trained athlete in the school is more able to manage his sex life than the boy who does none of these things, provided the latter keeps his body healthy. On the contrary, he may find it more difficult. A full, interesting and active life away from the glamour of false living is, of course, more likely to ease matters than the reverse. There will always be an over-plus of energy, which must be controlled by conscious direction, just as any other of life's activities must be consciously controlled. Whilst accepting sublimation on the one hand, we must recognise that sex energy requires a good deal of active control."

"Do you consider masturbation a suitable outlet?"

"Perhaps; but I want notice of that question. I cannot answer it with a simple yes nor no. I can say this, however. I think we have made far too much trouble over masturbation—or self-stimulation, as I prefer to call it—in the past.

We have not distinguished between the sex play of infants, the self-stimulation of the adolescent, or the masturbation of the adult. They differ profoundly. In so far as adolescents are concerned there is undoubtedly a natural release to be found in occasional self-stimulation, provided it is done willingly, without fear or worry, and with no after-feeling of shame. Moreover, it must be accepted as an emotional outlet whilst the act is being performed."

"What do you mean by that?"

"I mean that it is no good a chap saying that he will do this and then, whilst he is doing it, tell himself that he ought not to be doing it or that he will go so far and no farther, and then finally, and in spite of his resolution to the contrary, have an ejaculation. That is bad. Rather must he do it, enjoy it and forget about it. Then it will have no adverse power over him, but become what it really is—a natural outlet for a state of intolerable tension. Done in this way the individual will release the strain and be able to get on with his work and, what is even more important, it will lose its power over him. Done in any other way he will feel tired and 'shagged', to use a schoolboy expression."

"That is rather an advanced view, isn't it? I can't imagine my schoolmasters approving it."

"Perhaps not, but a great many schoolmasters do accept this point of view and try to get it across to their boys. And I should say it is the accepted medical teaching now. Of course, like everything else, it has its dangers. There will always be the person who says that as there is nothing wrong with masturbation; we can all do it whenever we wish to; but that is not what I mean at all. People who talk like that are merely trying to find excuses for their own behaviour. It is only to be used as an outlet for natural tension, and not for a tension that is constantly being produced by thought or action. When used in any other way I should say that it was a symptom of something else—an indication of some underlying frustration, worry or anxiety which ought to be discovered and brought to light."

"You have discussed it from the point of view of the school-boy, would you allow its being used as an outlet for tension in young men?"

"Certainly. Combine it with an intelligent attitude to sex, a desire to discipline oneself and a respect for personality, and I should say it would tide a man over a difficult period of life."

"And you consider it would be better for a man to do that than to have connection?"

"No, of course not. The best use of sex energy is with a woman in marriage, but that isn't always possible. There may be a hundred and one reasons why coitus should not take place. In that case excessive tension can be relieved in the way I have suggested. That does not mean that a man can take his girl out every night and make love to her for an hour and then relieve his tension by having an ejaculation either at the time or later. That, I hope you will agree, is a complete misuse of sex energy; it is bad for him and bad for the girl."

"Yes, certainly. Are you sure that behaving in the way you suggest won't interfere with a man's capacity in marriage?"

"Absolutely. It will only cause difficulty in marriage if the man is convinced that, because he did it as a boy at school or when he was a young man, he did himself harm and weakened himself or injured himself permanently, and that can be quickly put right. In such cases the fellow is full of fear and anxiety, and directly he has a premature ejaculation—which probably happens in about 75 per cent. of cases anyway; he fears the worst and gets into an awful stew, and is quite convinced that his marriage is wrecked. You will find that such men have fought against the temptation for years, have dammed back their emotions and finally stopped all sex activity. That pleases them very much, because they think they have become masters of their own house, whereas in actual fact they have done nothing of the kind. They have either dammed down their sex emotion to such an extent that they eventually do become incapable of expressing themselves satisfactorily in marriage, in which case they often develop some strange illness or habit, or they do something which, in many ways, is much worse and indulge in mental masturbation."

"What is that?"

"The individual allows himself to imagine all sorts of sexual situations—to phantasy or day-dream, as we call it—and by this means obtain an erection, but he never allows himself to go quite far enough to have an ejaculation. That, to him, is the dangerous thing—the loss of semen. He doesn't realise that his sex organs make semen much as his salivary glands make saliva, and there is always plenty of that. The glands don't lose their capacity through use.

"I would add this, however, that just as the heart or lungs of an adolescent of sixteen or so are not developed, so are his sex organs not fully mature, and they had much better be left alone to manage themselves. The night loss is a natural outlet for excessive fluid. I would far rather deal with a person who has practised self-stimulation as an adolescent than one who says he has never done anything. The latter is far more likely to have difficulty in marriage than the former. We have got to realise that the problem of self-stimulation—apart from the release of tension I have discussed—is a psychological one, and not a physical one."

"How so?"

"It is Jung who points out that most of us grow up more quickly physically than emotionally. He says that our consciousness rises out of the depths of our unconscious mind, ' like separate islands which only gradually unite to form a continent '—a continuous consciousness.[1] A youth of marriageable age has only just started to emerge from what he calls ' the mists of original unconsciousness '. There's a passage in one of his books which illustrates his point of view. After pointing out that youth has wide regions which still lie in the shadow of unconsciousness, so that he possesses only a partial understanding of himself, Jung goes on to say that in reality he is only ' imperfectly informed as to the motives of others and of himself. As a rule he acts almost entirely from unconscious motives. He thinks he is acting consciously and wisely, but it remains a great and surprising discovery when he finds that what he thought was the final peak is in reality nothing but the lowest step of a very long approach. The greater the extent of the unconsciousness, the less is marriage a free choice; a fact that shows itself

[1] Jung, "Marriage". Contribution to Analytical Psychology.

subjectively in the sense of the driving power of fate so clearly felt when one is in love.'[1] So, you see, youth is constantly trying to run before he can walk; to use the physical in a complete sense before he is ready for the experience. He still has to learn to use his reason and his intellect, to exercise self-control and acquire a respect and reverence for his body and mind."

" I see. What about masturbation in adults ? "

" That is more difficult to answer. If it is done to release emotional tension, or as a substitute for coitus—as for instance when a married man is away from his wife for some time—and if it is then done in the way I have suggested, it is harmless. If, on the other hand, it is done *in preference* to the act of coitus, it is pathological, and the individual needs treatment. In this case sex is being used as an escape from reality, and there is failure to grow up and realise that its rightful use is in conjunction with one of the opposite sex. Sexual expression is never really being used on its highest level unless it is used between a mature man and woman who know what they are doing and have a creative and positive purpose before them. Thus it is misused whenever it causes harm to another or, of course, to oneself. It follows from this that all other sexual expression is a departure from the ideal, and that sex affairs between two people of the same sex are sterile and will always lead to trouble. Self-stimulation therefore is a departure from the ideal because the person is satisfying himself; he has turned in on himself."

" So even the adolescent isn't living up to the ideal ? "

" The adolescent isn't old enough to marry. He is immature, and his emotions and reactions are those of immaturity. There are many things we do in adolescence which we do not do when we grow up. That is one of them. Self-stimulation may be regarded as a normal activity of the adolescent, out of which he gradually passes through direction and control to marriage and the complete fulfilment of his sexual needs. His aim should be to reduce its frequency and minimise its importance."

" I see."

. . . . .

[1] Jung, " Marriage ". Contribution to Analytical Psychology.

"Do you mind discussing the matter from another angle for a moment?" Mr. Holmes said. "What you have just said may be good enough for some people, but how would you approach the problem from a religious point of view? What sort of advice would you give to a fellow who has a definite religious basis to his life? Sex is usually dealt with from the religious angle at school, and yet the results aren't very satisfactory."

"You are quite right. Too often sex and confirmation are still muddled up in an unhealthy relationship. An understanding of the religious approach necessitates some understanding of the composition and action of the mind. Not only are we born with a complicated system of instincts and emotions which work through the mind; but our whole personality is made up of these instincts, the mind itself, and our intelligence, all of which are acted upon by the environment in which we live. The mind is capable of knowing, feeling and deciding, and acts through the brain, but is not the brain. We are also given the ability to appreciate abstract principles, such as truth, beauty and goodness. Furthermore, most of us believe that we have souls, and realise that we can draw upon spiritual powers if we wish to do so. We do this in many ways; through communion with our friends, by reading; but the chief method is by prayer."

"That seems to mean harping on the very theme one wants to escape."

"That is just where so many people get confused. The method of praying is all-important: Prayer directed towards the actual condition that the individual is trying to change may do more harm than good, by simply concentrating the mind on the very thing that he wants to conquer. The mere reception of an impression or stimulus by the mind is not in itself evil or sinful; it is when we dwell upon the impression and allow our imagination free run that any conception of sin can enter into the problem. If we know that the reading of certain books, or the companionship of certain people, or some particular mode of life encourages the production of these undesirable stimuli, we must endeavour to rearrange our lives in such a way that their effect is minimised. It is no use trying to deal with an intolerable emotion when we are in its grip. We should be better advised to consider the problem dispassionately at some other time, and then formulate a course of action. We can then pray constructively and in a purposeful way towards maintaining the necessary strength of will to continue the course of action we have set ourselves. It is no use just asking to have the trouble taken away from us; we have to do something about it ourselves. It is Leslie Weatherhead, I think, who points out that in a battle between imagination and will, the former usually wins. And so we must endeavour to bring the imagination to our aid. This can usually be done by consciously allowing it to dwell on other matters in which we are interested. By these means we can obtain a considerable measure of control; but the process is difficult and needs considerable perseverance and understanding. We almost always need outside help. There is every reason why we should cultivate a wholesome outlook concerning the problems of sexual behaviour. Half our troubles arise because development in the realm of sexual morality has not kept pace with development in other branches of life."

" How do you mean ? "

" Women are demanding a place in the sun, to-day; they say they have a right to exercise other faculties than those of reproduction. The domination and superiority of man are gradually losing ground, and this necessarily creates situations which demand considerable readjustment. As you yourself have pointed out, we are living in an age when there's an enormous stimulus to sexual expression such as our grandparents never dreamed of. Our dances are provocative; our cinemas are an appeal to the emotions, whether of love or cruelty; our theatres are largely concerned with problems of sex; and our literature delves into the intimacies of the love life with amazing frankness. Even the use of the word love has lost its meaning. We talk about the ' love life ' of prostitutes; the love of man for man, or woman for woman; pre-marital love and married love. How can the ' love ' that a prostitute is forced to bestow on her passing visitor be compared with the passionate interchange of affection between two young lovers ? There is, too, an interest in the abnormal, as is shown by the mass of literature which deals with unhealthy sexual abnormalities and the widespread sale of anything pornographic."

"Yes, it is extraordinary what some fellows read. Most of the stuff is merely suggestive."

"That is just the point. They are really sexually starved. It is interesting to speculate on the effect that different types of sex books have on people. There is the gaudy little book that suggests so much and tells so little. There are those productions that arrive in secretive covers and are so very unsatisfactory because even our lowest emotions have their satiation point. Finally, there is the book that endeavours to speak constructively, wholesomely and scientifically. It is when we come to read with our intellect, for the sake of acquiring real knowledge, of climbing from the unconsciousness, that Jung speaks about, to the realm of Reason; of formulating a plan of life that is not destructive to our personality, that the perusal of such books is beneficial to us."

"But it isn't only the books which are suggestive, surely. I think that the way some women dress or don't dress is most provocative; with their rouge and lip-stick and all. They make life damned difficult for a fellow."

"But life wouldn't be any easier if you abolished cosmetics. We must learn to accept these changes naturally and healthily. We've got to put sex on to a higher level of consciousness; enjoy it by all means, but enjoy it beneficially; only then will it take its proper place in our lives."

"You think, then, that dress and rouge have a sexual significance?"

"Of course they have, and a perfectly natural one too, but we mustn't allow them to become an obsession. Again you must remember that different things attract different people. Some of us are stirred by a particular face or figure which leaves another unmoved. Some people like blondes, others brunettes; some prefer the tall, athletic type; others the short and dumpy. Hands, too, can be delightfully attractive or positively revolting. Hairy people are attractive to one person and repulsive to another. Some scents are intoxicating; others repugnant. Some eyes are arrestingly attractive; others the reverse. We can't help being stimulated by these various factors. The stimulus must be received in such a way that it is not destructive to the personality. It is the little things in life which are frequently so important. How often have you not found your emotion aroused by a pretty face only to have it immediately destroyed by the lady's voice?"

"That's true enough," Mr. Holmes said.

"We all have our particular likes and dislikes, and ought to recognise them. It would be ridiculous for a woman who was repelled by a squint, to marry a cross-eyed man. And some woman will like the squint."

"But such an attraction is a perversion, surely?"

"Maybe, but who is to say where normality ends and perversion begins when it comes to sexual attraction? Consciously or unconsciously, we are always exciting the emotions of those around us. The world would be very dull if there were no pretty women, no attractive men, no plays or pictures. Unfortunately, we have created a situation in which the strain and conflict are too great and for which we have provided no adequate relief; unless you consider that pre-marital relationships, homosexual practices, flirting and petting parties are a suitable relief. But they aren't; they are a misuse of sex. This is the 'modern nervousness' to which Freud refers. Yet we can't be surprised when people indulge in these activities if we take no steps to deal constructively with the problem."

. . . . .

"You haven't said anything about mutual stimulation yet," Mr. Holmes said.

"I have already suggested that it is a misuse of sex energy when I said that sex activity should only occur with a person of the opposite sex. Mutual stimulation is a baby habit indicating that the individual hasn't grown up emotionally, however physically perfect he or she may be. It is no doubt very enjoyable whilst it lasts, but it is a selfish and sterile relationship. It can lead to nothing but sorrow and quarrelling. In so far as the adolescent is concerned it is to be condemned absolutely, because once started it runs like wildfire through a form or school and, further, because it involves another person and tends to fix emotions at an immature level. We all pass through a stage when we are attracted to people of our own sex; there is nothing wrong in that—it is the basis of friendship, and quite natural. But the stage must be managed properly, and the personality of another person must not be abused any more than the personality of another should be abused in the heterosexual sphere. Once started, it is easy to continue, because the habit grows and there are plenty of people to practise on. In so far as my experience goes, I should say that here again mutual stimulation is an indication of some underlying disharmony; the elder boy, for instance, or, if you like it better, the leader and promoter of the affair—the masculine element—has not grown up properly and is, for some reason or other, unable to make a natural transference to heterosexuality, whereas the smaller pretty boy—the feminine element—is at first ignorant and then conscious of pleasure, excitement and power. He acquires a form of behaviour which makes him a menace in a school, because he goes out of his way to seduce his elders; he becomes a sort of prostitute."

"Would you expel the boys?"

"Certainly not. I would have every case looked into most carefully and would see to it that those concerned—because there is always more than two—were properly helped. A jaw from the headmaster is useless unless the headmaster is wise, in which case he doesn't give a jaw, although he eventually gets the whole story quite clearly put before him. He then decides what to do. Those needing it receive expert help. Occasionally it is necessary to remove an individual whose influence is really bad, but in that case it would be made clear to him and everyone else that he is being removed because he is ill and needs treatment and has let the school down, and not because he has committed a sex offence. Occasionally one finds a psychopathic personality in a school, in which case he or she may do untold harm before he is discovered and dealt with."

"What is a psychopathic personality?"

"The psychopathic personality is one of the hardest

types of personality to understand. It is an abnormal personality from the very beginning, the individual never developing a normal moral sense, and being unable to tell the difference between right and wrong. He is often very charming and intelligent, but highly dangerous, because he is completely amoral."

" What is to be done with such people ? "

" That depends upon the individual case, and is far too complex a subject for us to discuss now. The point is that they occur and must be watched for. The teacher of the future should know enough psychology to be able to tell the difference between the child who is just naughty through high spirits and the strongly introverted or extraverted temperament. They all require different handling. The master who expels boys for sexual offences without first seeking expert advice—and several of them still exist—needs a little treatment himself. There is no need for these conditions to exist in the school of to-day." [1]

Dr. Hansell looked at the clock. " Time for bed, I think. I hope I have helped a bit."

" Yes, rather. You have given me plenty to think about. Thanks very much."

[1] See Griffith, Edward F., " The Road to Maturity ", Methuen, 1947.

CHAPTER XV

"THE WAGES OF SIN"

MRS. BELLAMY had been quite right when she said that Betty Romney was worried over a man. Her affair with Montague Brain wasn't working to plan. And yet it had all seemed so simple when they had talked it over to begin with. They were both young—Monty was twenty-five and Betty twenty-one—they both had jobs in London, Monty in the City, where he had good prospects but a dull job, and Betty with a firm of solicitors who paid her a good wage, for she was as efficient as she was attractive. They had many common interests, such as dancing, music and the theatre; the same circle of friends, and the same likes and dislikes in food and drink. What more natural——! But let them tell the story for themselves——

"May I smoke?" Betty demanded as she walked restlessly about Dr. Hansell's consulting-room the day after the conference had ended.

"By all means, if it helps," Dr. Hansell answered, opening a drawer and producing a box of cigarettes which he kept for such emergencies.

"Thanks! I must talk to someone, and from what I hear of you from Wendy and Mrs. Bellamy, I think you'll understand. Monty and I have been living together for the last year; I don't mean actually living in the same house, but, well—how can I put it?"

"I understand well enough."

"I live at home, but do pretty well as I like, and Monty has been lucky enough to find a small flat of his own. I don't get on any too well at home as a matter of fact—Father is a bit sticky and Mother fusses too much, so I stay in town a good deal with a girl friend. The family want to marry me off, but I'm not too keen, especially as both my sisters have made a hash of matrimony. Besides, Monty and I don't believe in running into things like that. He thinks that people ought to try each other out first, and I agree with him. He gave me some books to read. I'm sure my sisters would have been wiser to have tried out their husbands first of all. Everyone knows that half the marriages that go wrong are messed up because people don't understand the physical side of life, and half the people who get married do so either because they have to or because they want to have sex experience and that is the only way they can get it legitimately. Most of them haven't got the courage to experiment for themselves first of all. Besides, Monty doesn't approve of babies; he says that the world is in such a muddle that it isn't right to bring children into it. In which case half the reason for marriage has disappeared."

" And you agree with him ? "

" Oh, yes. Don't you ? "

" Not altogether," Dr. Hansell said, smiling. " It is rather a negative philosophy of life, don't you think—a bit selfish ? "

" Oh, no. You've got it all wrong. Monty isn't selfish— not a bit of it. He'd sell his coat off his back for you."

" I see. And so you started your experiment a year ago ? "

" Yes."

" And it hasn't been a success from the physical point of view ? "

" No. But what makes you think that ? "

" You're trying so hard to justify your position. Besides, you're all strung up; you can't sit still for a moment. I would never expect to find a happily married woman behaving as you're behaving now, a year after her marriage."

" But we aren't married."

" Exactly ! But you're living as if you were—at least, you spend much of your time together."

" Oh yes, I often stay up for two or three nights at the flat, and we get away for week-ends occasionally."

" And it hasn't worked ? "

" No. I'm afraid it hasn't."

" Why not ? "

" Hundreds of reasons. It was all right for a bit, but I suppose I expected too much. I thought it would be grand, doing things for him, and helping in his work. He started off by letting me do a little typing, but now he doesn't seem to like me taking an interest in that side of his life. Most of the time we seem to be going to parties, and when we get back to the flat he is always making love to me."

"That was the main purpose of the arrangement, wasn't it?"

"But it doesn't work."

"Why not?"

"I can't explain." She stubbed out one cigarette, and lit another.

"Let me see if I can help," the doctor said, kindly. "You say that the physical side doesn't work. You mean by that, that you get very little satisfaction?"

The girl nodded.

"You expected a wonderful experience, which unfortunately you never achieved, I suppose?"

"It was all right at first. He was awfully kind and understanding. But it never meant anything to me. I expected too much. And he frightened me. He was so—violent. I never told him I didn't like it, but he seemed to sense it. That made matters worse, because we used to quarrel."

"Weren't you afraid of having a baby?"

"No. I wasn't afraid of that."

"What form of contraceptive did you use?"

"We didn't. I left all that to him."

"Surely you discussed the matter beforehand?"

"Oh yes. We agreed not to use anything. Monty said it would be all right."

"You mean you practised what is known at coitus interruptus?"

"I suppose so."

"But that isn't a normal method of performing the sex act; it's only practised with a view to preventing pregnancy."

"I know; but lots of people use it—at least, Monty says so. Isn't it safe?"

"No, I'm afraid it isn't. I thought you said you had read some books on the subject."

"So I have, but I didn't bother with them very much; Monty seemed to know all about it."

"THE WAGES OF SIN"

"But that is one of the main reasons why you didn't get any sensation. Coitus interruptus only works satisfactorily in a minority of couples."

"Why isn't it safe?"

"That will take me a minute or two to explain. You know that the male seed, or sperms, are manufactured in the testicles and the female eggs in the ovary?"

"Yes, and one egg bursts from the ovary every month and passes down the tube to the womb, where it grows into a baby if it is fertilised. If it isn't, it passes away in the period."

"That's very well explained," Dr. Hansell said. "Now the sperms are always being manufactured in enormous quantities, and are mixed with a fluid called the seminal fluid, which nourishes and protects them. The whole is called semen, which leaves the body through the tube called the urethra, which passes down the penis. This organ is capable of becoming stiff or erect, and thus of being introduced into the vagina or front passage of the woman. The discharge or ejaculation of semen is accompanied by feelings of considerable pleasure. You probably know all that."

"Most of it, I think."

"What you do not know, or don't seem to have realised the significance of, is that the semen may contain anything up to five hundred million sperms, one of which is capable of fertilising the egg. After fertilisation the other sperms all die off. Coitus interruptus, or 'being careful', as so many people term it, often fails because, even supposing the penis is removed most carefully from the vagina before ejaculation, that does not mean that a drop of the fluid has not already leaked down the urethra and so become deposited upon the walls of the vagina. This drop could easily contain several thousand sperms and, as I have said, one sperm is capable of fertilising an egg. This also explains how it is that in certain cases the sperms find their way up the whole length of the vagina, even when they are only deposited on the outside of the sex organs. Did you know that?"

"No."

"Another objection to coitus interruptus is that in most cases the woman fails to achieve her proper sensation. This is because sexual excitement fills the sex organs of both partners with blood and causes a state of engorgement which, while being quite obvious in the man, is by no means so obvious in the woman, since her sex organs are inside the body. The ejaculation in the man brings with it a feeling of satisfaction and relief from tension, leaving him momentarily tired, but profoundly contented. A similar experience should occur in the woman, and is known as the orgasm. The removal of the penis from the vagina at the critical moment frequently deprives the woman of that final stimulus which is so necessary to cause the orgasm. It seems to be more difficult for a woman to achieve a proper sensation than it is for a man."

" Why is that ? "

" Oh, there are a variety of reasons ; it is a most complicated matter, but the fact remains that if a woman does not achieve this relief, she is left in a state of tension.[1] If this continues for a long time, it affects her health, making her irritable, nervous and overstrung. A woman can feel sensation in two different places : the clitoris, which is a small, sensitive organ, rather like a tiny penis, situated between the inner lips of skin protecting the entrance to the vagina ; and secondly, inside the vagina itself. An experienced woman can often obtain several orgasms before the man has an ejaculation, if he is a good lover and able to exercise sufficient control and she doesn't hold herself back. Some women can achieve an orgasm by means of coitus interruptus, but even they will agree that the final mutual orgasm is far more satisfying. For women who have had little or no sex experience, I think coitus interruptus is most unsatisfactory and leads to much unhappiness, as in your own case. You found the relationship from which you expected so much devoid of all real satisfaction, and so you began to avoid its performance whenever possible because it only made you feel all strung up and horrid. Am I right ? "

The girl nodded her head.

" You seem to have escaped becoming pregnant, which is something to be thankful for."

She laughed bitterly. " I'm not so sure."

[1] See Chapter XIII.

"Surely——!"

"I'm not certain. My periods are always so irregular that I never worry very much if they're late, but I have been a bit anxious lately, as I am nearly three weeks overdue. And you say that this method fails very frequently?"

"In at least sixty per cent. of cases, I should think."

"Oh dear, and I haven't been feeling too well lately, either."

"There are dozens of reasons why women miss their periods, besides that of pregnancy," Dr. Hansell said.

"Yes, I know; but I was pretty certain before I ever got into this room."

"Well, we'd better try and find out," Dr. Hansell said. "If you will go into the other room, I expect I shall be able to decide."

"All right," Betty answered, getting up and going towards the door. "But what happens if I am pregnant, God knows. You will help me, won't you?"

"Don't let us meet trouble half-way," the doctor replied.

As he waited for the girl to get ready he began pacing the room. What a mess she had made of things! Why wouldn't people try and find out about these matters before making such important decisions? Was this disinclination to take advice one of the penalties of being young? Was it necessary for everyone to buy their experience so dearly? Where did the fault lie? With the parents who avoided discussing these matters, or with our system of education which provided no adequate information? Most general practitioners or medical officers of health could help by telling people where to get proper advice, but they didn't bother very much even when they were asked. The trouble was that most young people thought they knew everything, and wouldn't go to people for proper advice, or were afraid of being read a moral lecture. Oh well——! He shrugged his shoulders and went into the examination room. A quarter of an hour later the two had resumed their respective seats.

"What is the verdict?" Betty asked quietly.

"You're one of those people with whom it's impossible to be certain," Dr. Hansell replied. "The signs are very indefinite. If you are pregnant it's very early. However, don't worry yet, because I can settle the question quite simply by a test called the A.Z. test."[1]

"I don't think we need bother about that, Dr. Hansell. I'm quite sure in my own mind."

"But I am not, my dear; and if I can't tell you, I don't see how you can be so certain; that's not reasonable. Lots of women frighten themselves so much that their periods cease for the time being. You may be like that. I can give you a definite answer very quickly, but it is essential to be certain. The test only takes about two days, and consists of making a special analysis of the urine, so you must let me have a specimen."

"I see, but supposing I am pregnant, what am I to do?"

"You can marry Monty, can't you?"

"Nothing would induce me to. Any love that I had for him died long ago. I don't think I ever really loved him. God! What a fool I've been."

[1] The A.Z. test for pregnancy, named after Doctors Aschheim and Zondek who discovered it some years ago, depends upon the fact that the urine of every pregnant woman contains special chemicals (hormones) secreted by the ovaries and the placenta (after-birth), which are essential to keep the baby properly fixed in the womb. If there are not plenty of them the woman may abort (miscarry). The amount of these hormones can be determined by special tests made on the urine. If therefore the urine from a pregnant woman is injected into a small animal, such as a non-pregnant mouse or a rabbit, the whole process of preparing the special lining in the womb is speeded up and brought to a head in a few hours or days. If the animal is now killed and the ovaries examined the state of preparedness can easily be determined. If nothing is there, then the woman is not pregnant.

It has now been found possible to carry out the test in a modified form on a special type of frog which comes from South Africa. The hormone will cause the frog to lay her eggs within a few hours. This test has the added advantage of giving a quicker result and the frog does not have to be killed but can be used again in a month or so.

Such tests are done in various hospitals and laboratories all over the country. All that is necessary is to send a clean eight-ounce medicine bottle full of urine to the laboratory, together with the name, address and, if desired, a telephone number and presumed state of pregnancy, plus a thirty-shilling postal order, when an answer will be given by post or 'phone within forty-eight hours, stating whether the result is positive (pregnant) or negative.

The address of such a laboratory can be obtained from any doctor or from the Marriage Guidance Council, 78 Duke St., Grosvenor Square, London, W.1, or the Family Planning Association, 69 Eccleston Square, London, S.W.1, or from any of the branches of either of these organisations.

Dr. Hansell looked at her kindly. She was almost crying.

"I don't see what alternatives you've got, unless you go away and have the baby without anyone knowing anything about it."

"I could never keep it from my people—and I can't possibly let them know; they're terribly conventional."

"But why not marry Monty——?"

"I tell you I won't marry him. I hate him. Can't you get rid of it for me?"

"My dear girl, surely you know that abortion is illegal unless there is some medical reason for interference. Even then the legality is uncertain; and you are perfectly healthy."

"But lots of people get rid of babies, don't they? I've heard of people who have managed it."

"I daresay you have, but the operation is usually done by incompetent people and often leads to trouble; the women frequently become poisoned and often die."

"I think that would be easier than the disgrace."

"Now look here, young woman," Dr. Hansell said, a little more sternly: "you must try and pull yourself together. You have deliberately decided that the worst has occurred, but I am by no means so certain. Anyway, you have plenty of time to decide what action you are going to take. The first thing to do is to make absolutely certain; if you let me have that specimen tomorrow, I'll be able to give you an answer in a few days' time. Until then you can do nothing, so you may as well think the matter over, talk to Mr. Brain and, if you're a sensible girl, take your mother into your confidence."

"I could never do that, Dr. Hansell; it would kill her."

"My dear girl, do try and remember that mothers are far more understanding than most of you young people think. Only very rarely have I come across one who won't respond sensibly if the matter is put in the correct light. Would you like me to talk to her?"

"You can't do that," the girl answered quickly. "It is very kind of you, but you don't know Mother; she would never understand. No! I shall have to settle this by myself. Luckily I have some money of my own."

"Look here, my dear; don't be foolish. You are being thoroughly unreasonable and jumping to conclusions without sufficient evidence."

Betty looked dully at Dr. Hansell. "I know all right," she said at last. "I've known for some time, really."

"But I tell you——!"

"It's very kind of you to take so much trouble, Doctor, and I understand your position exactly. I'm afraid I haven't any great faith in your tests; I've made my bed, and I must lie on it."

She got up.

"My dear girl, for heaven's sake go slowly and think the matter over. Let me have the specimen, and come and see me again, will you?"

"I'll let you have the specimen if you want it, but I doubt if I shall come and see you again."

"Well, have a talk to Monty, then. Please!"

"I'll do that," Betty said at length. "But this is my affair. I went into it with my eyes open, and I have been a damned fool. I can hardly believe that I could have been so stupid. Monty has nothing to do with it—at least, he can't do anything about it that'll be any use. I know that he would marry me all right, but I'd rather die than be tied up to him for the rest of my life."

"But he is partly responsible for the trouble, and it is only right that he should shoulder some of the burden!" Dr. Hansell exclaimed. "I am dead against young men getting off scot free. He has a lot to answer for."

"Oh, I don't know; he did his best according to his lights. The mistake was mine in not finding out a bit more beforehand."

"Or your parents', possibly," Dr. Hansell said.

"Perhaps; they never told me a thing, neither did my sisters. I must be going. Thank you for your kindness. Please don't think ill of me."

"You will come and see me again?"

"I'll think about it."

"Have you any objection to my getting in touch with Monty?"

"I wouldn't like you to do that—and yet I don't know.

You might be able to stop him getting some other girl into a similar mess. He's all right really; just ignorant, like me."

She held out her hand. "Good-bye, Doctor, and thank you."

"Good-bye, my dear. I will ring up directly I hear anything."

"Thank you. If you don't mind, though, I would rather ring you up. I'll send the specimen in the morning. Good-bye."

Dr. Hansell frowned deeply as he shut his door. That sort of case worried him immensely. He felt so incapable. If she were pregnant—and he thought it more than likely—it seemed probable that she would try to find someone who would perform an abortion. He hated to think of the possible consequences. How ridiculous it all was! here was he, a respectable physician, debarred by his conscience and the antiquated laws of the country from doing anything to help the girl. And yet society tolerated an arrangement by which she could go to any man or woman who was only too willing to do the operation for her, provided she paid sufficiently well. Ridiculous! Monstrous! What fools parents were to allow their young people to grow up in such abysmal ignorance! Well, he had done his best, and perhaps he was worrying unnecessarily. He looked at his watch, made a hurried note to get in touch with Montague Brain, and rang the bell.

. . . . .

Montague Brain appeared the next day in response to a telephone request from Dr. Hansell's secretary.

"It's very good of you to come, Mr. Brain," the doctor said, indicating a vacant chair. "Please make yourself comfortable, and smoke if you feel inclined. Has Miss Romney been to see you?"

"Yes," the young man replied, filling his pipe. "But I couldn't get very much sense out of her, except that she thought she was going to have a baby; but she's always getting scared about that, in spite of all I do to reassure her. She said she'd been to see you, but I couldn't discover what you had told her exactly. She often gets upset nowadays:

I think a great deal of her trouble is physiological. I understand that women become emotionally upset at the periods, especially if these are irregular. I have frequently suggested to her that she should consult someone and get things put right, so I am glad she has been to see you."

Dr. Hansell grunted. "I'm afraid it's more serious than that," he said at length. "You will forgive me if I speak plainly?"

"By all means; I like plain speaking—one knows where one is."

"Judging by what Miss Romney has told me, Mr. Brain, you seem to be a young man with ideas, although some of them struck me as being a trifle pessimistic. Still, there is an underlying truth in what you say. Civilisation is certainly in a muddle; but, if I understand you, your solution lies in the direction of *laissez-faire*, of fiddling while Rome burns. To you everything is so hopeless that it is useless to do anything about it; but surely if we all behaved just as we liked, the world would be in a truly chaotic state."

"Well, it is pretty chaotic, isn't it?" the young man said vehemently. "Take this subject of sexual morality, for instance. The inherent evilness of sex has been impressed on us for so long that most of us have really come to fear it. Marriage is impossible until years after we are ready for it, and even then every obstacle is put in our way. If we live promiscuously we are dubbed anti-social; if we marry we soon get sick of the unequal struggle and come to hate what we originally loved. If we want to make a new start, we must first of all commit adultery, and hang out the family washing for a perverted public to gloat over with sadistic pleasure. If our co-partner is foolish enough to commit adultery whilst this dismembering process is going on, we are denied any relief whatsoever, and are doomed to maintain a farcical appearance of happy wedlock; it is a sham before God and man."

"Much that you say is true," Dr. Hansell replied; "but the cure proposed by most people seems little better than the disease. If we refrain from marriage because it is too difficult and dangerous, we put in its place a freedom of sexual behaviour which will allow people to 'enjoy themselves', to use your own phrase. But this method as often leads to misery. Our romance fall to bits, our desire for sex gratification is frequently unsatisfied, and, unless we are very lucky, we find ourselves landed with maintenance orders, illegitimate babies or venereal disease. In any case, we become soured, unhappy and disillusioned, and seek relief in further excitement in order to escape from reality."

" That is very true, but if, on the other hand, we wait for several years before making a 'happy marriage', we find that we have held ourselves in check for so long that our sexuality has become distorted. That, at least, is what I have discovered from my reading."

"You are quite right," Dr. Hansell said; "but such a marriage is merely another attempt at escape. We have not recognised the underlying cause of our sickness."

"And what is that?"

"The repression of the sex instincts."

"But surely——!"

"One moment! You are going to say, no doubt, that the sex instinct is no longer repressed, but before coming to that decision we must understand what the term means. The old idea behind the taboo on sexual behaviour was largely based upon the assumption that the sex instinct was solely a reproductive instinct; but it is quite obvious that women have all sorts of emotional feelings which are not directly connected with the desire for reproduction. Women desire sex experience for its own sake as much as men do, but it has been to men's advantage in the past to ignore this fact, although they will readily allow the truth of the contention in their own case. It would be ridiculous to suggest that every time a man desires union he wants to satisfy his reproductive instinct by creating new life. The suggestion has only to be made to see how stupid it is. And the same applies to women. The trouble is that we will not face the fact that the satisfaction derived from the sex act is natural and beneficial in itself. The matter is discussed by Freud, who says that man's sexual instinct is not 'primarily meant to serve purposes of reproduction but is intended to furnish certain forms of gratification'.[1] He points out that our

[1] "Modern Sexual Morality and Modern Nervousness", published by the Eugenic Publishing Co., New York, p. 16.

sexual instincts consist of many single component parts; the desire for children is one, and the desire for sexual enjoyment is another. There are other parts, such as the aggressive and vindictive tendencies, which have to be sacrificed for the good of civilisation."

" How can one do that ? "

" By transforming the specific sexual tendencies into other channels, though this transference is never complete and cannot go on for ever. Freud also points out that [1] ' a certain degree of direct sexual satisfaction appears to be absolutely necessary for by far the greater number of natures ', and frustration of the need is avenged by manifestations which ' we must regard as illness '. Further, it must always be remembered that the energy derived from the sex instinct varies in different individuals, and that an enormous amount can be used for other activities. The instinct ' possesses the ability to displace its aim without materially losing its intensity '.[2] This means that the original sexual aim can be exchanged for another aim, not necessarily sexual, but closely related to it. This is the meaning of sublimation. The opposite process—fixation—leads to the development of abnormalities. That the reproductive purpose of sex and the desire for sexual enjoyment can be separated is not only a psychological truth, but can be borne out in an entirely different field of scientific investigation—that of Biology. Biologically speaking, the sex act—the mating aspect—and the reproductive act need by no means function together; the one can be used without the other."

" I didn't know that, although it sounds reasonable enough."

" You can read all about it here," Dr. Hansell said, passing a little book across to Montague Brain. " Take it home and have a look at it." [3]

" Thanks, I will."

" Let us return to our social problem," the doctor said, " and the cures I have outlined. The present malaise is caused both by a misunderstanding of the nature of sex

---

[1] " Collected Papers ", vol. ii, p. 83.
[2] *Ibid.*
[3] " Sex ", by Dr. P. B. Wiesner.

and by an unnatural repression of the sex instinct. In the first case we have a freer mingling of the sexes and a laxity in sexual behaviour which shows itself in promiscuity and petting parties; examples, in themselves, of the minor abnormalities and illnesses to which Freud draws attention. Sex relationships before marriage are the inevitable result of the present economic conditions and our system of late marriage. In the second case we have the long-drawn-out repression that has created an unhealthy state, which the 'happy marriage' you mentioned just now frequently comes too late to save. I heard of a couple recently who had been engaged for four years, and had worked themselves up into such a state of tension that they became utterly antagonistic. Marriage for them would be a calamity—they had waited too long."

Montague Brain fidgeted uneasily.

"Now let us bring this down to a consideration of the immediate problem which brings you here—your relationship with Betty Romney. Should I be right if I summed up your attitude as follows? You decided about a year ago that the future of civilisation being so uncertain and your economic condition likely to remain much the same for the next few years, thereby making it impossible for you to support a wife, even had you wished to, you might as well try an experimental relationship which might, eventually, lead to marriage. You believed that since many people tripped up over the physical, the obvious solution was to make sure of the physical. If the affair failed, no great harm would have been done; you could both try again. Have I stated the case fairly?"

"Yes, I think so."

"But it hasn't worked, has it?"

"I don't know about that. It has worked very well in the sense that it has proved my point negatively. Betty and I thought we were suited to each other, but we aren't; we went into the matter with our eyes open."

"You did, you mean."

"That isn't altogether fair, Doctor. We talked it all over carefully to start off with, and I explained everything to her, to the best of my ability, before we ever did anything. We agreed that if it didn't work there would be no recriminations and we could each go our own way. That it hasn't worked is obvious, though I can't account for it, because we seemed to have everything in our favour. On the other hand, the original idea has worked, because we've proved that we are not suited to each other. We may have some temporary unpleasantness at the moment, but that will soon pass; at least we've avoided the awful fate of being tied together for the rest of our lives."

"And you're free to make the experiment with someone else?"

"Naturally."

"And will the result be the same?"

"Not necessarily."

"Oh, but I think it will."

"Why?"

"Because you've approached the whole matter from the wrong angle. You have said, 'To hell with repression, let's experiment with the physical and see whether we can make it work.' But of whom have you been thinking? You say you talked it all out beforehand; but from whose point of view? I think you must agree that the answer can be given in two words—Montague Brain. You've completely ignored the true meaning of sex. Besides, your actual practice of the physical leaves much to be desired. You've looked at the whole question from a man's point of view, and completely forgotten that there is a woman's point of view as well, and that it's likely to be a very different one from yours. Your whole aim—an unconscious aim, no doubt—has been towards your own satisfaction. You started off without getting any preliminary advice or instruction and that, I must say, appears to me to be well-nigh criminal in these days."

"I read a good deal."

"Well, it didn't do you very much good, so far as I can see. You don't appear to me to know the simplest principles of sex behaviour, if I may say so without offence; you've not yet learned that the sex life is a dual relationship based on mutual consideration and unselfishness. You've taken as much as you can from that girl, but what have you given her in return ? A home ? Comradeship ? Children ? A life in which her own personality can develop ? A sense of security ? No ! You have given her none of these things —things which are of paramount importance to a woman. And yet you suggest the relationship is comparable to marriage. Why, my dear sir, there is no connection between the two. In no single instance can the two be compared, except in so far as you have shared the same bed. You've given no thought to the effect of the experience on the other individual or, if you have thought at all, you've presumed that her reactions are the same as your own. But they aren't, and they never will be. The whole affair is only a few degrees better than prostitution."

" Oh, I say——"

" Indeed yes. In fact, I'm not sure that the prostitute isn't in a better position, because she does at least get paid. I'm sorry, but I cannot see that in any single respect has Betty Romney got anything out of the affair. To you, the whole business was a try-out of the physical, but no woman is really concerned with the physical alone. Some men can approach women through the physical, and come to appreciate mental and spiritual qualities later. Most women, on the other hand, are primarily attracted to men by their work, or their conversation—their personality, if you like—and reach the physical afterwards. Physical experience, to them, must go hand in hand with all the other things that have been lacking in your relationship. I don't mean to say that it's impossible for such a relationship as yours to work, but it must be based on different principles, and must certainly have some chance of working well from the physical point of view. Yours had none ! "

" You don't give me credit for very much, do you, Doctor ? "

Dr. Hansell laughed dryly. " Please don't misunderstand me. I don't wish to imply that you didn't try, to the very best of your ability, to make the experiment a success ; I'm sure you did. It's simply that you didn't think ; you didn't understand ; you thought it all so much simpler than it really was."

" Then you don't believe in these relationships ? "

"It is no use saying that. They are here amongst us, and it is no use pretending they aren't. They are a sign of the times. But of one thing I am quite sure, and that is that they do not provide an answer to our social problem. As a matter of fact it isn't a question of pre-marital relationships versus marriage, rather is it one of ignorance versus purpose and teaching. There is no reason why you and Betty Romney could not have made a success of your relationship if you had designed it to have some creative value—some meaning beyond your own self-seeking pleasures and some understanding of each other's emotional needs. To suggest that she knew what she was about is ridiculous. She was bemused by you; left everything to you, and didn't even read properly the books you lent her. Even if you had married under these conditions you would have made a muddle of it because your attitude is quite wrong. Had you had some decent marriage preparation and learnt to change your ideas you might then have made a quite successful marriage. All the ingredients were there. But I am afraid the damage is done now, and there is very little chance of altering it. Sex feeling is a very tricky thing. Once it goes wrong it is very difficult to get right again. I have seen dozens of young married people get into just such a mess as you two are in now, simply because they were not taught. In my opinion no sex relationship should occur between people until they have real knowledge and real help."

"In that case it is probably a good thing we can part whilst the going is good."

"Possibly, because you are no longer in love with each other. But what a travesty you have made of the affair—how soured and bitter one or both of you will become, and how unnecessary it all is! You have hurt each other abominably. And one affair like that leads to another. I've seen it happen again and again. The girl is left disillusioned and unhappy, feeling the need for something she hasn't got, and so she looks round for someone to give it her, and the whole show starts again. No permanence, no stability. No! There is nothing to be said for these ill-thought-out affairs, any more than there is anything to say for an ill-thought-out marriage; indeed, there is more chance of a marriage becoming an eventual success because the very fact of being tied together forces people to think things out and make the necessary adjustments. There's no such necessity in a pre-marital relationship. On the other hand, it could be argued that a pre-marital relationship is more likely to work well because there is no obligation on either partner to stay with the other, so that both have to be on their best behaviour; neither can have a sense of possession. These affairs fail through lack of understanding and preliminary education."

"Then you have a solution?"

"Oh yes, but I couldn't go into that now; it would take too long."

Montague Brain grunted. "Well, you may be right," he said. "What you have told me has upset me a good deal. I feel I've made a hash of things, and I had no intention of hurting Betty; I'm very fond of her."

"The blame isn't entirely yours," Dr. Hansell said kindly. "Miss Romney cannot altogether be exonerated, although I'm inclined to think that, in her case, her parents are chiefly at fault. They gave her no solid background on which to build her life or meet the problems which would inevitably arise. To let an attractive young woman like that loose on the world without making sure that she realises both her danger and her power is most reprehensible. But what can you expect, when her parents' educational endeavours were no more than a series of 'don'ts'? Added to which, matters were not improved by the unfortunate marriages of her sisters."

"I should think not, indeed," the young man exclaimed. "I have seldom come across people who bicker so much as that quartette. They would put anyone off marriage."

"So I gather. There is one matter I would like you to explain, Mr. Brain. Miss Romney says that you used no contraceptives—that you relied entirely on coitus interruptus. Surely, if you have read as much about this subject as you seem to imply, you realised that that method is most unsatisfactory?"

"As a matter of fact, Doctor, I've only read one or two books; but what I have read led me to think that most contraceptive methods were unsafe or unæsthetic, and I was pretty sure that Betty wouldn't learn anything for herself. I know a good many men who say that coitus interruptus is all right. Am I wrong?"

"I'm afraid you are," Dr. Hansell said, proceeding to give the explanations that had been necessary when talking to Betty Romney. "So, you see," he concluded, "your very method of coitus practically doomed your experiment from the start. Although you got some satisfaction, the girl got none. Even so, your background was all wrong, and I don't think the use of contraceptives would have solved your difficulties."

"Do you think there is anything in what she says about being pregnant?"

"It is possible," Dr. Hansell replied, "but I don't know yet for certain. However, I shall know definitely in a day or two, as I am having a special test carried out."

"My God! I hope there's nothing like that?" Montague Brain exclaimed; "it would be a calamity if she were pregnant."

"What would you do?"

"Marry her, I suppose, but I doubt if she would agree. No! The only thing to do would be to get rid of it; plenty of girls do so, I believe."

"Abortion is a very serious matter, Mr. Brain," Dr. Hansell said. "All you young people seem to regard it far too lightly. Do you realise that a lot of healthy women die every year simply because they go to the abortionist, and that one of the chief causes of sterility is infection of the female genital tract following on abortion and sepsis?"

"No, I can't say I do."

"Well, it is a fact, and it is people like you who contribute to the problem. To you, and people like you, sex is a mere personal matter; you do not realise that your behaviour affects society as a whole; that what you each do affects the other and ultimately the State."

"I should have said an affair like that is entirely our own affair."

"Precisely. And if everyone begins to think like that and behave like that the whole social structure is undermined as more and more people get swept into the stream. We have no right to regard these matters from a purely personal angle, nor, for that matter, can the State any longer ignore the needs of young people, nor the frightful moral muddle in which we live at present."

"Well, I certainly do seem to have made a mess of things, don't I?" the young man said. "And I kidded myself I knew a thing or two."

Dr. Hansell laughed. "You are no better and no worse than thousands of other young men," he said kindly. "You are really suffering from the effects of a social disease—moral hypocrisy. Whilst people agree that sex is essential to life and that passion is a normal part of sex, they will not look at it creatively and realise that it has no real meaning for human beings when it is used as a mere physical activity. And the last thing they will do is to talk about it intelligently and openly."

"But what exactly do you mean by sex?"

"Most people apply the term to the physical relationship alone," Dr. Hansell said. "But an understanding of sex means an understanding of the energy and power of those instincts which have to do with Love in its widest sense; love of oneself, love of friends, love of parents and children, love of humanity in general and devotion to ideals. This was ably pointed out by Freud many years ago, but has not yet sunk into the public conscience. Sex is concerned with all activities; all emotions, desires and feelings; and its power influences our relationships with each other as well as with society in general. And so, to understand the underlying causes of many of our present troubles, whether individual or national, it is necessary to enlist the aid of the scientist, the biologist, the psychologist and the student of physiology, as well as the moralist, the philosopher and the student of social economics. In some way or other we have got to get rid of the idea that sex is something nasty, of which one must be ashamed, and replace it with the idea that sex is good and beautiful and creative and closely related to all that is highest and best in men and women; that it is concerned with the welfare of the community in general; that it is something to be taught about, and learned about, intelligently. How many people do you find discussing the matter sensibly? In how many homes do you ever hear the subject mentioned except in a coarse fashion or with bated breath? But there is no more need to be ashamed of sex than there is to look at a naked body and say that it is disgusting. It is true that the contemplation of a nude picture or person may arouse sensual thoughts, but so may the reading of certain passages from the Bible. It is not the object which is sensual or disgusting, nor yet the mind which receives the impression of the objects, but the individuality of the person who distorts the impression. In itself, the sex instinct is neither good nor bad, moral or amoral, but just a crude force to be used for our improvement or destruction. It is part of the raw material necessary for the formation of character. To some it is an ever-present source of difficulty that needs constant regulation and supervision; to others it hardly presents itself as a problem at all; much in the same way that jealousy in some is an all-consuming fire, and in others a mere name."

"But how is one to regulate it, if it's an 'all-consuming fire'?"

"By trying to understand it. It only becomes an all-consuming fire when it is misused, misdirected and repressed. The saints and prophets of old who took themselves off to the desert in order to subdue the flesh only made matters worse for themselves; they lived in a perpetual torment. Many people live like that to-day, and yet it is wrong and quite unnecessary. Man is provided with intelligence and will, by which he can modify and redirect his sexual energy; but he can't abolish it. Instead of the old negative idea of the inherent evil of sex, we must put in its place a constructive ideal of the essential goodness and worthiness of the instinct which, if rightly used, can become one of our most valued possessions. Its wrongful use can produce nothing but sadness and remorse. Our whole development depends upon our ability to manage it properly, and that, I admit, is very difficult. But we must always remember that our individual actions have social repercussions that we do not always appreciate at the time. The sex instinct must be used as an artist uses colour—creatively.

Were the artist deprived of his sex desires he would no longer be able to create a masterpiece. And just as the true artist would never prostitute his art for self-seeking ends, so must you and I learn never to use our sex activity to please the self. The canvas upon which you work is the personality of your partner—a living, sensitive thing, responsive to the slightest touch, the merest word thrown out in jest. And so you must not daub your paint indiscriminately; there must be a plan and an ideal behind your work. If your methods are all wrong and your aim is misdirected, you'll merely make a mess of things. That, unfortunately, is what you've been doing with Miss Romney."

"Yes, I see that now. What would you advise me to do?"

"Nothing for the moment; except to keep in touch with her. Tell her that you've been to see me and will do anything you can to help her. Impress upon her the need for delay and show her that you understand in some measure."

"I'll try to do that; I'm very grateful to you, Doctor. I wish to God I'd had the sense to come to you to start off with."

"That's what you all say," Dr. Hansell replied, with a smile. "We can only hope that it's not too late and that something can be saved from the wreck. We shall all three have to work together. I'll let you know as soon as I have any definite news."

. . . . .

"You have seen the body of the deceased, Mr. Romney, and identify it as being that of your daughter Betty?" the coroner was saying, as Dr. Hansell entered the court a few days later.

"That is so. She was my youngest child."

"Can you tell me when you last saw your daughter alive?"

"Five days before her death; on Saturday the fifteenth, to be exact."

"Was she in good health?"

"She appeared to be perfectly well, and told her mother and myself that she was going to stay with some friends in the country."

"Are these friends known to you?"

"Oh yes."

"Was your daughter in the habit of paying visits in that fashion?"

"Certainly; we never interfered with her movements; in fact we rather encouraged her to make her own friends and lead her own life."

"I see. She was twenty-two, I think?"

"Yes."

"Did she have any occupation?"

"Yes, she was secretary to Messrs. Player and Forethought of Gray's Inn Road. It was our hope, however, that she would marry."

"Was she engaged?"

"Not to my knowledge."

"Will you tell me in your own way of the events that led up to this tragedy, in so far as you are aware of them?"

"I'm afraid there is very little I can tell. She never said or did anything to indicate that she was in any trouble. Neither her mother nor I noticed anything wrong. She had rather a reserved manner, but always appeared happy. When she was away from home she frequently did not communicate with us for several days at a time, and we did not worry so long as we knew where she was. We were not surprised therefore when we didn't hear from her on this occasion. Wishing to communicate with her on Wednesday the twentieth, however, about some arrangements I was making for some theatre seats, I rang her up, and was surprised to discover that she was not staying in the house. As a matter of fact it transpired that her friends had not seen her, or heard from her, for two or three months. I was naturally annoyed, because I realised that she had been deceiving us for some purpose. You see, she had led us to believe that she had frequently stayed with these friends during the past year. I rang up one or two other people on the off-chance that she might be there, but could get no information as to her whereabouts. We were still wondering what to do when we were informed by the police that the poor child was in the hospital. When we arrived she was unconscious, and died about a quarter of an hour later. I'm afraid that is all I can tell you."

"Thank you, Mr. Romney. I am obliged for your clear statement. I have only two further questions to put to you. Did you make your daughter an allowance?"

"She had a small income of approximately a hundred a year in her own right, which I supplemented whenever necessary. As a matter of fact I gave her twenty-five pounds about a fortnight ago."

"Indeed. Did you give it to her on your own initiative or did she ask you for it?"

"She asked for it."

"Was that unusual?"

"No, we had a sort of tacit understanding that she could have another hundred a year or so from me, whenever she wanted it."

"What about her friends?"

"She seemed to have plenty of friends of both sexes and they frequently came to the house for meals or tennis."

"Do you know a Mr. Montague Brain?"

"Certainly. He has been to the house frequently with Betty."

"Did you approve of their friendship?"

"I saw no reason to do otherwise. He always struck me as being a nice young man, though a trifle self-opinionated."

"Thank you, Mr. Romney."

Turning to the foreman of the jury, the coroner enquired whether they wished to put any questions. After glancing at his companions the foreman replied in the negative.

"Then that will be all for the moment, I think," the coroner said, addressing Mr. Romney, who, bowing slightly, left the witness-box. His place was taken by a police constable, who, after taking the oath, opened a note-book and began to read.

"On the night of Monday the eighteenth at 11.15 p.m. I was proceeding on my usual beat when I observed a young woman holding on to some railings. Her appearance led me to suppose that she was in distress, so I approached her and enquired if anything was wrong. 'The pain is awful,' she whispered. 'Where is the pain?' I enquired. 'In my stomach,' she said, and more or less crumpled up in my arms. I asked her where she lived and what her name was, but she appeared to be too ill to understand what I was talking about. I accordingly thought it my duty to put her in a passing taxi and take her to the hospital, which was only a short distance away, there being no ambulance available. I had some difficulty in accomplishing my purpose, but managed to get her into the taxi with the help of the driver and a passing pedestrian. She never said a word whilst we were driving to the hospital, only moaned a little now and then. We had to carry her into the casualty department, where she was seen by the doctor."

"You acted very wisely," the coroner remarked. "Did you make any further attempt to find out who she was?"

"Yes, sir. I searched her bag, but it contained nothing except a ten-shilling note, some coppers, a powder-box and one or two keys. I asked the nurse to search her clothing, but she couldn't find any clue to identify her."

"Didn't the girl say anything else?"

"She mumbled one or two words, but I couldn't catch their meaning."

"I believe you were present later on when she made a statement."

"Yes, sir, on the Wednesday afternoon at three p.m., to be exact."

"Who else was present?"

"The doctor and the ward sister."

The coroner passed a paper to the constable. "Is that the statement?"

"Yes, sir, written down by the doctor and witnessed by all three."

"And that is your signature?"

"Yes, sir."

"I suppose everything possible was done to try and trace her relatives?"

"Yes, sir, but it wasn't until the afore-mentioned statement was made that we were able to communicate with them."

"Thank you; that will be all, unless the jury wish to ask you any questions."

The jury not wishing to avail themselves of this opportunity, the policeman retired and the next witness, a thick, stocky young man with a cheerful face, was called.

"What are your full names, please?"

"William Everard Winter-Wait."

"And you are a registered medical practitioner?"

"Yes, sir."

"And you are one of the casualty officers at the hospital?"

"That is correct."

"Will you kindly tell the jury all you know of this case in as untechnical language as possible?"

"On the night of Monday the eighteenth I was called to Casualty at about 11.30 p.m. to see a woman who had been brought in. When I arrived I found the girl whom I now know to be Miss Romney. She was obviously in a serious condition, being cold, collapsed and practically unconscious. I admitted her immediately. On further examination her condition was diagnosed as acute peritonitis. After some hours she had improved sufficiently to justify an exploratory operation being performed. This was done at 4 p.m. by Mr. Bliss-Venables, one of the honorary surgeons to the hospital. Unfortunately, however, the condition was such that very little could be done. The patient rallied slightly during the following day, but relapsed again during the night of Tuesday the nineteenth. During all this time she remained unconscious, or rambled so incoherently that it was impossible to make out what she was talking about. However, she suddenly became quite sensible about 3 p.m. on Wednesday afternoon and, although very weak, said that she wished to make a statement. This was made very slowly, so that I was able to write it down in the presence of the sister and the constable. It is that statement which you now have before you."

"Thank you. Please proceed."

"The effort of making the statement seemed to exhaust the girl, and in spite of everything being done for her benefit, she again relapsed into unconsciousness and died at 4 p.m.—about a quarter of an hour after her parents arrived at the hospital."

"I understand that a post-mortem examination was made."

"Yes, sir. I have the report here." The doctor produced a paper.

" Will you kindly tell us the relevant facts ? "

" The examination showed that the girl was suffering from generalised peritonitis due to an infection spreading from the womb, which was found to have a perforating wound at its lower end. The whole organ was in a very unhealthy state. In my opinion the patient died from shock following septicæmia, due to an infection arising from the wound in the womb."

" Was there any evidence of pregnancy ? "

" The organs were in such a bad state that it is almost impossible to say definitely, without further microscopical investigation, which is now being carried out. All that I can say at present is that their state, together with the obvious signs of interference, makes it practically certain that an attempt had been made by some incompetent person to perform an abortion. In any case, the pregnancy, if there was one, was very early."

" Can you form any opinion as to the time of the interference ? "

" It would be difficult to give a definite date, but a few days would suffice ; these conditions frequently spread very rapidly."

" Thank you. Perhaps you will kindly read the statement made by the deceased, since it is your own handwriting."

The doctor took the paper from the coroner, and cleared his throat. " ' My name is Betty Romney,' he read. " ' I am twenty-two years old and live at 18, West Partington Avenue, Henwick. You say I am very ill. I think I am going to die, and would like to make a statement so that no one will get into trouble. This is no one's fault but my own. I knew what I was about all the time. I was going to have a baby which I did not want. Neither did I wish to marry Monty, although he has frequently asked me to do so.' " The doctor paused and looked at the coroner. " I asked her who Monty was. ' Montague Brain,' she replied. ' A friend of mine.' ' Is he the cause of your present trouble ? ' I asked. ' Yes,' she said. Realising that this answer could be interpreted in two ways, I continued my questioning. ' Do you mean that he caused this condition ? ' I asked. ' Oh no, he knows nothing about this—nothing at all.' 'You mean that he is the cause of the pregnancy?' 'Yes.' 'Then how did you get into your present state?' 'I went to someone who did it for me. I told my people that I was going to stay with friends in the country, so as not to worry them, but actually I went to an hotel, where I stayed under the name of Watkins. A day or two after I had been to the person I felt hot and funny, so I decided to go for a walk. I walked for a long time and had a lot of pain and felt sick and don't remember much more. I would like to see my mother and father.' I replied that they were being fetched, and asked her the name of the person to whom she went, but she refused to tell me. 'It doesn't matter,' she said; 'I don't want to cause more trouble. Tell Dr. Hansell that I'm sorry I didn't take his advice.' That is all," the doctor concluded, returning the paper to the coroner.

"Thank you, Doctor; your evidence has been very clear. There seems to be little doubt from this statement," he continued, addressing the jury, "that this is another of those distressing cases of attempted abortion which are becoming far too frequent. You will observe that the girl takes all the responsibility for her own actions, and it is highly improbable that the police will be able to trace the perpetrator of this outrage. I may say, however, that they have not yet completed their enquiries. In fact, I gather that they wish for an adjournment of this inquest until they have had more time to investigate the affair. Am I right, Sergeant?" he enquired from an officer sitting just in front of him.

"That is so," the officer replied.

"Very good. Before adjourning, however, I think we had better hear the evidence of Mr. Montague Brain and Dr. Hansell, both of whom are referred to in the girl's statement."

Montague Brain came into the witness-box, looking pale and drawn.

"I will not trouble you more than is necessary, Mr. Brain," the coroner said, after the young man had taken the oath, "but I think it advisable to hear what you have to say, if only for your own sake."

"Thank you, sir. I shall be pleased to tell you all I can."

"You knew Miss Romney well, I gather?"

"Yes sir. We have been friends for a couple of years."

"Were you engaged to be married?"

"Not exactly. Neither of us wished to marry to start with, and later on I think she was unwilling to make any definite arrangement."

"Why?"

"I don't think she was certain in her own mind."

"Would it be fair to say that you were more in love with her than she with you?"

"That may be so, but we were very fond of each other and had much in common."

"You saw a good deal of each other, I presume?"

"That is so."

"And I gather that intimacy occurred on several occasions."

"Yes."

"Were you aware of her condition?"

"Yes; she told me of her fears, and I tried to persuade her to marry me straight away, but she refused."

"Why?"

"I can only say that I don't think she was sure of herself. You see, we hadn't been getting on very well recently, but I felt that everything would be all right if only we were properly married."

"Her feelings had changed towards you, then?"

"I think it was on account of the secrecy of the affair, rather than any actual change in her affections. I realise now that we made a mistake. She had become nervous and overstrung and would not listen to me."

"When did you see her last?"

"On the evening of Monday the eleventh. She came to my rooms after she had seen Dr. Hansell and said she was sure she was pregnant and that she would have to do something about it. I tried to dissuade her from doing anything drastic till we knew for certain, and she left me promising to think it over."

"Were you not surprised to hear nothing further from her?"

"She wrote a note the next day, saying that she was going away for a few days and would ring me up when she came back, so I naturally did nothing. I have the note here if you would care to see it."

"Thank you." The note was passed to the coroner, who read it carefully and passed it to the foreman of the jury.

"Thank you, Mr. Brain. I don't think I need detain you any longer, unless the jury wish to ask you any questions."

As no questions were forthcoming, Montague Brain returned to his seat, and Dr. Hansell was called.

"I shall be obliged if you will tell me what you know of this case, Dr. Hansell," the coroner said, when the formalities had been completed.

"Very little, I'm afraid," the doctor replied. "Miss Romney came to see me some days ago, because she thought she was pregnant, and wanted my advice about her relationship with Mr. Brain, whom I also saw at a later date. I was unable to form an opinion as to whether she was actually pregnant or not, but I arranged to make certain laboratory tests. I told her that I would be able to give her a definite answer in a few days. I must explain that the test is a very reliable one and a positive result can be obtained very soon after conception has occurred. The nature of the case indicated that if a pregnancy had occurred it would be about three weeks old, which would certainly be shown by the test. Although the girl was in a very over-wrought state and talked about doing away with herself, I hoped I had persuaded her to refrain from coming to any decision until the result of the test was known. I explained to her that there were many other causes which might bring about her present condition, of which worry was one, and I tried to persuade her to take her mother into her confidence, but this she refused to do. She appeared to be satisfied with my advice and promised to ring me up in a few days. As she did not do this, I endeavoured to communicate with her when the result of the test came through—that is to say on the day of her death."

"What was the result of the test?"

"It was negative."

The coroner looked up quickly and stared at Dr. Hansell.

"Negative! Then the girl was not pregnant at all," he said at last.

"That is so."

"Are you certain that the test is reliable?"

"I believe it is accurate in ninety-nine cases out of a hundred."

"If what you say is correct, the operation, if we can call it an operation, was performed unnecessarily?"

"That is so."

"How do you account for the girl's insistence on being pregnant?"

"I've known such cases to occur before, especially through fear or worry, as in this case."

"Thank you, Dr. Hansell."

Dr. Winter-Wait, on being recalled, said that the condition could have been caused through interference whether the girl was pregnant or not.

The coroner held a short conference with the police sergeant and then addressed the jury.

"You will have listened to the unfolding of this sad story with very mixed feelings. You will have been distressed at the thought of a young life being ended so unnecessarily; angry when you contemplate the gross incompetence and stupidity of some unknown individual; and your sympathy will, I feel sure, go out in full measure to her parents in this terrible and unforeseen trouble that has come upon them.

"I feel that I cannot let the matter rest there, however. Cases of death from abortion following criminal interference are becoming increasingly frequent; and it is a well-known fact that many thousands of cases occur every year of which we know nothing. This evil practice causes suffering and ill-health to many women. The causes of this serious increase are numerous and altogether outside the province of this court to consider. However, I cannot refrain from drawing your attention to two facts which seem to have some bearing on the problem. The first is that as the law stands at present, and it has not been altered since the middle of last century, an abortion performed before the seventh month is illegal, however skilfully the operation is carried out, and however eminent the surgeon. It is obvious that with the possibility of a long trial, and even imprisonment, facing anyone who performs these operations, the average medical practitioner, who is rightly jealous of his or her reputation, is going to avoid such cases. Similarly, hospitals are not very willing to accept such patients even when there are the clearest medical indications for interference, because of the present uncertain state of the law. Thus the practice is driven underground, and comes into the hands of the type of person who has obviously interfered with this poor girl.

" You must not think that because this court and similar courts throughout the country are frequently investigating the results of abortion in unmarried girls, that the practice is limited to this type of case. On the contrary, I must remind you that there is ample evidence that the majority of abortions occur in married women, usually in women who have had several children. But, to quote from a recent Government report: ' abortion is responsible for a greater proportion of the deaths among the unmarried class, and is largely responsible for the higher maternal mortality rate of unmarried women.' [1]

" Neither is the practice restricted to any particular class, but is a condition affecting all social grades. In the eight years from 1926 to 1933 deaths from abortion numbered little short of 3,000,[2] of which 65 per cent. were due to septic abortion—that is to say abortion in which some interference had presumably occurred. The report to which I have just referred states that ' abortion is an important factor in the puerperal mortality rate of the country, since approximately 14 per cent. of all puerperal deaths are due to this cause.' [3]

" In the second place I must remind you that should any of you feel that the number of deaths I have quoted seems comparatively small compared, for instance, with the figures

[1] Report on Maternal Mortality, 1937, p. 222.
It is stated in the same report that in one area where 93 cases of abortion were carefully investigated by the authorities, only 13 of the women were pregnant for the first time, whereas 50 of the remaining 80 had had from one to three children ; " The married women numbered 85, the single 13 and three were widows ".[*]

[*] Ibid., p. 199.
[2] Report on Maternal Mortality, 1937, p. 212.
[3] Ibid., p. 222.

for road deaths; it is estimated on good authority that one pregnancy in every five terminates in an abortion, which of course is not necessarily criminal.[1] The loss of these unborn children, which must run into thousands a year, and the deaths of so many mothers, is almost a national calamity at the present time. In connection with this I feel it my duty to draw your attention to a further extract from the official report I have just quoted. 'The dangers associated with artificially induced abortion do not appear to be sufficiently realised, and there is urgent need for the education of women respecting the damage to health and the danger to life from attempts to terminate pregnancy artificially.' [2] This is only too true, but I would not limit the need for such education to women only. I think that men, in particular, should be thoroughly instructed in the dangers women run by some thoughtless action on their part.

" Finally, I cannot help feeling that this case should be a warning to those unfortunate women who have taken risks which lead them to suppose that they are pregnant. Had this unfortunate young lady listened to the advice given to her by the doctor, or, better still, had she understood the significance of the whole relationship into which she entered, it is possible that we should not have been called together to-day. The enquiry is adjourned until this day week at the same time, in order to give the police an opportunity of making further enquiries. I must thank you, ladies and gentlemen, for your patient assistance."

[1] Bourne and Williams, " Recent Advances in Obstetrics and Gynecology ".
[2] Report on Maternal Mortality, p. 221.

EPILOGUE

WHERE have we got to? What conclusions are to be drawn by a consideration of all the matters we have discussed in this book? Is there anything more to be said? The first thought that may strike the reader is that the book is largely concerned with material things; with techniques and procedures; with the function of sex on the physical level, and he may well ask himself whether the removal of these abuses, even if that were possible, together with an improvement in our economic conditions, will be enough. I doubt it, not without a change of heart. True, it is suggested that man will never reach perfection whilst he regards sex as a mere physical activity and woman as someone to be picked up and discarded as he chooses; that he will get nowhere whilst he uses someone else's body for his own amusement, and that only when the physical is linked to the spiritual will sexual fulfilment be properly appreciated. Is this enough, however? Is not something else needed? I think it is. That something is a capacity to appreciate moral truth and give integrity and purpose to actions which can otherwise become isolated and devoid of meaning. This requires a degree of spiritual awareness which many people seem to ignore or don't even possess. But if this element of our make-up is absent the individual has no incentive to feel responsibility for his actions—there is no positive direction to his life.

This inability to accept responsibility or refusal to acknowledge that, having entered into some relationship with a person, we have some responsibility towards that person, is one of the chief characteristics of our age and is at the root of much bad behaviour in the personal relationships of men and women. People embark on an affair far too lightly and then, when things go wrong, throw it up, leave the other in the lurch, or in some way or other avoid recognising their responsibility, escaping as quickly as possible. They enter the relationship without due forethought, and they get out of it without recognising the effect of their action on the other and without doing everything possible to put the situation right. Sometimes, of course, the situation has gone so far that it cannot be put right, in which case it must be accepted, dealt with and forgotten. Some people's life-pattern is such that they must act in this self-seeking fashion. They do much harm and cause much misery. The incidents and stories recounted in this book are not isolated, they are a common occurrence throughout the whole of society, and create an enormous amount of misery which could be largely avoided if society would take more positive steps to deal with the underlying causes. So much that goes by the name of love nowadays is not love at all but mere selfish amusement combined, in some cases, with mechanical efficiency. The achievement of mechanical perfection, however, is not enough. Love, and all that is meant by love, must spread over the man-woman relationship as an all-pervading tenderness, which concerns itself entirely with the well-being of the other person. Sex must be raised from the primitive to the sublime; from the urge to penetrate and be possessed, to hurt and be hurt, to the surrender of the self in the contemplation of the other's joy, for, as Middleton Murry well says: " Sex fulfilment depends upon the man preferring the woman's delight to his own ",[1] and, one must add, to the woman preferring his delight to her own. Such love can only be possible when it is mutual; there can be no holding back, no reservation, no " if " or " but ", no seeking after one's own pleasure; all carnal feeling—all lust —must be translated into a love so perfect, so full of sensation and feeling, so tender and passionate, so technically perfect and emotionally complete that it defies description. In this way the primitive drive of sex can be translated into a positive and creative power which pervades the life of two united individuals and becomes the expression of a mutual fellowship which the two have established.

The achievement of such perfection, however, takes time, and it must be worked for and thought about. Unfortu-

[1] Murry, J. Middleton, "Adam and Eve", Andrew Dakers. Ltd., 1944, p. 144.

nately it is only experienced by a small proportion of people, for even to-day the spirit is at war with the flesh and something is held back or kept in reserve. Many a young woman, having ventured into the unexplored garden of love with her young man and feeling assured that everything will be all right because they "love each other so much", finds that everything is all wrong; that her man, knowing that he can now let himself go with a clear conscience, is overcome by his primitive feelings in the presence of so much beauty and is turned into a possessive beast, or his self-centredness is so great that he is impotent and cannot fulfil himself or express himself adequately. In all such cases the flesh is still warring with the spirit, in the sense that his conscience is disturbed by the memory of some past escapade, some ugly thought, some sinful lust of the flesh, or some guilty feeling which deprives his love of natural spontaneity. No longer is it necessary to agree with D. H. Lawrence when he says that such experience is necessary to youth and talks about the "ecstasies and agonies of love, the agonies and ecstasies of fear and doubt".[1] Have we not seen in the course of reading this book that many of the conditions which produced these ecstasies and frustrations can now be prevented by an intelligent approach to marriage, thus enabling a couple to avoid many of the pitfalls Lawrence was writing about, and reach a perfection of love far greater than was possible in his day? Moreover, by taking thought early enough, and approaching the whole subject openly and sensibly, we can do much to prevent the onset of fear and the development of those aggressive and primitive desires which are the accompaniment of fear and frustration.

Whilst technical perfection by itself can, in certain cases, provide great satisfaction, no lasting fulfilment will be possible until the flesh, united with the spirit, is swept to the higher-levels of experience, from whence, cleansed of all impurities, it can return to enrich the personality of the loved one. To some such talk is meaningless; to others it is the essence of life, but I doubt if it is ever reached without toil and trouble. There is no easy road to true happiness in love, and because so many people will not accept this simple

[1] "The Fantasia of the Unconscious".

truth they fall by the wayside, frightened of the difficulties, fearful of the implications and unable to accept the responsibilities which are the inevitable consequence of sexual activity.

If one is to talk or teach about marriage, therefore, one must be prepared to discuss the relationship of sex, not only to the spiritual life of man, but to religion as we know it to-day. Sex and religion are so closely linked in the minds of many people that it is impossible to talk of one without reference to the other. To the materialist this relationship is of little consequence. To the religiously minded person it is of paramount importance. Whilst the former tends to throw over all standards that have a religious flavour, the latter tends to view all efforts at sex enlightenment as dangerous and likely to undermine true morality. For the former all that is necessary in the physical relationship is technical efficiency, sufficient to produce a mutual orgasm; for the latter the attitude of mind in which the couple approach the whole relationship is of far greater importance than any technical ability. In truth, of course, neither is right. Only those who accept the discoveries of science on the one hand and relate them to the spiritual nature of man on the other have much hope of reaching a balanced matrimonial life. The relationship between sex and the spirit is, therefore, fundamental to man, for every man has a soul.

The pity of it is that the two ever came to be separated, but, as has been suggested in earlier chapters, the reason is to be found far back in the history of the Christian Church, and even in the pre-Christian era. Belief that the world would soon be changed by the second coming of Our Lord persisted for years after His death, and encouraged the early Christians to think more of spiritual than physical matters. After all, they had to do something about the licentiousness and cruelty which surrounded them. Being unable to accept a sexuality so out of keeping with what they had been taught regarding the value of human personality, it was only natural that they should combat these evil forces by a refusal to have anything to do with a power whose expression seemed to produce everything that was ugly and shameful. However much we may criticise St. Paul for his attitude to sex, it was only natural that he should condemn behaviour so utterly alien to his whole philosophy of life. Although he recognised the force of the sex urge and the necessity for its expression, he didn't assign it a very high place in life; those that couldn't contain themselves were advised to marry in order to avoid worse evils, which wasn't very encouraging advice to those who possessed a normal sex appetite. This attitude was made worse in later years by Christian teachers, who lauded celibacy and virginity and took a somewhat poor view of those who found it necessary to express their physical needs in marriage.

Eventually, not only were the priests prevented from marrying, but more and more people of both sexes were forced into monasteries, partly to escape the ravages around them, partly to read and work and partly to improve their chances of reaching spiritual perfection. This was a disastrous policy from many points of view and did a great deal of harm. Writing in 1869 Francis Galton pointed out that the celibacy enjoined by religious orders on those who inhabited the nunneries and monasteries had a serious effect on society as a whole. " Whenever a man or woman was possessed by a gentle nature that fitted him or her to deeds of charity, to meditation, to literature, or to art, the social condition of the time was such that they had no refuge elsewhere than in the bosom of the Church. But the Church chose to preach and exact celibacy. The consequence was that these gentle natures had no continuance and thus by a policy so singularly unwise and suicidal, the Church brutalised the breed of our forefathers. She acted precisely as if she had aimed at selecting the rudest portion of the community to be, alone, the parents of future generations. She practised the arts which breeders would use, who aimed at creating ferocious, currish and stupid natures. No wonder that club law prevailed for centuries over Europe; the wonder rather is that enough good remained in the veins of Europeans to enable their race to rise to its very moderate level of natural morality." [1]

If only someone had had the vision to elaborate the positive relationship between sex and the spirit which Christ

[1] Galton Francis, " Hereditary Genius ", p. 343.

had indicated, and had made people realise that this powerful urge could be used creatively in marriage, and that through its proper release men and women could learn to love each other on a higher plane, the whole history of our civilisation might have been altered. A wonderful chance was missed, and has only now presented itself again. And yet we need not be surprised that whilst Christ understood these things His followers did not. Theirs was a very primitive society, lacking in knowledge of sex psychology and, what is even more important, in the knowledge of effective contraception. And so, instead of being raised to the heights, sex became a deep and awful mystery; unmanageable and devastating in its expression—a sin against God and man. And yet, as Middleton Murry says, the sex act is " the supreme opportunity for the complete fusion of the spiritual and the physical ". When it is a mere physical act it is followed by a sense of sadness and degradation, however experienced the lovers may be, but as an act of human love it is an ascent of pure delight, from which there is no reaction. " It is quite independent of the purely personal satisfaction of orgasm; it is essentially the supreme psycho-spiritual communion." [1]

So far as one can judge, the Church could never accept this summing up; indeed, she has hardly accepted it yet, and this is one of the main reasons why she has lost her influence over so many people to-day. I cannot agree with Lawrence, however, that Jesus denied or despised sex. On the contrary, there is evidence that He believed profoundly in marriage and the home and taught man to respect woman as his equal, to share things with her and to love her. Many of His acts and sayings indicate that He had a profound understanding of the human sex problem. His followers, however, instead of keeping to His simple teaching, developed a series of mysterious elaborations which have fuddled the minds of thinking people for centuries and gave the priests an immense and, to a large extent, improper hold over the people. To offend against their laws was tantamount to excommunication or death. Much of their teaching was antagonistic to the idea of healthy home life and natural generation. Christ had an understanding of sex far and

[1] " Adam and Eve ", p. 160.

away beyond that of His followers. He went to weddings and encouraged people to enjoy themselves; He forgave prostitutes and gave them fresh hope and He talked with the woman of Samaria, with whom no good Jew should have spoken. He even recognised biological differences in the sex make-up of people. "For there are some eunuchs, which were so born from their mother's womb; and there are some eunuchs which were made eunuchs of men; and there be eunuchs, which have made themselves eunuchs for the Kingdom of Heaven's sake. He that is able to receive, let him receive it." [1]

We know well that some people are born with a faulty constitution which profoundly affects their physical and emotional life; that others by upbringing or accident or disease are impotent or sterile, while others are celibate of their own volition, " for the Kingdom of Heaven's sake ". One of His last sayings was concerned with love and home: " Woman, behold thy son," He said to His mother, and to the disciple whom He loved " Behold thy mother! And from that hour the disciple took her into his own home." [2]

There is nothing in all this to indicate that He condemned the home or family or sex. On the contrary, although He was Himself celibate, He had a profound understanding of sex, and indicated that there is a place for both the married and the single. Each has his own vocation and his own rewards. In each case sex must be understood and positively directed. In so far as the man–woman relationship is concerned, sexual love united to spiritual feeling can transform the whole relationship, strengthen home and family life and enable people to attain a rich fulfilment of their personalities. That surely, was His teaching.

Any criticism of the Churches that I have made is done deliberately in order to encourage people to think and talk about these matters, for only thus shall we progress. Nor I hope am I being unfair; I do not intend to be, but I do feel that a little more clarity of thought and practice is essential. For instance, here is a point bearing upon what Francis Galton was saying about heredity. I understand

---

[1] St. Matthew, Chap. 19. v. 10-12.
[2] St. John, Chap. 19, v. 27.

that the Roman Catholic Church has little to say for the science of eugenics. Their policy regarding childbearing is to encourage it in every possible way, for souls are of value. Nothing must be done to interfere with childbearing however maimed in mind the couple may be. Considerations of a hereditary nature do not come in. If they did they could not possibly countenance the breeding of some of the material which is being bred at the present time—notably in parts of Ireland. And yet, when it comes to accepting a man or woman into a celibate society, whether it be monastery or nunnery, careful enquiry is made into the antecedents of the novice to make certain that she, for instance, comes from a good healthy stock and there is no history of serious illness, physical or mental, in the family background. If there is, or if she herself is unfit—and she has to have a strict medical examination—she is rejected. Such people when they take their final vows are " married to Christ " in the spiritual sense and are given a ring. How comes it that so much care is taken over the choice of a bride for Christ and so little over the selection of parents and the breeding of children? If the one is right why not the other? To the outsider there seems to be here some confusion both in thought and practice.

The positive statements on the Christian position regarding sex and marriage quoted in Chapter I [1] deserve a wider publicity because they do not appear to have been accepted by the general body of Christian people. The matter is urgent, however, because the failure of both Church and State to formulate a constructive policy is having a grave effect upon family life and preventing young people from constructing a sex ethic which is based upon all that is highest and best in human nature. But this is not all. Not only are we in a position to accept sex as a positive contribution to human happiness. We possess the capacity of regulating populations throughout the world, of encouraging the production of good, healthy, virile and intelligent people and of limiting the production of less suitable persons. Those couples who can show a good record of emotional stability, physical health and good socialising qualities should be encouraged

[1] P. 17.

to breed, and really adequate allowances should be made to them, whereas everything should be done to prevent and discourage the breeding of unsuitable stock. Whilst we do not know everything about heredity and genetic breeding, we do know quite enough to determine who are likely to produce the best children, and they should be encouraged to breed. Honesty, enlightenment and constructive teaching are the chief necessities to-day. Marriages will continue to break down until we revolutionise our ideas regarding the responsibility which society has to those who marry. Marriage preparation must start at an early age, and we must do everything that we can to give people sufficient understanding of their own and other people's psychological make-up that they can determine, in some measure, their motives and the type of individual best suited to their particular personality.

Whilst the effect of uniting psychologically maladjusted types in marriage is becoming more obvious, this matter will require far more thought and consideration than has been given to it in the past. No amount of sex instruction will compensate for this serious underlying antipathy, and every attempt must be made to show young people how to recognise unsuitable types. On the other hand, an accurate knowledge of physical reactions and the varying needs of the sexes will go far to bring about adjustment and harmony in a marriage which might otherwise break down. There are some who think that all marriages should at first be solemnised by the State, and only those wishing to take further lifelong vows, in accordance with Christian ideas of marriage, should be allowed to marry in church. Such an arrangement has much to commend it, but, in my opinion, no arrangements will be satisfactory until it is recognised that every couple marrying according to the laws of Church or State should have adequate marriage preparation, including a visit to the doctor. The pre-marital consultation with the doctor is an essential forerunner to satisfactory sexual intercourse and eventual marriage stability. Many people marry in church because the State ceremony is so incredibly dull and materialistic. Would it not be possible to devise a marriage service that could be held in a Registrar's Office and, whilst avoiding controversial issues relating to religion, was simple and dignified and gave form and substance to a ceremony which, to many a couple, is the most important single event in their lives ? Bridesmaids and a wedding dress and a simple ceremony would go far to remove the dislike that so many people have to the State marriage.

We live in an era which is full of immense possibilities for advancing human happiness. Now, for the first time since Christ lived, are we given the opportunity of uniting the sex and spiritual life of man into a creative activity which will make marriage in the future one of the deepest and finest expressions of the human personality. We can rebuild broken populations, decrease excess in childbirth, extend the duration of life and encourage the production only of those who are fit and worthy of world citizenship. We can educate towards sexual happiness and contentment and bring emotional release to millions of men and women. The possibility is there. Have we the capacity to see or the courage to act ?

Sexual energy is a life force, one of the inborn urges of man, and needs creative outlet. It cannot be repressed, denied, controlled, ignored, frowned upon or debased without doing harm to the individual concerned. Life flows freely when and only when it is transformed and fitted into the whole personality of man, not just accepted on the feeling level or considered as an intellectual entity, but integrated into every department of man's being, which means, to use Jungian terminology, that man must live equally as a thinking, feeling, sensing and intuitive person. All the teaching in the world whether by book or word of mouth ; all the anatomical knowledge, biological instruction and technical information—all the materialistic approach, in other words—will be useless unless the heart is in its right place ; unless there is spiritual acceptance and understanding. Much can be done to prevent injuries being caused to people through ignorance and much more education will have to be done along these lines until we reach that state of maturity in which sex is accepted on its proper level—as an activity acceptable to God and ordained by God. That is how it was regarded by the wise men of the East many centuries ago and that is what we have now lost, thus making it something to feel ashamed of or guilty about. Sex, for the majority of people, is still spiritually taboo. Thus do we suffer from anxiety, for that which should be freed is held back. What I said about St. Paul a short while back is, therefore, but a superficial analysis of the situation and needs some further amplification. Just as there are opposites in everything else in life, such as left and right, good and evil, just and unjust, so is there that which is called flesh—which includes all that is material, seeable and measurable—and spirit, which is not to be seen, but includes mind, emotion, thought and creative idea.

The first is physical and conscious, the second is spiritual and unconscious. These two war, the one with the other, inside every single person, however clever, brilliant, weak, horrid, charming or powerful he may be. Not until they have been brought into a positive relationship to each other and learnt how to respect and value the other will there be any chance of harmony and balance in the individual life. This may occur early or late in life and there are many ways of achieving it, but occur it must, otherwise the individual will go to pieces and all that surrounds that person—all that he loves and respects—will be affected by that upset. That is the problem of broken relationships and no amount of guidance or teaching or re-education or anything else will do any good unless the spirit is willing. That surely is what St. Paul was saying and what we have ignored. So concerned are we with material things that we ignore that which is spiritual, that is to say, we refuse to look inside ourselves and take stock of what is going on there. The purpose of psychotherapy is to enable people, ordinary everyday people, to obtain this insight and is one of the means by which man can achieve wholeness and fullness of life. Such help, properly given at the proper time by a competent person, will achieve wonders. We are all anxious and frustrated in some degree, and some need considerable help, some need a little. Some need it early in life, some later on; but we all need it. In so far as my knowledge goes it is the lack of psychological insight which is the chief cause of marital disharmony, and it is by psychological means—by talks, interviews and, occasionally, by a more prolonged analysis—that the marriage may be saved. With it must be combined much technical material that is mentioned in this book. Neither is sufficient in itself. Each must partner the other.

Physical love is instinctive energy in which sex plays a great part and has many facets like self-love, love for parents and children, friendship, and love of humanity in general. That is the Eros of Plato. But it is not what St. Paul was talking about, although Freud in one of his early papers suggests that it was. St. Paul actually told people that the things of the flesh were of secondary importance to those of the spirit because of the belief in the early second coming of Our Lord when, presumably, we would no longer need our physical bodies. Let them concentrate rather on understanding one another on the spiritual level, in which case Love became Agape—a thing of the spirit.[1] Only by such love could people be in accord, and do not we know in our heart of hearts that he was right? But, he said, if you find it difficult to live solely on that level then by all means marry and have sexual union. Thus what he said hundreds of years ago and what Christ taught about sex and love is precisely the same as is being said by a large section of modern psychological teaching to-day. There is no discord here and there need be no disagreement. Our task to-day, therefore, is to present these truths as a unity so that people may bring up their children in the knowledge and love of the God which is both within and without, accepting that which is physical as something which is only good and holy when it is not only understood, but enjoyed as a creative activity of the human personality. Passion transformed into love is no weak and washy thing, but an adventurous activity of the soul.

After some consideration I have decided to add no more bibliography than is contained in the text. Those in search of further information can consult some of my other books,

---

[1] See an article of mine first published in the Middlesex Hospital Journal in December, 1947, entitled: "Anxiety Neurosis in Modern Life", and now obtainable as a pamphlet from the Marriage Guidance Council Book Room, 78 Duke Street, London, W.1.

notably " Modern Marriage " and " Sex and Citizenship ", both of which contain extensive bibliographies, or they can apply to the Marriage Guidance Council Book Room, 78 Duke Street, London, W.1, or Delisle Limited, 122 City Road, London, E.C.1, who have extensive lists. That much of the material of this book is controversial I am well aware and, indeed, I intend it to be, because I believe society will have to pay an increasing amount of attention to the subjects discussed in this book, much of which is still either unknown, ignored or glossed over with varying unsatisfactory results both to the individual and the nation. No such discussion is possible without factual knowledge.

I have added a short index sufficient, I hope, to help the reader to refer to the major problems discussed. I believe it is usual in such books as this to state that the characters mentioned in the book do not refer to any living person. That I cannot say, for my characters could well be called Everyman and Everywoman. The names, of course, are entirely fictitious; the people might just as well be given letters of the alphabet, but I think Lady Burr sounds nicer than Lady B. and Dr. Hansell better than Dr. H. So far as I am aware there is no society for Human Betterment—which, perhaps, is just as well!

INDEX

Abortion, 40, 112, 190–194, 248–280
  and Bourne case, 112
  and maternal mortality, 279
Abstention, 26, 39, 212
  effect of, on sperms, 200
Adolescence, 213, 231–247
Artificial insemination, 207–210
  indications for A.I.D., 208
  indications for A.I.H., 207

Behaviour, standards of, 16, 87, 236, 281
Betrothal, 95

Celibacy, 212, 285
Cervical erosion, 201
Children and divorce, 129
  and unhappy homes, 159, 214
  when to start them, 138
Chromosomes, 63
Church and divorce, 101–113
Coitus interruptus, 23–26, 36, 44, 120, 186, 251
Collusion, 100, 114, 117
Condonation, 115
Consummation, 118–124
Continence, 6, 89
Contraception, 5, 14, 21–31, 32–46, 71, 85, 131, 211, 222
  and abortion, 250
  and divorce, 120–124
  and heredity, 42
  and local authorities, 46
  and marriage preparation, 130, 222
  and quality of children, 91
  and Roman Catholic Church, 27–31
  and sterility, 203
  and the Church, 211
  harmful effects of, 10
Cowen v. Cowen, 120, 187

Denning Committee, 100, 114, 116, 117
Desertion, 116

Divorce, 75, 100–129
  and children, 129
  and House of Lords, 107, 124
  and medical examinations, 126, 127
  and money, 115
  and Roman Catholics, 108
  and sex, 101
  psychological aspects of, 100, 111–113, 124

Emotional release, 81, 89, 98, 111, 122, 179, 234, 264
Engagement, 96, 136

Family, the, 84–92
  the, and marriage preparation, 213
Frigidity, 183

Herbert Act, the, 119
Heredity, 42, 62, 70, 92, 171, 285, 287
Homosexuality, 169
  types of, 176
Hormones, 89, 196–198, 232
  ovarian, 196, 197
  pituitary, 196
  testicular, 197
Hymen and divorce, 126
  before marriage, 132

Illegitimacy, 83
Innocent party, the, 113
Intelligence, 67

King's Proctor, 117

Lipoidal examination, 205
Love, 93, 157, 227, 267, 282

Male infertility, 198
Marital disharmony, 54, 93, 102, 165

INDEX

Marriage and homosexuality, 172
  in Register Offices, 107
  preparation, 94–96, 123, 125, 130–139, 213–230
  purpose of, 49–54, 89, 132–135, 260, 264
Masturbation, 206, 237, 238, 246
  and Roman Catholics, 206
Maternal mortality, 279
Mating, 54, 57, 88, 123, 219
Menstruation, 253
Mental deficiency, 58–72
Moral standards, alteration in, 1–4, 15, 54, 212

Non-co-operating partners, 128
Nullity, 119, 126–128

Orgasm, 135, 185, 202, 220, 252
Ovulation, 133

Parents and marriage preparation, 217, 224
  and schools, 94–96
  and sex education, 214, 268
Post-coital test, 204
Prediction tests, 216
Pregnancy diagnosis test, 254, 277
Pre-marital consultation, 215
Psychology and divorce, 111–113, 124
  and marriage, 221
  and masturbation, 241
  and sex, 236, 281

Quality of children, 91

Re-marriage, 113
Retroversion, 200
Rh factor, 209
Roman Catholics and contraception, 27–31
  and divorce, 108
  sterility, 206

Sex and divorce, 101, 110
  and religion, 17–21, 47–57, 101, 238, 242, 284–291
  and reproduction, 219
  education, 40, 48, 88, 93, 125, 174, 213, 237
  equality, 243
  inhibiting factors, 224
  purpose of, 10, 18, 51–53, 88, 97–99, 132, 185, 212, 224–226, 234
Sex relationships and nullity, 118
  before marriage, 77–84, 94, 232, 262, 283
  best time for, 133
  duration of, 228
  outside marriage, 140–168
  stages of, 229
  transformation of, 260
Safe period, 27
Science, use of, 20
Self-control, 44, 237
Separation, 85
Social conventions, 90–92, 96
Sperm counts, 199
  discovery of, 196
  manufacture of, 240
  mobility of, 200
  types of, 199
Sterility, 195–205
  causes of, 198
  psychological aspects of, 201
  tests for, 196, 204
Sterilization, 39

Trial marriage, 125
Tubes, examination of, 203

Venereal disease, 83, 84

Womb, size of, 201
Women, changing attitude to, 243

For Product Safety Concerns and Information please contact our EU
representative GPSR@taylorandfrancis.com
Taylor & Francis Verlag GmbH, Kaufingerstraße 24, 80331 München, Germany

www.ingramcontent.com/pod-product-compliance
Lightning Source LLC
Chambersburg PA
CBHW061432300426
44114CB00014B/1648